D0915894

THE "HOW TO" GRANTS MANUAL

THE "HOW TO" GRANTS MANUAL

Successful Grantseeking Techniques for Obtaining Public and Private Grants

David G. Bauer

American
Council on
Education

NEW YORK

Macmillan
Publishing
Company

Collier Macmillan Publishers
LONDON

The American Council on Education/Macmillan Series on Higher Education

Macmillan Publishing Company
A Division of Macmillan, Inc.
866 Third Avenue, New York, N.Y. 10022

Collier Macmillan Canada, Inc.

Library of Congress Catalog Card Number: 84–12282

Printed in the United States of America

printing number
1   2   3   4   5   6   7   8   9   10

Library of Congress Cataloging in Publication Data
Main entry under title:

The "How to" grants manual.

   (The American Council on Education/Macmillan series on
higher education)
   1. Fund raising. 2. Grants-in-aid. 3. Corporations,
Nonprofit. I. David G. Bauer Associates. II. American
Council on Education. III. Series.
HG177.H68   1984   658.1'5224   84–12282
ISBN 0-02-902430-7 (Macmillan)

Contents

Preface

This "*How To*" *Grants Manual* is a compilation of years of effort and experience to systematize the process of grant seeking for nonprofit agencies in the United States. Having instructed over five thousand grant seekers in hundreds of seminars, I am sensitive to the problems faced keeping in control of grant seeking, instead of having the grant seeking control you. Whether you are a one-person grants office, a part-time grants person, or have a staff of twenty, this manual will help you improve your grants investment return.

This book will save you hours of precious time and increase your monetary return by thousands of dollars. By applying this systematic approach to the grants area, you will project a professional image to funding sources through your ability to organize your proposal efforts.

Special thanks must be given to the American Council on Education, the State University of New York College of Technology, and the Public Management Institute for the opportunities they have provided by assisting in the development and sharing these techniques.

This manual will give you insight into the grants marketplace, where competition is keen, owing to the increased expertise of grant writers. The system outlined in this manual provides techniques that I know will work to help you obtain the grants you desire. Although the grants marketplace changes almost daily, this manual will enable you to locate and secure funds, whether they be federal or private.

In order to reduce the time spent on researching possible funding sources for projects that involve higher education, I suggest you locate the companion piece to this manual, *The Complete Grants Sourcebook for Higher Education* (New York: ACE/Macmillan, forthcoming). While you will discover some similar worksheets in the books, the sourcebook represents thousands of hours of research to help find the best funding sources. Use of the techniques in this book will increase your chances of success with funders.

Introduction

WHY SEEK GRANTS? IS ALL THE EFFORT WORTH IT? WHO NEEDS GRANTS?

Understanding the importance of grant seeking to nonprofit organizations in the United States requires some knowledge of the marketplace. The following points should be kept in mind:

- There are over 300,000 nonprofit organizations (NPOs) competing for grant funds in the United States.

- New federal regulations allow not-for-profits and profit-making companies to compete for the same dollars, which makes the grant-seeking process more competitive. There are even "Small Business Set-Asides" in the grants arena, which makes it more difficult for nonprofits to secure their "fair share" of necessary funds to maintain their existence.

- Reaganomics has forecast a cut of 25 billion dollars in direct grants to NPOs by 1985.

To be competitive in the grants world requires knowledge and insight into what is happening in the grant-funding area and why. Each of the major areas of grant funding are dealt with in detail in this book.

The importance of the written proposal or grant to the not-for-profit world is staggering:

- *$20 to 30 billion* of the federal government budget is awarded through a grants mechanism—be it a block grant or a categorical grant.

- *$3.46 billion* went to nonprofits in 1983 from private foundations in the form of grants.

- *$3.10 billion* went to nonprofits from corporations, a similar award procedure.

Nonprofit organizations turn to the grants mechanism for everything from bricks and mortar, new projects, and extension of services to paying last year's phone bill deficit.

The grants mechanism provides the funding source with the key to unlocking the world's largest reserve of collective and individual genius and putting that collective intelligence against any one of the multitude of problems that plague the world of modern man. To unlock this reserve, a funding source announces its attention to direct funds to specific areas of concerns that the funding source feels should be addressed.

The NPO uses all of its resources to develop an approach to solving the stated problem or areas of concern. How you find the grant opportunities that are *right* for your organization, and how you can bring the process to a positive conclusion are the concerns of this manual.

This resource manual and its systematic approach are based upon a "winning approach" to grant seeking. The funding sources have a certain perspective on what they want for their money. This perspective is based upon their values and how they perceive the monies they are charged with dispensing. Whether they are corporate board members, foundation trustees, or government officials, they have interpreted their charge or job through their own beliefs and values.

The key to using this book is to understand that the grants system is reflective of producing a match between what the funding source wants and what your organization can provide. *Note* that I did not say what you *need*; not many people care about what *you need*, unless it matches with what *they need*.

This manual will help you pinpoint what you need and develop strategies on how to develop the interest of others in projects or grants that would benefit both of you.

This requires more analysis before you write your proposal and more tailoring of your proposal to each funding source. The result is well worth the extra effort.

Rather than investing time in a grants effort that generates a 2 percent success rate, you can improve your time investment and obtain a 50 percent success rate through this systematic approach. The "secret ingredient" in this system is confidence—*yes,* confidence.

Following these steps will provide you with the knowledge that you need when approaching each funding source.

You will avoid a hastily prepared approach that is based on your needs and not on those of the funding source. You will not send the same proposal to a list of funding sources, you will develop a tailored approach. Or, as a women in my grants class said: "I used to go after grants with a shotgun; now I use a rifle and spend time aligning my telescopic site."

Successful grant seeking involves doing your "homework." This book is dedicated to providing the direction and shortcuts to do the work of grant seeking in as time-efficient a manner as possible.

While many grant seekers *begin* with the proposal, the systematic approach of this manual does not address the actual proposal until Chapter 15. The purpose of this book is to increase the probability of getting your proposal awarded and most successful veteran grant seekers agree that much of the work required for a funded proposal is done *before* the proposal is written.

This manual is organized upon the following key concept: your ability to communicate with a potential funder, show them your ideas and approaches to the solution of their problem, and co-opt or draw them into the decision on which approach to utilize will drastically increase your grants success rate.

There are several theories that can be used to substantiate why a pre-proposal contact with the funding source results in success. One theory that is particularly useful in explaining how to be more successful is Festinger's Theory of Cognitive Dissonance.

Dissonance is defined as the static that is produced in individuals when they are presented with information (facts) that is not in agreement (matched) with what they have decided is true (reality). Since each person bases his or her reality on his beliefs or values, we are then influenced by those values and view, or compare, the world to what we *believe to be true.*

This means that a potential funder has an existing value system of which you must be aware. Failure to be sensitive to this value system and neglecting to view your project from the funder's perspective can cause dissonance. This means that your preferred solution to the problem may meet with a negative response to your request—not because it would not produce the anticipated results, but because the funding source has a problem accepting that approach because of the static it produces in themselves.

This theory explains why it is important to learn about your funders before you approach them for funds. You can reduce the probability of causing dissonance (static) by planning. You can increase your success by knowing the funder's values and:

- taking a person with you who has similar values to that of the funding source;

- wearing the "right" clothing; and

- selecting an approach they would like.

While it is not always possible to contact funding sources before you develop your proposal, funders leave a trail of information about their values. You can find out what they value by:

- reviewing who and what they have funded, and

- analyzing their choices in selecting staff (reviewers, etc.).

Finally, as you read this text, remember how your value system works to provide you with selective discrimination to avoid producing dissonance. You may decide that you do not like what you are reading in this manual. Before you question the facts presented herein or the validity of this systematic approach, ask yourself if you are experiencing cognitive dissonance. Your success in the "grants world" will depend on how sensitive you are to the funder's values.

Remember the Golden Rule: "She or he who has the gold rules."

Note: When you match your project with an interested funder, think seriously of the reduction of dissonance with how the funder perceives you, your proposal, and your organization. Expressing your rights, freedoms and opinions may conflict with the "Golden Rule."

MAY YOUR GRANTS EFFORTS BE REWARDING!

THE "HOW TO" GRANTS MANUAL

PART ONE

How To Get Ready To Seek Grant Support For Your Organization

CHAPTER 1

Organizing a Proposal-Development Workbook

    The steps necessary to produce a grant application are very logical and follow a definite order. Many people seeking grants find the process complex and difficult to deal with because they are overwhelmed with the totality of the task or end result. As a result of this feeling, they avoid approaching proposal development until it is too late to do an adequate job.

    Allen Lakein, in his book, *How To Get Control of Your Time and Your Life* (New York: New American Library, 1974), discusses a theory that you can utilize to get your grant-writing process under control and organized. His "Swiss Cheese" concept divides a difficult task into parts. Lakein's example of a mouse confronted by the job of carrying away a huge piece of cheese is analogous to the feeling a grant seeker has when presented with the prospect of creating a grant proposal—*overwhelmed!*

    To avoid this feeling, Lakein suggests that the mouse would best be advised to divide the big piece of cheese into parts. Avoid being overwhelmed by the whole task by completing the smaller parts. By eating holes and dividing the cheese into manageable parts you get "Swiss Cheese."

Bauer Associates have applied this concept to your grant-seeking efforts by creating a set of Swiss Cheese tabs (see Fig. 1.1). These tabs are similar to Lakein's mouse eating holes in the cheese. We have divided the task of developing a proposal into thirty (30) steps. By addressing each step in the grant-seeking process, you organize your approach, control the process, and lower your anxiety level.

This manual is based on this concept. Take your proposal a piece at a time and the process will not overwhelm you. The Swiss Cheese Book approach can save you *50 percent* of the time involved in proposal preparation.

I have found it a great help in making the grants process more understandable and manageable. Make a Swiss Cheese Book for each of the major areas for which your organization is planning to seek funding through utilizing a grants mechanism.

For example, a nonprofit organization working with senior citizens might have several Swiss Cheese Books/Proposal Organizing Workbooks to address:

- Transportation

- Health

- Nutrition

- Recreation

Your Swiss Cheese Book/Proposal Development Workbook should be a three-ring binder with tabs dividing up the task of a full-scale proposal. To follow the above example, when you read a research article on nutrition for the elderly, make a copy or summarize it and place it under the tab for "Documenting Need/Needs Assessment."

When a politician visits your center and expresses a concern for the elderly, get a letter of support for your work and put this politician on an advisory committee. File a copy of the endorsement under the tab "Advocates," and the name, address, and telephone number under "Advisory Committee."

FIGURE 1.1.   Proposal Development Workbook (Swiss Cheese Book).

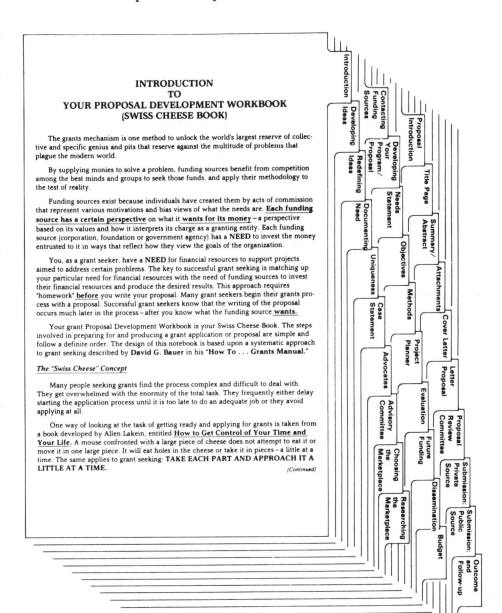

INTRODUCTION
TO
YOUR PROPOSAL DEVELOPMENT WORKBOOK
(SWISS CHEESE BOOK)

The grants mechanism is one method to unlock the world's largest reserve of collective and specific genius and pits that reserve against the multitude of problems that plague the modern world.

By supplying monies to solve a problem, funding sources benefit from competition among the best minds and groups to seek those funds, and apply their methodology to the test of reality.

Funding sources exist because individuals have created them by acts of commission that represent various motivations and bias views of what the needs are. **Each funding source has a certain perspective** on what it **wants for its money** – a perspective based on its values and how it interprets its charge as a granting entity. Each funding source (corporation, foundation or government agency) has a **NEED** to invest the money entrusted to it in ways that reflect how they view the goals of the organization.

You, as a grant seeker, have a **NEED** for financial resources to support projects aimed to address certain problems. The key to successful grant seeking is matching up your particular need for financial resources with the need of funding sources to invest their financial resources and produce the desired results. This approach requires "homework" **before** you write your proposal. Many grant seekers begin their grants process with a proposal. Successful grant seekers know that the writing of the proposal occurs much later in the process – after you know what the funding source **wants.**

Your grant Proposal Development Workbook is your Swiss Cheese Book. The steps involved in preparing for and producing a grant application or proposal are simple and follow a definite order. The design of this notebook is based upon a systematic approach to grant seeking described by **David G. Bauer** in his "How To . . . Grants Manual."

The "Swiss Cheese" Concept

Many people seeking grants find the process complex and difficult to deal with. They get overwhelmed with the enormity of the total task. They frequently either delay starting the application process until it is too late to do an adequate job or they avoid applying at all.

One way of looking at the task of getting ready and applying for grants is taken from a book developed by Allen Lakein, entitled **How to Get Control of Your Time and Your Life**. A mouse confronted with a large piece of cheese does not attempt to eat it or move it in one large piece. It will eat holes in the cheese or take it in pieces – a little at a time. The same applies to grant seeking: TAKE EACH PART AND APPROACH IT A LITTLE AT A TIME.   *(Continued)*

Review the list of tabs after you have read this manual. You may want to eliminate or combine some areas to tailor the concept to your organization. (Sets of thirty tabs can be purchased from Bauer Associates at a reasonable cost.)

SUGGESTED TABS

1. Organizing A Proposal Workbook
2. Developing and Evaluating Proposal Ideas
3. Redefining Proposal Ideas to Find More Funding Sources
4. Documenting Need/Needs Assessment
5. Uniquenesses/Capitalizing on Your Differences
6. Your Case Statement
7. Advocates: How to Use Them
8. Advisory Committee: How to Develop Community Support

In addition, you will want tabs for the research and contacts in the marketplace you choose.

FOR GOVERNMENT FUNDING SOURCES

14. Federal Grants Research Form
15. Selecting the Appropriate Government Funding Program
16. How to Contact Government Funding Sources
17. The Project Planner

FOR PRIVATE FUNDING SOURCES

23. How to Record Research and Information
24. Private Funding Source Research Tools
25. Locating and Selecting the Appropriate Private Funding Sources
26. How to Contact a Private Funding Source
27. The Letter Proposal
28. Submission and Who to Contact on Follow-Up

Your Proposal Development Workbook acts as a file for your proposal ideas. A potential funding source will be very impressed if you respond to a question by referring to your Proposal Development Workbook instead of a tattered pile of file folders and loose pages of notes.

One grant seeker using this successful process, called our office to tell us how great it was to see the look on a potential funder's face when she was asked, "Why should we give the money to your organization when there are hundreds of others who are asking for this grant?" She opened her Proposal Development Workbook to the tab on uniquenesses and presented a list of fifty reasons why her organization was uniquely suited to carry out the proposed project—with the best five reasons circled.

The Proposal Development Workbook is one step in the process of making your grants effort more cost- and time-effective. If you thought that proposal preparation was a Herculean task—last-minute, forty-eight-hour miracle—think again. This manual and its usefulness are based on the assumption that proposal preparation is an organized approach that utilizes adequate development time and provides support to the mission and the image of the organization.

Those grant seekers who prepare proposals overnight pose a threat to the image of your organization in the eyes of a funder, and develop the fear of proposal preparation in your staff.

This manual uses time-proven steps to allow you to improve your image with funding sources (known as "positioning" in marketing talk, but it really works when you present your organization as an honest, organized, well-planned agency—even if it is not totally true). One hastily written proposal (overnight wonder) with budget transpositions and typographical errors will affect your image negatively for many years.

Organizing your Proposal Development Workbook is a process that, once initiated, promotes development of project ideas, location of funding sources, and writing proposals. It is a proactive process.

Finding a funding opportunity and developing a proposal is a *reactive process* that puts you under someone else's time frame and adds to the existing pressure that deadlines normally create.

The grants process can be *made* to work for you and your organization.

CHAPTER 2

Developing and Evaluating Proposal Ideas

The underlying theme or philosophy of this manual is based on the concept that when you ask someone (funder) for support (grant), you must look at your organization and your request from their perspective. It is the "Golden Rule"—not the one you were taught in grade school, but the rule for grant seeking: "He or she who has the gold rules."

The least we can do is try to determine what the grantor values, likes, and dislikes, and avoid those areas that may be potentially negative, while we highlight the areas that make us look competent to the grantor.

Most grant seekers write the proposal first, which does not allow sufficient flexibility to tailor or select alternative approaches (solutions) to the problem. A funder, while very definitely concerned about the problem, may find your approach (solution) very unpalatable.

The process outlined in this chapter recommends that you develop several alternatives to solve the problem (perform your research, develop your model, or solve your space problems, etc.).

By providing the funding source with several approaches, you develop credibility and present an image of analysis as a basis for your approach—*not a bias and preference of your project staff.*

The worksheets in this chapter will provide you with three useful tools:

1. Idea generation;
2. A system to summarize your best ideas and assess organizational commitment to the project; and
3. Cost/benefit analysis of your best ideas/approaches.

One of the best techniques for developing sound proposal ideas and alternatives is to *brainstorm* the idea with your staff and peers. This has the added benefit of tapping the collective genius of the group. You build support for the proposal since you invited your staff to share in the idea generation. Thus, the project becomes "our" project and your staff will be more willing and eager to work at night and on weekends to meet the deadlines (when numerous proposals are worked on).

Brainstorming is a simple technique of quickly generating a long list of creative ideas. To obtain maximum benefit from this idea-generating process, break your participants into groups of five to eight individuals, and:

1. Appoint a neutral group leader to facilitate the process (encouraging and prodding other members, checking the time).
2. Appoint a recorder.
3. Set a time limit (ten minutes will be plenty).
4. State one question or problem (e.g., reducing student dropouts, increasing attendance, keeping pregnant teenagers in school, increasing student interest in certain subject areas).
5. Ask group members to generate and present as many answers or possible solutions to the problem as possible, within a time limit.
6. Encourage group members to "piggyback" on each other's ideas (suggesting a new idea that adds to one already given).
7. Record all answers; combining those that are similar.

Note: One crucial rule of brainstorming is to avoid any evaluation or discussion of ideas until the process is over.

An important rule in brainstorming is that the recorder can ask to have an idea repeated, but should allow no comments by others (e.g., "We can't do that!" or "That's stupid!").

Brainstorming/Wish List Summary Form for Proposed Project

This worksheet could be subtitled "Pre-proposal Summary." When you have ideas you would like funded, project directors can fill out "Idea Summary Forms," rather than write full-scale proposals. These forms can then be discussed by a "Proposal Review Committee," staff, or the administrators, and returned for modification.

There are many benefits to this:

- Projects can be quickly summarized; *more ideas* for projects are generated.

- The increase in the number of ideas lends itself to an *increase in the number of fundable projects.*

- There is a *greater chance of combining two or three good ideas into one "great" one.*

- Because project designers have not invested a great deal of time in writing a proposal for their idea, they are less *defensive when their project summary is criticized or modified;* subsequent improvements are therefore easier to make.

Many organizations find it useful to copy this form in bulk on both sides of one sheet of paper, and then distribute copies to their staff. This can be of benefit when proposals must be approved before they can be written. This sheet also has the advantage of becoming a valuable way of coordinating contact with funding sources. Many grant-seeking organizations find themselves unknowingly discredited by unauthorized staff contact with funding sources. While these contacts are usually made by zealous, well-intentioned staff members, the mistakes staff may make and the first impression they may leave are a potentially indelible source of embarassment.

This form can be used to insure that the individuals who are required to sign your proposal at submittal time know (in advance) that the proposed project is coming.

I recommend that you have your key people (person) make comments concerning areas they question or object to in the right-

PRE-PROPOSAL REVIEW AND APPROVAL FORM

PROBLEM AREA: A POSSIBLE SOLUTION IS:	COMMENTS

Resources Needed (approximately)
 	
1. Total Estimated Dollar Cost: $_____
 	
2. Matching or Inkind Commitment: $_____
 	
3. Estimated Time Needed For Proposal Process: _____
     Pre-proposal Date _____
     Contacting Funders (completed B) ___ : _____
     Proposal Submission _____
     Project Start-up _____
 	
4. Individuals in Charge: (Project Director)
     _____
 	
     Co-workers _____
 	
     _____
 	
5. How Does This Project Relate To The Mission Or
     Goal Of Agency:
     _____
 	
     _____
 	
SUMMARIZE:
 	
   Objectives:
 	
   Methods:	

PRE-PROPOSAL REVIEW AND APPROVAL FORM (Cont.)

PROBLEM AREA:	A POSSIBLE SOLUTION IS:	COMMENTS
Estimate Non-Personnel Resources Needed:		
Travel _____		
Supplies _____		
Printing _____		
Postage _____		
Other _____		
6. Estimated Equipment Costs: $_____		
7. Facilities Needed: _____		
Square Ft. _____		
Desired Location _____		
Special Considerations _____		
_____		
_____		
_____		
8. Project Personnel Needed: _____		

Title	Salary Range	Name (if known)	

hand margin of the form. Then have them initial the form—giving their consent or approval to proceed. This insures that the time, money, and resources spent in the proposal-preparation process will not be met with a negative response and result in a failure to have your proposal signed when it is completed.

This process allows your decision makers to comment on:

- Matching funds commitment;
- Space and resource allocations;
- Coordination of contact and use of funding sources;
- Organizational mission, etc.

The explanation of how this project relates to the mission or purpose of your organization is of critical importance. Funding sources are wary of groups that write proposals simply to "get" money. It may be advisable to review the chapter on "Case Statement." Several organizations give prospective grant seekers a copy of the "Case Statement" or mission statement when they distribute a pre-proposal review form.

Cost/Benefit Analysis Worksheet

An important aspect of any fundable idea is its economic feasibility. Funding sources want to know that you've chosen methods that will produce the best results for the least amount of money. The cost/benefit analysis worksheet will assist you in demonstrating economic accountability.

Column One. Complete this column with brief descriptions of each method you are considering. For example, a project to feed senior citizens could range from a meals-on-wheels program, to congregate feeding, to a food cooperative for the elderly. Choose two or three possible approaches that will fulfill the goals of the project.

Column Two. Record here the estimated price or cost of each idea or set of methods. This figure will be found on your Pre-Proposal Review and Approval Form.

COST/BENEFIT ANALYSIS WORKSHEET

1. SUMMARY OF IDEA AND METHODOLOGY	2. COST	3. # OF PERSONS SERVED	4. COST PERSONS SERVED	5. POSITIVE POINTS	6. NEGATIVE POINTS	7. RATING

14

Column Three. Utilize this column to estimate the number of individuals, persons, or clients who will be affected by a particular methodology (idea or approach).

Column Four. Enter the estimated cost per person or client served. This is essential, since funding sources are wary about sponsoring projects that possess an unrealistic cost per individual served. Projects with a high cost per person have great difficulty securing funding and are considered a waste of money by many funders.

Column Five. This column provides the opportunity to summarize the advantages of each idea of set of methods. This approach has resulted in funders considering the support of a more costly approach because the advantages outweigh the expense.

Column Six. In this column, the disadvantages or drawbacks to each approach can be highlighted. This increases your credibility with the funder, as you develop their confidence in your honesty.

Column Seven. The seventh column is used to rate each approach. Your objective is to present the problem and several alternative solutions while allowing the funding source to:

- Feel confident that you have analyzed the situation carefully.

- Observe your flexibility and see the pros and cons of each approach.

- Make a choice of the approach they favor (now you have the advantage of writing the approach the funding source agrees to).

You should use this worksheet each time you refine your project ideas. You can also bring a completed "Cost/Benefit Analysis Worksheets" to preliminary meetings with funding officials. They will be impressed by the fact that you considered their financial interest while designing your project.

Remember that many grant officials are executives of profit-making companies. They're very sensitive to cost-efficiency in all investments they make. Take this into account when refining your project ideas; it will help you win more grant funds.

CHAPTER 3

Redefining Proposal Ideas To Find More Funding Sources

Most grant seekers have a myopic view of their proposal idea. They define the idea in a narrow perspective—like looking at the world with tunnel vision. They fail to see that their project can be related to many funders. To expand your funding horizons, think of the project in as many ways as possible to uncover potential funding sources that may not be obvious when you look at only one way of defining the project.

Look at the project from at least four perspectives or categories and analyze possible connections to the project:

1. *Subject Areas,* the most common perspective: Does the project deal with education, labor, etc.?
2. *Constituency Group:* What type of constituency or target groups could benefit from the project?
3. *Type of Grant:* Can you do a pilot project instead of a needs assessment?
4. *Project Location:* How you define the geographic boundaries of the project affects the funding sources greatly.

```
+-------------------------------------------------------------------------+
|                      REDEFINING YOUR PROJECT                            |
|                                                                         |
+-------------------------------------------------------------------------+
| PROJECT:                                                                |
+-------------------------------------------------------------------------+
|                          Education                                      |
|                                                                         |
|   _____ Elementary and Secondary          _____ Vocational    |
|                                                                         |
|   _____ College                           _____ Continuing    |
|                                                                         |
|   _____ Adult                             _____ Other:        |
|                                                                         |
|   Relationship/Connection to your project:                             |
|                                                                         |
|                                                                         |
|                                                                         |
|                                                                         |
|                                                                         |
|                                                                         |
|                                                                         |
+-------------------------------------------------------------------------+
|                          Humanities                                     |
|                                                                         |
|   _____ Art                               _____ Opera         |
|                                                                         |
|   _____ Museum                            _____ Theater       |
|                                                                         |
|   _____ Music                             _____ Other:        |
|                                                                         |
|   Relationship/Connection to your project:                             |
|                                                                         |
|                                                                         |
|                                                                         |
|                                                                         |
|                                                                         |
|                                                                         |
|                                                                         |
+-------------------------------------------------------------------------+
```

REDEFINING YOUR PROJECT (Cont.)

PROJECT:

Sciences

_____ Physical Science - astronomy and space,
             earth science _____

_____ Life Science - nutrition, environmental,
             agriculture _____

_____ Social Sciences - anthropology, sociology

_____ Business - labor, unions, management

Relation/Connection to your project:

Constituency Groups

_____ Youth   _____ Other:

_____ Women   _____

_____ Handicapped   _____

_____ Native American   _____

_____ Blacks   _____

_____ Hispanics   _____

_____ Orientals   _____

_____ Elderly   _____

Relation/Connection to your project:

REDEFINING YOUR PROJECT (Cont.)	
TYPE OF GRANT - Look at these kinds of grants and check any that may be useful in funding all or part of your project.	EXPLAIN RELATION/CONNECTION OF YOUR PROJECT - How can you use this type of funding?
_____ Block - Federal funds to state agencies. _____ Research - What parts of your grant can be defined as pure or applied research. _____ Consortium - Team up with another organization in your field. _____ Construction - Bricks and mortar. _____ Continuing Education - Will this project and results be useful to a college as Continuing Education?	_____ Demonstration - Proving or demonstrating a new approach or method. _____ Discretionary - Some funding sources have funds to use at their discretion if you show them a reason to fund. _____ Planning - Can your project be more successful if you get a grant to plan an approach to the problem? _____ Training - Does your project have components that call for education/training of participants, staff, volunteers? _____ Equipment - What types/kinds and amount of equipment will be needed. _____ Other
PROJECT LOCATION - Many funders are interested in your project as it relates to their geographical interests.	EXPLAIN RELATION/CONNECTION TO YOUR PROJECT
_____ City - Community Foundations, etc.: City Government _____ Community-wide - Corporate and Special Interest Foundations; County Government. _____ County - Borough	_____ State - State Governments Sources; Block Grant From Federal Level _____ Regional - Federal and State Regional Commission/Offices _____ National - Federal Sources and Foundations and Corporations with national scope.

Carefully examine each of these categories. Each time you discover another way to look at the project, you will have uncovered additional funding sources that may become interested in your project.

In viewing the worksheets, check the subcategories that might apply to the project and use the accompanying work space for notes.

The final step is explaining the connection or relationship to the project. There is space on the worksheet for this activity.

CHAPTER 4

Needs Assessment

This section is vital to your decision to proceed and invest your time and effort into developing this proposal any further. Most grant writers make statements like, "Everyone knows the need for—!"

The needs assessment is critical to your ability to create a motivating and interesting proposal. Many grant seekers place undue emphasis on the development of the methodology, or how you will solve the problem.

First, a funding source must clearly see that there is a *pressing problem or need that must be addressed.* The needs-assessment section (pp. 22–25) will provide the back-up for the development of a convincing and motivating needs statement in a final proposal.

At this point, you make a copy of any pertinent article, study, quote, or statistic that is related to the problem area you will address. Developing the needs assessment is analogous to a lawyer developing background information for a case. This information will be reviewed and certain data selected for use. A good lawyer will select from this data base the information that will sway a particular jury toward his or her side of the argument.

The purpose of the needs assessment is to provide you with a command of the facts to document the need. You will select infor-

21

NEEDS ASSESSMENT

TYPE OF APPROACH	ADVANTAGES	DISADVANTAGES
1. Key Informant - Solicit information from individuals whose testimony or description of what exists for the client population or state-of-affairs is credible - either by their position in the community or through their experience and/or expertise. Includes: elected officials, agency heads (police chiefs, juvenile delinquency, parole officers, etc.). Funders may value their opinions/insights.	° easy to design ° costs very little ° you control input by what you ask and whom ° excellent way to position your organization with important people (shows you're working on common problem/concern)	° Most funding sources know you have selected and included comments of those individuals sympathetic to your cause. You may be leaving out parts of the population who have not been visible and caused problems that were noticed, commented on.
2. Community Forum - Host or sponsor public meetings. You publicize the opportunity to present views of populace. You also invite key individuals to speak. Funder may like the grass roots image this creates.	° easy to arrange ° costs very little ° increases your visibility in the community ° promotes active involvement of the populace	° Site of forum has proformed effect on number and type of representation. ° You can lose control of the group and have a small vocal minority slant results or turn meeting into a forum for complaints.

NEEDS ASSESSMENT (Cont.)

TYPE OF APPROACH	ADVANTAGES	DISADVANTAGES
3. Case Studies/Examples - An excellent approach to assist the funder in appreciating what representative members of the client population are up against. Select individuals from the needs population or client group and provide analytical, realistic description of their problem/situation, their use of your services, need for them, etc.	° easy to arrange ° costs very little ° increases sensitivity to the client's "real world" ° very moving and motivating	° Your selection of a "typical" client may be biased and represent a minority of cases. ° You must describe one "real" person - not a composite of several put into one "example." The anonymity of the person must be insured.
4. Statistical Analysis - Most funders like to see a few well chosen statistics. With this approach, you utilize existing data: ° census data/records ° Govt. studies/reports ° reports and research articles to develop a statistical picture of the needs population	° there is an abundance of studies and data ° little cost to access data ° allows for flexibility in drawing and developing conclusions ° analysis of data is catalytic in producing more projects and proposals as staff "sees" the need	° can be very time-consuming ° bias of staff show up in studies quoted ° feelings on funder's part that you can prove anything with statistics ° if original data has questionable validity, your extrapolation will be inaccurate.

NEEDS ASSESSMENT (Cont.)

TYPE OF APPROACH	ADVANTAGES	DISADVANTAGES
5. Survey - Very commonly used approach to gathering data on the needs population, this approach has usefulness even when the survey is carried out with volunteers and with limited statistical validity. Accurate surveys may entail control groups, establishing random samples, and use of computers and statistical analysis. However, acknowledgment by you that the results of your survey cannot be extrapolated beyond the sample group will prove more than adequate in most situations.	° high credibility with funders ° excellent flexibility in design of survey to get at problem areas and document exactly what you want to document	° takes time to do survey properly

NEEDS ASSESSMENT WORKSHEET

WHAT INFORMATION DO WE NEED TO DOCUMENT THE PROBLEM?	WHICH APPROACHES TO NEEDS ASSESSMENTS ARE BEST FOR US AND/OR PREFERRED BY FUNDER: KEY INFORMANT: ___ COMMUNITY FORUM: ___ CASE STUDIES: ___ SOCIAL INDICATORS: ___ SURVEY: ___

DATA TO BE GATHERED	HOW IT WILL BE GATHERED	WHO WILL DO IT	DATE DUE	COST	CONSORTIUM AGENCIES INVOLVED

mation from this data base that is necessary to develop a needs statement depending on the known viewpoints and biases of those who will read and act on the proposal.

The key to needs assessment is *choosing the approach.* There are five basic needs-assessment approaches:

1. *Key Informant:* testimony from people who know about the problem.
2. *Community Forum:* public meetings to get testimony on the problem.
3. *Case Studies:* example of clients in a need population.
4. *Social Indicators:* use of data from public records to depict need.
5. *Survey:* random selection of population to answer questions related to need.

The worksheets on the previous pages will help you decide which one to adopt for your organization. Information is provided for each approach, followed by some questions to assist you in choosing the best one.

It will enhance your "fundability" or ability to attract funds for this project if you provide the funding source with well-documented needs for the project.

The needs assessment should be done prior to contacting the funding source or writing the proposal.

The information from your needs assessment should provide an accurate and compelling need that must be addressed. Most proposals lack "urgency," they sound like, "If you can't afford to fund the project this year, how about next year?" The urgency is reflective of the immediacy of the need. The funding source should feel that they must fund the project now, or things will be worse by next year.

Take a few minutes to look at the various types of needs assessments to determine the approach that is right for you. You may decide that you need to write a small grant first to fund the needs assessment. This is made easier by telling the funding source that they will be ultimately responsible for all the funds that result from this excellent needs statement that will attract other funders in a final proposal.

Please note that some funding sources do not talk about needs, but refer to a search of literature in the field, or review of related literature or studies. These are a form of approach #4, social indicators. The key here is to do a thorough search of studies so that you appear to be the "expert." There are several computerized searching tools you can review in the research section. You must use the most recent studies to show you have "state-of-the-art" knowledge.

One problem encountered in this review of studies is that of causing dissonance in the funding source or the individual they hire to review your proposal by citing researchers you prefer or feel are the most influential in the field, when they favor some other researcher.

CHAPTER 5

Capitalizing on Your Differences

Many grant seekers forget that the funding source has to choose among many prospective grantees and that the successful grantee must *stand out* from the rest of the competition. How can you increase your ability to project an image that puts you "a cut above the rest"?

One method is to show the funding source that you are different from "the crowd." You are the logical choice to fund because you are *different* from others in your field. Your differences, or uniqueness, make you the logical choice for investment of their grant dollars.

Many of our seminar participants have a great deal of trouble here. They respond with "I'm just another college, hospital, association for _____." This is generally not true. Examine what you do that is different from the others; your staff, location, building, special areas of interest, and the like. You could make being similar to many others a uniqueness by explaining that you are uniquely suited for funding because:

- We are similar in make-up to *x* percent of the others in the United States;

- A pilot project done here could be replicated in other similar organizations in the United States.

These are rather weak uniquenesses. A little time spent on this chapter and its exercises for developing a list of those special qualities that your organization can capitalize upon will be a very worthwhile investment.

Keep the information you develop here in your Proposal Development Workbook (Swiss Cheese Book). It will then be ready when needed in writing letters or proposals, and in making personal contacts.

In order to be prepared with answers to the question, "Why should we give the money to your organization instead of another in your field?," brainstorm a list of responses to the question. Use the following activity to add a little excitement and flavor to a staff meeting, board meeting, or with a volunteer group or advisory committee.

The Uniqueness Exercise

This exercise will result in:

- A list of those factors that make your organization unique.

- The ability to select those uniquenesses that have particular appeal to a funding source.

- A staff that refocuses on your unique qualities, placing you above the "others."

This exercise can be successful with a variety of groups. It is especially useful to do this with:

- staff

- volunteers

- clients

- board members

Exchanging the lists among the groups will develop more unique characteristics.

EXERCISE INSTRUCTIONS

1. Give the group Sheet A (p. 31); remind the group of the rules for brainstorming from Chapter 2; set a time limit for brainstorming. Use Question 1 or 2 and record the answer.

2. Combine the answers to Question 1 or 2 provided by individuals and/or groups.

3. Ask each person to look at the list and:

- rank-order their preferences 1 to _____?

- give each individual ten points and request them to allocate their ten points over the entire list; this will produce a weighted list.

Use your completed list to select uniquenesses that will convince a funder that their money will go farther with you. For example:

- Your staff has _____ years' experience.

- Your buildings are centrally located.

- Special equipment is available.

- Your needs population and geographics are broad.

In addition to use in the grants area, your uniquenesses are valuable in:

- training and recruiting staff, board members, and volunteers;

- developing case statements (Chapter 6);

- direct mail, wills and bequests, other fund-raising techniques.

SHEET A: OUR UNIQUENESSES

Our organization has many unique qualities. These positive qualities can be utilized to convince a funding source that they are investing in the right individuals when they grant your organization money.

This exercise will result in a combined list of qualities that make you stand out from the competition for grant funds. Your leader will tell you when to begin recording your responses to Question 1.

Question 1: *What makes our organization/college good at what we do?*

Question 2: *Why will a funding source (donor) give a grant to us instead of some other organization in our field (what makes us a good investment—what are the advantages of funding us)?*

CHAPTER 6

Your Case Statement

Your case statement, or mission statement, is a key ingredient in presenting your case for funding or in the awarding of a grant to your organization. When you present your application for funding, your approach is that:

- There is a compelling need.

- Your organization is uniquely suited to carry out the project.

- It is your purpose or mission to carry out this project—verified by your "case statement."

The case statement provides the funding source with written documentation that the purpose (reason to exist) of your organization and this project are a perfect match.

Your case statement consists of:

1. *How and why your organization got started*—(what social problems or reasons for starting existed). *Note:* societal need today is more valuable than number of years you've existed. One funding source remarked to me that the organizations she had the greatest doubts about were those that have been around a long

WORKSHEET

1. How and Why Your Organization Got Started.

   Year _____ Prime Movers/Founders _____

   Societal Need: _____

   _____

2. Today – Changes From Original Mission: _____

   _____

   Societal Need Changes: _____

   _____

   Current Priorities: _____

   _____

   Clients: _____

   Staff: _____

   Buildings: _____

3. Future: Where Will Your Organization Be Five Years From Now? Change
            in Mission: _____

   _____

   Changes in Need: _____

   _____

   Changes in Facilities and Staff: _____

   _____

4. Optional – What Opportunities Exist or Will Exist To Move You Toward
              Your Plans/Goals.

   A. _____

   B. _____

   C. _____

time. She felt that they generally were bureaucratic, had a tendency to lose sight of their mission or purpose, and generally had more "dead wood" on the payroll.

2. *What is your organization doing today?* Have you deviated from the past? Why? What effect has the passage of time had on

your mission and reason for being? What are the current priorities, programs, clients, staff, buildings, and uniquenesses (Chapter 5)?

3. *Where are you going in the future?* What is your five-year plan? Ten-year plan? Or longer, if you have one? Since funding sources are investing in you, they want their project to be placed with a winner who will still be around when the funding runs out.

Show the funding source that you are worthy of funding and that the project that they have invested in will continue to benefit people due to your long-range planning and ability to secure future funding to carry on.

The worksheet on page 33 is designed to assist you in determining the factors that should be included in your case statement. If you already have a case statement, review it to see if you can update or tailor the statement for the grants marketplace.

If you have a ten-page mission statement, use this worksheet to edit it and reduce it to one concise page.

CHAPTER 7

Advocates

HOW TO USE THEM

The politics of grant seeking is a fascinating area that spells M-O-N-E-Y for those that master the art and develop their political skills. Do not be frightened! The politics of grant seeking is understandable and can be an organized process.

Many people develop a sick feeling in the pit of their stomach when the word politics is used, so we will use the term *advocates*. Those people who know your organization and identify with your cause, mission, or your staff need to know how they can be of service to you. *They can always say no!*

This chapter suggests that you consider exploring the area of advocacy and how you can help people help you. The worksheets develop a systematic approach so that you know who your contacts are. You may find that there are supporters you did not even realize you knew.

You will develop a list of the people you can utilize as advocates. This list will be valuable since you can then select people to:

- write endorsement letters (see worksheet, p. 40);
- talk to funding sources for you; set up appointments;

- utilize advocates' expertise (finance, marketing, etc.);
- accompany you to meet with potential funders.

Use the worksheets below to increase your advocacy potential. Several organizations have placed the results of this process on a microprocessor. When a potential funding source is located through research, the data base is consulted to see if you have any advocates who know the funding source. There may be:

- members on both your organization's and the funding source's boards;
- an advocate who can get you "in" to talk to funder;
- an advocate who could write a letter to a "friend" on the board.

One successful method in using your advocates is to divide them into two major categories:

- *Inside your organization:* Employees, board of trustees, advisory committee members, volunteers, former staff, former clients, and the like.
- *Outside your organization:* Associations and groups you belong to, experts in the field, politicians, religious leaders, community leaders, and so forth.

Next, using those individuals who are inside your organization, follow these steps:
1. Pass out the advocacy worksheet (see p. 37) to the individuals you have identified (this may be done in a group or individually).
2. Read the section explaining how the information they provide will be used; you will have better results.
   Note: Several organizations have had very good results when introducing this advocacy concept attached to a major project of the organization that has widespread support. It may be necessary to list several of your most logical funding sources and ask the clear question:

Do you know any of these funding executives or board members?

LIST: _____

_____

_____

3. Record the information in your computer and/or files.
4. When a match between a potential funder and an advocate is made, call your contact person and discuss the possibility of having him or her help you in meeting the funding source or board member/trustee.

When you locate a funding contact using the Webbing Form (p. 38) ask the person completing the form to set up an appointment for you with the funder, through the contact. If appropriate, ask the person making the appointment if he or she can come with you to the meeting. This will add credibility to your presentation.

Keep all returned forms on file and update periodically. This is a good activity for volunteers to handle. Expand your advocates and you expand your universe of potential funders with whom you are able to communicate. Bauer Associates has available an inexpensive computer program for your microprocessor that allows for storing and using this information. Care must be taken to safeguard this information. Through use of a small, personal computer, you can safeguard the program and data by performing your own security. Make a copy and store it in a safe place.

Use of larger central computing facilities greatly reduces security. *Remember:* you are storing personal information that is *privileged,* and you must not allow any access to it, or you violate your advocate's trust.

Use the Advocate Planning Sheet on p. 39.

Draft of Possible Advocacy Worksheet

We are requesting your assistance in completing this survey of potential ways that you may wish to assist _____ in continuing our mission to _____. In particular, our organization's ability to attract grants from funding sources is increased by 300 percent

POSSIBLE WEBBING FORM

YOUR NAME: PHONE #:

ADDRESS:

1. What foundation or corporation boards are you or your spouse on?

2. Do you know anyone who is on a foundation or corporation board?

3. Does your spouse know anyone on a foundation or corporation board?

4. Do you know any government funding contacts? (Have you served on any
    government committees?)

5. Have you ever helped a not-for-profit organization get a grant? (Who
    and When?)

            NOTE: It is optional to ask for personal data.

6. Fraternal groups, social clubs, service organizations that you are
    involved in.

Other questions you may ask include: educational background, military
background, religious affiliation, political preference, job title and
description, and information on ability to travel for business.

(greatly) if we can talk informally with a funding official (or board
member) before we submit a formal proposal.

We are asking you to help us identify those linkages that you
may have with a potential funding source. If our research indicates that a funding source you have identified has a record of

ADVOCATE PLANNING SHEET

PROJECT TITLE: _____ PROJECT DIRECTOR: _____

Select from this list the ways to utilize advocates that will advance this project.

° Endorsement Letters	° Set up your appointment
° Testimonials	° Accompany you to see funding source
° Letters of Introduction	° Go see funder for you

TECHNIQUES FOR THIS PROJECT	ADVOCATE TO BE USED	WHO WILL CONTACT ADVOCATE AND WHEN	DESIRED OUTCOME	DATE COMPLETED

providing grant support for one of (your organization's) projects we would:

- Contact you and explain the project.

- Discuss how you could assist us, for example:
  a. by writing an endorsement letter,
  b. in getting to talk to the funder.

- Have your complete approval before any action was taken.

This information is critical to allow us to utilize every advantage we can find in this very competitive marketplace. A simple phone call can result in our proposal actually being read, not left in a pile. In considering our need, remember our pledge to never use your name or linkage without your consent.

These linkages are worth hundreds of thousands of dollars each year from foundations, corporations, and the government.

Thank you for your cooperation.

Endorsement Letter Worksheet

An advocate may not provide you with a useful endorsement letter unless they know what you are looking for. A well-intentioned endorsement that focuses on the wrong aspects of your project causes turmoil because:

- You may not be able to include the endorsement in your proposal, which may prove embarrassing.

- It is difficult to correct the letter, return it with comments, and ask for another.

To avoid these problems, give the advocate a basic summary or outline of what "they" might consider including.

Note: put in any pertinent facts or statistics, and once they are stated in the endorsement letter, they are a fact that you can quote (e.g., using your program graduates has increased services by 20 percent with no increase in cost).

Include:

- Facts/statistics.

- Length of time they have worked with you (number of hours, awards earned).

- Summary of their committee work and their major accomplishments (give away any credit you can).

The advocate should be able to retype and sign the "outline."

Be sure to include the advocates' addresses and any instructions that the funding source may require.

CHAPTER 8

Advisory Committees

How to Develop
Community Support

Some funding sources require that you demonstrate community support for your proposal. The funding source may want to see this support in the form of advisory committees, resolutions, and minutes of meetings or letters of endorsement.

The following worksheets are designed for you to review as you consider community support and how it will increase your fundability.

By using your Proposal Development Workbook (Chapter 1) for community support, you can put together an advisory committee and benefit from their input on brainstorming project ideas, needs-assessment techniques, letters of endorsement, and other helpful tasks. Many grant writers start the process of applying for a grant so near the deadline date that advisory committees are a token and, in most cases, never meet or provide input. It is not uncommon for funding-source representatives to ask to meet with committee members when they arrive for a site visit. By utilizing the Swiss Cheese Concept, you can deal creatively with this area of community support and have *legitimate* minutes of *actual* meetings with your committee.

HOW TO DEVELOP COMMUNITY SUPPORT

PROJECT TITLE: _____ PROJECT DIRECTOR: _____

_____ DATE: _____

#	TECHNIQUES	APPLICABILITY TO THIS PROJECT	WHO WILL CALL MEETING	MEMBERS OF COMMITTEE	DATES
1	ADVISORY COMMITTEE brainstorm uniquenesses of your organization (chapter 5)				
2	ADVISORY COMMITTEE work on setting up needs assessment (brings them closer and more aware of the need, more commitment)				
3	Use your ADVISORY COMMITTEE to brainstorm your project ideas				

HOW TO DEVELOP COMMUNITY SUPPORT (Cont.)

#	TECHNIQUES	APPLICABILITY TO THIS PROJECT	WHO WILL CALL MEETING	MEMBERS OF COMMITTEE	DATES
4	Use your committee to develop a public relations package and produce it (printers, media representative) NEWSPAPER COVERAGE for your organization -- press releases, interviews, etc. RADIO - TELEVISION COVERAGE public-service announcements on talk shows, etc.				
5	Have an artist perform or an open house for key people* in the community				

*Public officials, Congresspeople, potential advocates, and others.

CHAPTER 9

Choosing the Correct Marketplace

Many prospective and oftentimes overzealous grant seekers launch their research effort too quickly. The approach that maximizes your grants potential requires the kind of planning that is described in the preceding chapters. Developing funding that will promote a professional image for your organization requires an approach to researching funding sources that:

- Is based upon a win-win attitude. Your research must provide the depth of information so that you know your project meets the funding source's needs (values) while moving your organization ahead toward meeting its mission, and providing benefits to people (clients): the funder *wins;* your organization *wins;* your clients *win.*

- Provides you the confidence to present yourself as worthy of funding. You will have done your research "homework." You have taken the time to find the "right" funder. They will see that you are confident and hear it in your voice.

You are not going to send a mass-produced copy of a proposal to hundreds of funding sources. You will have a tailored approach based on your research.

To locate funding sources that are interested in you and your proposal idea, compare your project to the funding source's interests. Different types of categories of funding sources have *distinct funding characterisitics.*

After your project has been redefined, you can begin to narrow down the search for the correct funding source. How do you know where to go, which type of funding source is the "right" one to approach? Since we know that certain factors predetermine how a funding source will "view the world," you must match or compare your proposal idea with those likely to be thought of by the funding source as *outstanding*—"just what they were looking for."

Look at each of the following types of marketplaces for your grant/contract before you spend time researching individual funding sources.

General Grants Marketplace Information

Twenty-five to 35 *billion* dollars is disseminated by the grants mechanism each year in the United States to 300,000 not-for-profit organizations (501-C3 Tax Exempt groups).

- The federal government disseminated 40 billion dollars in 1980, which went down in 1983 to 20–25 billion dollars, and is holding at this level for 1984.

- Foundations contributed 3.46 billion dollars in 1983, a 9.5 percent increase over 1982 (inflation was 3.4 percent). The year 1984 will show a similar tendency to keep pace with inflation.

- Corporations contributed 3.10 billion in 1983, a 5.1 percent increase over the 1982 total. 1984 will have similar increases.

The questions are:

- What proposals are best for each type of funding source?
- How do you find out about the grants?
- Which sources are best for your type of organization?
- How do you apply?

Government Agencies

From the general marketplace facts, you must look at government funding sources as your first choice for grant monies. While President Reagan has made budget cuts in federal programs, the federal government grants four times more money than foundations and corporations combined. A budget cut in federal programs by 15 percent does not eliminate them as prospects for grant seeking. Of much greater importance are the changes in how the federal government will disseminate the grant funds. Remember:

- The federal government is the largest single funding source in the world (20–25 billion/year).

- Many foundations and corporations will fund only those grant seekers who have exhausted the possibility of a federal grant.

- Reaganomics has forecast a decrease in direct federal grants to nonprofit organizations by 25 billion by 1985 (is this possible?).

What is the government's mechanism and current changes? The government has had some type of grants mechanism in place since the United States was founded. Reaganomics has had and will continue to have an effect on the availability of government funding. Most knowledgeable consultants have different opinions as to how much and how many programs the federal government can eliminate or pass on to the states and nonprofit organizations to carry out. But there is little doubt that the federal government cannot eliminate the federal role or responsibility relative to the grants mechanism.

There is a need for a national focus on research and demonstration projects. The waste and duplication that would result from delegating these responsibilities to the individual states are obvious to most politicians and bureaucrats. To return to the 1940s, when research was funded by foundations, can only be viewed by looking at the marketplace facts on dollars available. Foundations and corporations cannot afford to replace the National Science Foundation, National Cancer Institute, etc.

Most people would agree that balancing the federal budget at the expense of research dollars for our health problems— diabetes, heart disease, cancer, programs for the elderly, and the like—is not acceptable. All of the events of today's grants world should be viewed with:

- A historical perspective—How did we get to this place and time through the grants process?

- A future perspective—What will the changes in economics, population, age patterns, and the political scene bring to the grants marketplace?

Project Grants or Categorical Grants

These grant opportunities are designed to promote proposals within narrow government guidelines. They address a specific area with which a federal program is concerned, for example, drug-abuse prevention, nutrition education for the elderly, or research on certain types of disease. The government decides what problems need to be corrected and you, the prospective grantee, design an approach to solve or reduce the problems.

Project grants are given out by various agencies under congressionally authorized programs. Grants are awarded to the organizations that submit the best proposals that meet announced program guidelines. Most programs require outside review panels to evaluate the project. Because project design is left to the grant seekers, this has been the most popular kind of government grant. Since these grants fall under definite categories for funding, a whole series of categorical grants developed, with each grant category having its own federal office to administer it.

HISTORICAL PERSPECTIVE

Historically the government grants mechanism as we know it increased in usage the 1960s with the Kennedy and Johnson administrations. Most grants under their "New Frontier" and "Great Society" programs were administered on the federal level. Early programs were of the project-grant type and followed a definite categorical funding pattern. In the 1970s, however, there began a growing trend toward local and regional distribution of federal government grant dollars. This "New Federalism" or "Revenue Sharing" is a trend away from categorical grants to formula or block grants (explanation to follow). In practical terms, this shift means that under block grants, more local political considerations must be taken into account when applying for federal grant dollars. For this reason, it is often a good idea to get to know not only funding officials in Washington, but also in the state capital and regional government offices.

Government funding agencies using the categorical and project grants approach require grant seekers to fill out long, standardized applications. This makes it difficult, but not impossible, to tailor proposal contents to the needs of the granting agency. These applications differ in format from agency to agency, and are generally tedious, complicated, and time-consuming.

Once they are submitted, there is generally a long review process, staff review for mechanical details, and peer review of proposal content. Government grants require frequent reports and keeping accurate project records.

REAGANOMICS AND CATEGORICAL GRANTS

The categorical-grants funding mechanism has been attacked by Reaganomics. The current administration philosophy of "the government governs best—which governs least" does not support a federally controlled system of categories and project areas controlled by Washington bureaucrats. The administration's goal of cutting 25 billion grant dollars before 1985 has actually been fairly accurate. 1980 saw 40 billion dollars in federal grants, while 1983 and 1984 will see the grants mechanism dispense about 25 billion dollars each year.

Do not be deceived by the press and media. Some government granting programs actually have more grant funds in 1983 than they had in 1982. What it all boils down to is that *you must check out each federal granting program individually. Some are drastically affected or eliminated by the block grant concept; others have added funds.*

FUTURE PERSPECTIVE

The categorical funding mechanism has been repeatedly used to provide a mechanism to deal with societal problems. New diseases like AIDS (Acquired Immune Deficiency Syndrome) and societal problems will continue to encourage use of the categorical grants mechanism. (*Note:* 1983 has seen more grant set-asides for small business and profit-making organizations. A percentage of designated federal agencies' grants must go to these set-aside programs.)

Formula Grants

The term "formula grants" refers to granting programs under which funds are allocated according to a set of criteria (formula). This mechanism has been used to pump money into the economy; CETA (Comprehensive Employment Training Act) and the 1983 "jobs bill" are examples.

Criteria for allocation may be census data, unemployment figures, number of handicapped, veterans, and the like, that a state, city, or region may have.

The funds go through an intermediary, such as a state, city, or county government, before reaching the nonprofit groups. The formula grants mechanism is another example of the "New Federalism." While the general rules are developed at the federal level, the rules can be interpreted and local political input can considerably alter the federal program.

Block Grants

The block-grant concept is an extension of both the "New Federalism" and "Formula Grants" movements to shift the decision-making process on how to spend federal money to the local level. Over ninety categorical-grant programs have been combined into less than a dozen block grants. The philosophy is this: Why should the federal government tell a local government what it needs to spend its money on? In following the block-grant concept, federal work forces can be reduced since the criteria for funding are:
1. How much of the available categorical funding did each state receive in 1981?
2. Take the amount received and divide by total amount of funds available under that category of funding, thereby calculating each state's percentage.
3. Take each state's percentage and apply it to the current appropriation.
4. Send the money to the state with any criteria or limitations that still accompany the money.

This system requires far fewer workers than categorical funding with an office and staff for each program; for example, if your state applied for grant funds for teenage pregnancy in 1981, and received some, that would increase your percentage of available funds under the block grant for health. The advantage of this system is that it is simple for government to figure out who gets what, since they have all the records on grants awarded by category and address. Its disadvantages are as follows:

1. Grants going to a state in 1981 did not mean to a state agency, it meant to any nonprofit organization in that state who received federal funds. Yet the block grant goes to a designated state agency. This means that your state gets rewarded for everyone's efforts, but your organization may not get funded again under the state-controlled block grant.

2. The rules that govern the distribution of the block-grant funds allow states flexibility. One state's guidelines instruct grantees that:

a. 50 percent of all block-grant monies will go to state-affiliated agencies.

b. The remaining 50 percent will be distributed among eligible recipients. An eligible recipient is defined as a not-for-profit organization in that state. The fine print stipulates that state agencies and affiliates are eligible to apply for this 50 percent as well as the 50 percent set aside for them in the first guideline (above).

Contracts

In recent years the differences between a grant and a contract have become fewer and fewer. Indeed, after hours of negotiation with a Federal Agency on your grant, you may end up with a contract officer with whom you have to finalize your budget. The basic difference between a grant and a contract is that a contract tells you precisely what the government wants done and you bid on accomplishing that task. You must prove that you have the ability to perform the contract and the lowest price. There is decidedly less flexibility in creating the approach to the problem or work tasks with a contract than there is with a grant.

Contracts are publicized or advertised in a different way from grants. They are governed by different rules, and are awarded on a lowest-bid basis from those contractors deemed qualified to do the specified work.

The contracts "game" requires a track record and expertise. The best way to break into this marketplace is to identify a successful bidder and approach them as a possible subcontractor. This way, you gain experience, confidence, and contacts.

The statistics quoted in this chapter *do not* include the government contracts monies. The variety and number of government contracts are staggering. The amount of money that the government spends on contracts stretches the imagination. Recent exposés on the thousand-dollar-part that can be purchased in a hardware store for fifty cents are an indication of the problems of administering the contract estimates and the contractors.

There are several types of contracts including fixed cost, cost reimbursable, and those that allow the contractor to add on additional costs incurred during the contract. Contracts have been increasingly pursued by nonprofit groups in recent years. The problems that nonprofits encounter in bidding on contracts have been reduced through developing separate profit and nonprofit agencies to avoid problems or security agreements, academic freedom, patent, copyrights, and the like.

State Government Grants

With the current movement toward elimination of categorical grants and the shift to block grants to states, the state-government grants area has increased rapidly. This places grant funds closer to you, the ultimate recipient, requires less long-distance travel, and allows you to use your local politicians to make your case heard. These advantages are counterbalanced when you consider that states can now set their own priorities for the grants, add additional restrictions, and bring in to play a review system of state bureaucrats and more political appointees.

Under the new block grants, states are required to sponsor open meetings to allow individuals to comment on what priorities and problems should be addressed with the federal monies. While this rule went into effect in fiscal year 1982-83, it was suspended for one year owing to difficulties it would cause the states. Some states scheduled these open meetings, and others will have to comply in 1984. You should attend these hearings and testify to the needs and viewpoints your organization values. The state is not bound by federal law to listen to you or do anything other than hold these hearings. (*Note:* While states have their own monies, granting programs, and rules when utilizing block-grant monies from the federal government, the states guarantee that the eventual user of those funds will follow all the federal rules, circulars, compliances, etc.)

Sometimes this new system may prove a blessing, and other

times you may not fare well. Your choice is to influence the political process on the state level, or move to another state whose priorities are more in line with yours.

The Foundation Marketplace

There are approximately 21,967 private foundations in the United States with 48.2 billion dollars in assets. Though these figures may seem staggering to the novice grant seeker, there is some consolation in the following:

- 15 percent of the foundations (3,368) account for 92 percent of all assets.

- Approximately 15 percent or 3,368 foundations give 82 percent of all grants dollars awarded.

- The average grant size of a foundation with $20 to $100 million in assets is in the $20,000–$25,000 range.

- Only 32,165 grants for more than $5,000 were given last year by 465 foundations.

Therefore, a small percentage of the foundations have most of the assets and a relatively high average grant size. What about the other 20,000+ foundations? Consider: the remaining foundations have an average grant size of less than $2,000 and they award hundreds of thousands of grants each year.

Selecting the right foundation marketplace and requesting a logical grant size from a potential funder involve having knowledge of the types of foundations. Each type or category of foundation will be outlined with pertinent characterisitics described. At the end of this chapter, you will see how this information is utilized to develop an easy-to-use funding matrix. This matrix will serve as a convenient guide to which criteria will be valued for each type of the five basic classifications of foundations:

1. Community Foundations;
2. National Foundations (multipurpose);
3. "Special-Purpose" Foundations;

4. Family Foundations;
5. Corporate Foundations.

COMMUNITY FOUNDATIONS

This group of 300 foundations represents the newest and fastest growing area in the foundation marketplace. The main purpose of community foundations is to provide a grants mechanism to address problems and areas of interest that affect the geographic area the foundation was created to serve.

These foundations have no connection with the United Way fund drives and are not in competition with their neighboring United Way organizations. Actually, community foundations are frequent grantors to agencies supported by the United Way. While both groups seek to enrich the community and address its problems, the community foundations' usual mechanism for building their funding base is to establish endowments. In this way, local citizens can leave a bequest to the community foundation that will insure that the interest from the bequest stays in the community for which the individual has a concern. This way of developing assets is very different from the United Way approach of payroll deduction, cash contribution, and corporate solicitation. Their assets are approximately two billion dollars and are growing daily. As the name implies, these foundations are primarily interested in the local needs of their communities and have been designed to promote this limited geographic area. The primary beneficiary of community-foundation grants is the health area, followed by social welfare, education, and arts and culture.

Most community foundations have been initiated by public-spirited citizens who leave money in a bequest to the foundation for specific types of local projects. Since the monies are held separately for donor interests, the majority of this group are classified as public charities. The foundation can abide by donor wishes or reflect changes in the needs and interests of the community. The community foundation's reason to exist is to deal with local need. They will fund causes that other foundations would not think of funding. If your organization's purposes relate to local need, even last year's deficit can be fundable if it means keeping you in business. You can get funding for a needs assessment. You can approach these foundations with the argument that a good needs assessment will result in attracting monies from other sources to the community. Convince the community foundation that their needs-assessment grant will be responsible for all the funds that are generated from your higher-quality proposal. If you are not sure if there is a community foundation in your area, write:

The Council on Foundations
888 7th Avenue
New York, NY 10019

If the answer is no, get the council's book on how to start one in your area. Better than that, get a grant to start one. You will never be sorry and your community will benefit for many years—and you gain another prospective funding source.

The ten largest community foundations are:

		Assets
1.	San Francisco Foundation	$377,540,812
2.	New York Community Trust	$350,000,000
3.	Cleveland Foundation	$250,393,712
4.	Chicago Community Trust	$126,723,307
5.	Permanent Charity Foundation of Boston	$ 72,218,291
6.	Committee Foundation of Texas	$ 68,958,000
7.	St. Paul Foundation	$ 58,825,415
8.	Hartford Foundation for Public Giving	$ 59,203,545
9.	Pittsburgh Foundation	$ 62,003,570
10.	Columbus Foundation	$ 58,895,715

(*Note:* There are several community foundations that define "community" in a variety of geographic parameters; for example, the California Foundation and the Rhode Island Foundation use large state areas, and others use city limits.)

NATIONAL GENERAL-PURPOSE FOUNDATIONS

When you think of foundations, the names the Rockefeller Foundation and the Ford Foundation usually come to mind. Although these large foundations number only a few hundred, they have two-thirds of all assets among the 21,967 foundations and account for over 50 percent of the grant dollars. Some foundations in this group have a philanthropic interest in one or more subject areas, give across the United States, and have a general scope to their giving pattern and interests than most of the other types of foundations.

This group prefers proposals that have the potential to impact on a broader scale. They prefer model, creative, innovative projects that can demonstrate the way for other groups to replicate the approach and solve their problems. Since they like to promote change, they do not fund deficits, operating income, or the many necessary but not highly visible or creative functions of your organization.

SPECIAL-PURPOSE FOUNDATIONS

Several hundred foundations fall into the "special-purpose" category. How you define "special-purpose" could increase this number by thousands. For our definition, "special-purpose" includes those foundations whose funding record consistently supports a specific area of funding and their funding represents a significant contribution in that specific area. For example, the Robert Wood Johnson Foundation specializes in the health area. The key is to fit your group and project into the area of specialization. This group evaluates your request on the potential impact your grant will have on their special area of interest.

FAMILY FOUNDATIONS

There are 20,000+ foundations in this category. They are hard to categorize by interests, but represent the values of family groups or members. These family members may be living or those whose interests have been memorialized by creation of a foundation. Most family foundations have geographic preferences and may act as a small-scale, special-purpose foundation. Many are operated by family members who change their giving patterns and funding priority frequently.

This group of foundations is the most susceptible to the influence of board members, their friends, and popular "causes." Your ability to link your organization to "friends" of the foundation is very important to insure that your proposal at least receives attention. Since these foundations can and do change their priorities it is helpful to have a contact who keeps you informed about the current year's funding goals.

CORPORATE FOUNDATIONS

The number of corporations that utilize a corporate foundation to administer their charitable contributions and grants programs is increasing. While exact figures are unavailable, in a 1983 Conference Board survey of 467 companies, half reported having a foundation.

While much can be said about the role that a corporate foundation plays in comparison to regular corporate giving, the fact is recognized that the ability to develop and stabilize a corporate philanthropy program is enhanced through a corporate-foundation structure. In 1982, two-thirds of the corporate foundations donated more money than they received. The ability to utilize foundation assets in times of reduced corporate profits leads to a more uniform and stable approach to corporate social philanthropy than the "see-saw" effect of relying solely on a percentage of company profit.

Since corporate foundations are an extension of the profit-making company, they tend to view the world as any company would. Many fund grants only in areas where they have factories or a special interest in the community. The corporation must see a benefit in funding your project. Making the grant benefit the corporation, the workers, or the ability of the corporation to attract high-quality personnel to the community are some of the concerns that corporations may exhibit in making grant choices. In many cases, there is little difference between corporate giving and corporate-foundation giving. Some corporations make grants through both mechanisms.

CORPORATE PHILANTHROPY

There are over 2.3 million for-profit corporations in the United States. There are many misconceptions concerning the giving patterns of these corporations.

- Only 31 percent of the corporations make corporate contributions to nonprofit organizations.

- Of those that do contribute, less than 10 percent make grants of over $500 a year.

Careful selection of corporations is suggested to avoid the embarrassment that can be caused by asking for a grant from a corporation that has never given one, or has never granted one of the size you are requesting.

Corporations contributed $3.10 billion to nonprofit organizations in 1982. Inflation was approximately 3.4 percent in 1983. Corporate giving was up 5.1 percent. This increase occurred while corporate profits declined by 24.7 percent. This was the third year in a row that contributions were up and profits were down.

In 1981, corporations were allowed to give up to 5 percent of their pre-tax profits to charitable groups. The average was 1.24 percent of pre-tax net income for all American business. President Reagan has reduced federal grants by over $15 billion and appeared on nationwide television to appeal to corporations to pick up the humanities and arts programs. The reaction in industrial circles was, "Why should we pick up programs the government feels are not necessary?"

The lack of sensitivity to corporate giving by the Reagan administration was shown when the president raised the pre-tax allowable donation to 10 percent of pre-tax profits. The national average moved up from the 1981 figure of 1.24 percent to the 1982 figure of 1.69 percent (a new high). This is far from the allowable 5 percent of 1981 or the 10 percent of 1982.

WHY DO CORPORATIONS GIVE?

Corporations give for a variety of reasons:
1. Some give based on a feeling of social philanthropic responsibility.
2. Some give tax-exempt gifts of money and products to help themselves:
   - Buy improved relationships with employees, the community and the union.
   - Gain marketplace advantages through product research

opportunities and the positioning of products in lucrative areas.

Corporate giving can usually be described in a "this-for-that" syndrome. They purchase what they want. They do not usually give away money; they invest it. For example:

- Education received 36.7 percent of corporate contributions.

- Health and welfare received 33.6 percent.

- Arts and culture received 11.9 percent.

Corporations have a giving pattern that is related to the geographic concerns of their workers and factories. You can learn far more about their profitability and their contributions through purchasing a share or two of their stock, than in purchasing expensive books on corporate philanthropy. Ask your Chamber of Commerce for a list of the corporations in your area. They are listed by the number of employees. Select those companies you can relate to by programs that benefit workers or research that relates to their products.

To approach corporate funding sources, you must relate your request to:

- Help in attaining corporate goals: manpower training; availability of resources.

- Employee or management benefits: health programs; cultural programs; recreation facilities.

- Improvement of the environment around the corporation: programs that affect transportation, communication, ecology.

- Improved corporate image: better reputation in the community.

When you evaluate your potential for getting corporate grants, determine what these "returns on investment" are, and emphasize them in your presentations to corporate funding officials.

Another interesting aspect of corporate philanthropy is what might be called the "school of fish syndrome." Corporations do not like to be the first to fund a project. They are afraid to drift away from the protection of the "school of fish." They are extremely sensitive to what their competition is doing. This can work in favor of the successful grant seeker. Once one corporation gives you a grant, others will tend to follow (to be in the "school of fish"). In addition, if a corporation grants to another organization in your field, your chances of getting a grant from a competing corporation increase. Corporations do not want to be first to take a chance, but then again, they do not want to get left behind.

CORPORATIONS

Compared to foundations and government-granting agencies, corporations have very unstructured application procedures. Personal contact, crucial to success in any grant solicitation, is especially important here. Corporate grant seeking almost always involves personal contact, followed by a businesslike proposal, and completed through negotiation with decision-making executives. You must appeal to the business sense of every corporate grant maker you contact; always show them in concrete terms how their grant will benefit the firm.

Summary of Grants Marketplace

Now you have a basic idea of the type of funding sources that make up the grants marketplace. You need a *Time-Saving Tool* to help you select the correct marketplace and also to give you an idea of the strengths and weaknesses of your project as you approach each potential funding area.

You now know from the general description of the marketplace that the federal-grants area must be approached first. You must play the odds that favor the 22-billion-dollar marketplace. Do not forget to track the possible block grants down from the federal level to the local or state level.

The greater the potential for developing a model that impacts a large area or great number of people, the more interest you will generate from federal and state funding sources. After you have reviewed the funding potential with the government sources or you have found that you are ineligible for funding from these sources, you will want to try the private-sector marketplace.

The private-sector marketplace can be approached logically after utilizing the worksheet that follows. List your project on a copy of the worksheet and rate your project by how closely it meets the criteria for each type of funding.

PRIVATE-SECTOR SUPPORT

FOUNDATIONS/CORPORATIONS

Project Title: _____

	COMMUNITY FOUNDATION	NATIONAL FOUNDATION	SPECIAL PURPOSE	FAMILY FOUNDATION	CORPORATE SOURCES
"THE NEED"	Local needs only	National needs, widespread	Need in their "specialty"	Geographic concerns usually	Needs of workers or product concerns
"YOUR PROJECT METHODS"	No experiments – time tested, proven approaches	Unique, cost-effective	Viewed as special to this area	Depends on what the board likes	Proven safe project methods, more unique research protocols
YOUR FRIENDS -- CONTACTS WITH FUNDERS	Very important local contacts	Important	Important, especially in field of interest	Very important -- gives you hidden agenda	Very important -- gives money to those they trust
GRANTS EXPERIENCE	Credibility and need can overcome lack of experience	Important, like to work with others	Not as important as the potential contribution	Not critical	Important -- expect experience

PART TWO

Government Funding Sources

CHAPTER 10

Researching the Government Marketplace

Public funding, or government funding, is comprised of:

- *Federal funds:* grants and contracts that are received directly from federal agencies by your organization.

- *State funds:* These consist of: (a) state granting programs that distribute funds generated from state revenues other than federal revenue-sharing monies; and (b) state block grant programs that distribute federal revenue sharing and block grant funds.

- *County/borough and city funds:* these provide grants to your specific area. They consist of funds from the parking meter fund to pass through monies from state and federal government.

How do you research and track these funds? The worksheet entitled Federal Research Tools (pp. 66–67) outlines some of the more useful resources for locating these funds.

65

FEDERAL RESEARCH TOOLS

NAME	DESCRIPTION	WHERE TO GET IT	COST
Catalogue of Federal Domestic Assistance (212)275-3054	The official information on all government programs created by law. It does not mean funds have been appropriated. (See sample entry in Figure 10.1.)	Supt. of Documents, U.S. Government Printing Office, Washington, D.C. 20402	$32.00/yr.
Federal Assistance Program Retrieval System (FAPRS)	A retrieval system that uses key words to match with federal granting programs to give the user the CFDA programs that are related to the desired grants area. (See sample entry.)	Call your Congressperson and ask how to do a FAPRS search. *They may do it for you at no cost.	*
Federal Register (202)275-3054	Official news publication for the federal government; makes public all meetings, announcements of granting programs, regulations and deadlines. (See sample entry in Figure 10.2.)	Supt. of Documents, U.S. Government Printing Office, Washington, D.C. 20402	$300.00/yr.
U.S. Government Manual (202)275-3054	Official handbook of the federal government. Describes all federal agencies and gives names of officials. (See sample entry in Figure 10.3.)	Supt. of Documents, U.S. Government Printing Office, Washington, D.C. 20402	

FEDERAL RESEARCH TOOLS (Cont.)

NAME	DESCRIPTION	WHERE TO GET IT	COST
Agency Newsletters and Publications RFP's & Guidelines	Many federal agencies publish newsletters to inform you about the availability of funds and program accomplishments. You can receive application materials, requests for proposals. (See sample in Figure 12.1.)		Usually free
Federal Executive Telephone Directory (202)333-8620	Includes names, addresses, and phone numbers of federal government agencies and key personnel.	Federal Telephone Directory, 1058 Thomas Jefferson St., NW, Washington, D.C. 20013	$129.00/yr.
Commerce Business Daily (202)275-3054	The mechanism to announce the accepting of bids on government contracts. (See Figure 10.4.)	Supt. of Documents, U.S. Government Printing Office, Washington, D.C. 20402	$160.00/yr.
Congressional Record (202)275-3054	Day-to-day proceedings of the Senate and House of Representatives; includes all written information for the record. (All grant-program money appropriated by Congress)	Supt. of Documents, U.S. Government Printing Office, Washington, D.C. 20402	$218.00/yr.
Listings of Government Depository Libraries	Provides locations of large public and university libraries that receive government publications (e.g., CFDA).	Chief of the Library Department of Public Documents U.S. Government Printing Office, Washington, D.C. 20402	

Approaching Federal Funding

You need to keep in mind that grant seeking follows an orderly progression. You use your Pre-Proposal Review and Approval Form (p. 11) to begin your search for funding. From the idea and from your redefinition of your idea, you develop a list of key words to use in your search.

Since almost all federal funding documents use key words and subject areas as a way to find granting programs, use your redefinition sheets and the Federal Grants Research Form (pp. 69–70) to assist you.

As you look at examples of the research on federal and state funding sources, you will see that the information to complete these research sheets is readily available. Do not stop with the first few sources that sound or look good. Remember that you want the best funding source. Complete your research.

Federal Grants Research Form

Choosing a federal grant prospect requires persistence. Personal contacts must be made, gathered, and recorded. With even a few proposals, the information you were sure you would remember gets lost in the confusion.

The Federal Grants Research Form allows you to keep track of the grant programs you set out to investigate. Copy this form and pass out a sufficient number to your grants researchers so that your data gathering will be consistent and complete.

The key to providing your organization with federal funding is a combination of determination, hard work, and homework. The homework consists of systematic research, record keeping, and follow-up. There are several ways one can look at this research and record-keeping function:

1. If anything happens to you, your contacts and your projects will be able to live on.
2. As one grant seeker reported in a grants seminar, "The only way I can extort my unusually high salary is to keep all the

FEDERAL GRANTS RESEARCH FORM

Project Title _____ | Source
                                                          | & Date
CFDA # _____ Title _____ |

Federal Agency _____

Authorizing Legislation # _____

Information Contacts: Federal/State

Name _____ Title _____

Address _____

Telephone _____

Regulations/Guidelines   Sent for: _____ Rec'd: _____

Application Kit   Sent for: _____ Rec'd: _____

Restrictions that must be observed

_____

Eligibility _____

_____

Formula/Matching Requirements: _____

Past Years' Peer Reviewers   Sent for: _____ Rec'd: _____

Comments on Peer Reviewers Analyzed & Attached: _____

_____

List of Agency Grantees requested (date) _____

Rec'd: _____ Observations-type of recipient _____

_____

Financial Data: Obligation Levels

19____ $ _____   19____ $ _____

19____ $ _____   19____ $ _____

(Cont.)

research and contacts in my head. They pray that nothing happens to me back at my organization."

You can decide which of these two diverse approaches you prefer to side with.

FEDERAL GRANTS RESEARCH FORM (Cont.)

Trend: Up _____   Down _____   Stable _____ | Source |
                                                              | & Date |
        Average Grant Size $ _____   Grant Range _____ to_____| |____

Deadline Dates: 19 _____   19 _____

Number of Proposals Req'd: _____   Bound: _____

Time Frame for Decision: _____

_____

Record of Contacts About This Program:

Date	Our Person	Federal Contact	Outcomes

How to Use the Catalogue of Federal Domestic Assistance (CFDA)

STEP 1: LOOK AT THE INDEXES

- *Agency Program Index*—difficult to deal with; gives you code of types of funds each agency program funds.

- *Applicant Eligibility Index*—allows you to look up a program to see if you are an eligible applicant (you must know the program first; this is not a great help).

- *Deadline Index*—look up the deadline dates for programs to see if they have a multiple deadline system.

- *Functional Index*—programs can be divided by the function they provide in each program area.

- *Popular Name Index*—lists programs by common usage name (the name most often referred to by agencies and applicants); this is good to check when you don't find a federal program under what you thought its name was.

- *Subject Index*—this is the most commonly used index, since most people express their interests in this way (according to subject).

STEP 2

Using redefinition sheets and key words, look for programs that would be interested in your project idea. Briefly outline the best ones on research sheets. Be sure to write down the CFDA number that references the program. (Familiarize yourself with the Federal Grants Research Form and the following guidelines for "Reading the CFDA."

READING THE CFDA

Samples of the catalogue (see Fig. 10.1) have been selected to demonstrate the features of each program you have located through the indexes. In the first example, CFDA Number 45.128 PROMOTION OF THE HUMANITIES—PLANNING AND ASSESSMENT STUDIES PROGRAM, reader aides have been placed in the left margin. These numbers will not appear on any of the other ex-

FIGURE 10.1. Sample CFDA entries.

than 60 percent of the costs for Collaborative Projects and no more than 80 percent for Institutes for Teachers.

Length and Time Phasing of Assistance: A. Institutes for Teachers: Generally from one to three years. B. Collaborative Projects: At least two years. Funds must be expended during the grant period. Funds are released as required.

POST ASSISTANCE REQUIREMENTS:

Reports: Progress reports are required at least semi-annually. Reports on project expenditures are required quarterly. Final progress and expenitures reports are due within 90 days after completion or termination of project support by NEH.

Audits: Final audits may be made at the direction of the Chairman of the Endowment for up to 3 years after the grant period. In accordance with the provisions of Attachment P to Circular A-102, "Uniform Requirements for Grants to State and Local Governments," audits shall bemade of organizations carrying out this program at least once every two years. These audits will be made in accordance with the General Accounting Office guidelines, "Standards for Audit of Government Organizations, Programs, Activities and Functions," and additional OMB guidance.

Records: Any and all records and journals required for audit under generally accepted accounting systems must be retained for up to three years from the date of submission of the final expenditures report.

FINANCIAL INFORMATION:

Account Identification: 59-0200-0-1-503.

Obligations: (Grants) FY 82 $4,762,000; FY 83 est $4,790,000; and FY 84 est $4,355,000.

Range and Average of Financial Assistance: As appropriate to the scope and purposes of the project.

PROGRAM ACCOMPLISHMENTS: In fiscal year 1983, it is estimated that approximately 60 grants selected from 250 applications will be made, thereby benefiting 2,500 teachers and more than 200,000 students. In fiscal year 1984, it is estimated that about 55 grants will be awarded from about 250 applications.

REGULATIONS, GUIDELINES, AND LITERATURE: 45 CFR 1100 AND 1105. A program announcement and guidelines as well as a publication entitled, "Overview of Endowment Programs for 1982-83" are available upon request from the National Endowment for the Humanities, Room 409, Washington, DC 20506. Available from the Superintendent of Documents, U.S. Government Printing Office, Washington, DC 20402 are: The Endowment's official publication, "Humanities" by subscription (6 issues annually, $14.00 domestic, $17.25 foreign) and the Endowment's Seventeenth Annual Report - Fiscal Year 1982 ($9.50 domestic, $11.90 foreign).

INFORMATION CONTACTS:

Regional or Local Office: None.

Headquarters Office: Carolyn Reid-Wallace, Assistant Director, Instruction in Elementary and Secondary Schools, National Endowment for the Humanities, Room 302, Washington, DC 20506. Telephone: (202) 786-0373. Endowment staff should be sent preliminary appplicatons at least ten weeks in advance of final application deadline for eligibility review.

RELATED PROGRAMS: 45.111, Promotion of the Humanities—Exemplary Projects, Nontraditional Programs, and Teaching Materials; 45.150, Promotion of the Humanities—Central Disciplines in Undergraduate Education.

EXAMPLES OF FUNDED PROJECTS: (1) An award to the University of New Mexico for intensive graduate level study in Hispanic colonial civilization to 30 teachers and curriculum directors from Arizona and New Mexico. (2) A grant to Rutgers University for 60 high school English teachers to study in a graduate institution a number of classic and modern literary texts having themes which will assist them in planning their own classes. (3) The Missouri Historical Society received a grant to support a 15-month coperative project to work with a local university and area schools to develop ten history units emphasizing the relationship between local and national events. (4) The City University of New York was awarded NEH funds for a project to implement the study of Latin in the New York City elementary schools through teacher

training in Latin language and culture and development of a Latin curriculum for grades four, five and six. (5) The University of Virginia, under an NEH grant, offered a four-week summer institute for high school teachers on the meaning of the American Revolution and the "new political science" embodied in the Constitution; lecturer and discussions treated Locke, Montesquiew, Tocqueville, and the "Federalist Papers."

CRITERIA FOR SELECTING PROPOSALS: Proposals are read and evaluated on their promise for improving the teaching and learning of the humanities at the elementary and secondary level. Intelligence and imagination in conception, intellectual substance, thoroughness in planning, strength of staff, degree of commitment, involvement of participants, demonstration of need, and many other factors are considered. See the program guidelines for specific criteria.

45.128 PROMOTION OF THE HUMANITIES— PLANNING AND ASSESSMENT STUDIES PROGRAM

① **FEDERAL AGENCY:** NATIONAL ENDOWMENT FOR THE HUMANITIES, NATIONAL FOUNDATION ON THE ARTS AND THE HUMANITIES.

② **AUTHORIZATION:** National Foundation on the Arts and the Humanities Act of 1965; Public Law 89-209 as amended; 20 U.S.C. 951 et seq.

③ **OBJECTIVES:** To inform NEH's own planning and to be of assistance to other cultural and educational institutions by supporting research and development activities which: (1) gather basic information about conditions in the nation's educational cultural institutions and organizations; (2) articulate problems and suggest potential solutions for pressing policy issues affecting the vitality of the humanities; or (3) result in analytical tools for measuring the vitality of particular sectors or areas of the humanities or that enable key types of humanities groups, institutions, or organizations to assess more effectively their services and programs.

④ **TYPES OF ASSISTANCE:** Project Grants.

USES AND USE RESTRICTIONS: Assessment studies provide the humanities community, including NEH, with necessary information about needs and available programming.

⑤ **ELIGIBILITY REQUIREMENTS:**

Applicant Eligibility: Entities of State and local government, U.S. citizens and residents, U.S. profit and nonprofit organizations, and public and private academic institutions at all educational levels are eligible. Foreign institutions are not eligible and foreign nationals are also ineligible unless affiliated with a U.S. institution or organization, or a resident within the U.S. for three consecutive years prior to the time of application.

Beneficiary Eligibility: Same as Applicant Eligibility.

Credentials/Documentation: Costs will be determined in accordance with OMB Circular No. A-87 for entities of State and local government and OMB Circular No. A-21 for educational institutions.

⑥ **APPLICATION AND AWARD PROCESS:**

Preapplication Coordination: Preliminary inquiry to program office before submission of proposal is essential. OMB Circular No. A-102 applies for this program.

Application Procedure: Application forms will be made available if preliminary inquiry indicates basis for an application. This program is subject to the provisions of OMB Circular No. A-110.

Award Procedure: Applications are reviewed by experts in the subject area and other appropriate individuals. Awards are made by the Chairman of the National Endowment for the Humanities after recommendation by the National Council on the Humanities.

Deadlines: One annually. February 1 prior to NEH National Council meeting which convenes in May and August 1 prior to the NEH Council meeting in February. Special competitions are announced.

Range of Approval/Disapproval Time: Variable: average four months.

Appeals: None, but applicant may reapply with a revised proposal.

Renewals: Applications for renewal are processed as new applications.

ASSISTANCE CONSIDERATIONS:

Formula and Matching Requirements: Cost sharing by applicant institution is expected; 10 percent of grant funds as cost sharing is recommended.

Length and Time Phasing of Assistance: Funds must be expended during the grant period. Funds are released as required.

POST ASSISTANCE REQUIREMENTS:

Reports: Progress reports are required at least annually but no more frequently than quarterly. Reports on project expenditures are required quarterly. Final progress and expenditures reports are due within 90 days after completion or termination of project support by NEH.

Audits: As determined by the Endowment. In accordance with the provisions of Attachment P to Circular A-102, "Uniform Requirements for Grants to State and Local Governments" audits shall be made of organizations carrying out this program at least once every two years. These audits will be made in accordance with the General Accounting Office guidelines, "Standards for Audit of Government Organizations, Programs, Activities and Functions," and additional OMB guidance.

Records: To be retained by the grantee for three years from the date of submission of the final expenditures report.

FINANCIAL INFORMATION:

Account Identification: 59-0200-0-1-503.

Obligations: (Grants and Contracts) FY 82 $845,000; FY 83 est $730,000; and FY 84 est $700,000.

Range and Average of Financial Assistance: $3,000 to $150,000; $50,000.

PROGRAM ACCOMPLISHMENTS: During fiscal year 1982, 44 applications were received and eighteen planning and assessment studies were initiated. This includes a survey of State education agency policies affecting the humanities in elementary and secondary schools, the 1982 Survey of Earned Doctorates, and the Higher Education Panel, a rapid response survey system managed by the American Council on Education. Program emphases for fiscal year 1982 included: analyses of the humanities labor force, funding patterns in the humanities, the financial status of humanities institutions and trends in the demand for and usage of humanities resources. Program priorities for fiscal year 1983 include trends in financial support for the humanities; elementary and secondary and early undergraduate education in the humanities; the state of scholarly communication; and career patterns of individuals trained or employed in the humanities.

REGULATIONS, GUIDELINES, AND LITERATURE: 45 CFR 1100 and 1105. A program announcement and guidelines as well as a publication entitled, "Overview of Endowment Programs for 1982-83" are available upon request from the National Endowment for the Humanities, Room 409, Washington, DC 20506. Available from the Superintendent of Documents, U.S. Government Printing Office, Washington, DC 20402 are: The Endowment's official publication, "Humanities" by subscription (6 issues annually, $14.00 domestic, $17.25 foreign) and the Endowment's Seventeenth Annual Report - Fiscal Year 1982 ($9.50 domestic, $11.90 foreign).

INFORMATION CONTACTS:

Regional or Local Office: Not applicable.

Headquarters Office: Arnita Jones, Program Officer, Planning and Assessment Studies, Office of Planning and Policy Assessment, National Endowment for the Humanities, Room 402, Washington, DC 20506. Telephone: (202) 786-0420.

RELATED PROGRAMS: None.

EXAMPLES OF FUNDED PROJECTS: (1) A survey of state education agencies' policies affecting the teaching of the humanities in elementary and secondary schools. (2) A study of trends in the humanities at the nation's twoyear colleges. (3) A conference on cost-cutting measures that may be implemented by small humanities journals. (4) An on-going survey system based on a sample of the nation's colleges and universities which is used to gather information on current policy issues. (5) A study of adult education in the humanities.

CRITERIA FOR SELECTING PROPOSALS: Planning and Assessment Studies projects should meet the following criteria: (1) clearly relate to important information or policy concerns in the humanities; (2) employ research methods most appropriate to the nature of the inquiry; and (3) provide well-designed dissemination plans that will allow the project's findings to have maximum impact. Priority is given to those projects that effectively exploit available data resources.

45.129 PROMOTION OF THE HUMANITIES— STATE PROGRAMS

FEDERAL AGENCY: NATIONAL ENDOWMENT FOR THE HUMANITIES, NATIONAL FOUNDATION ON THE ARTS AND THE HUMANITIES

AUTHORIZATION: National Foundation on the Arts and Humanities Act of 1965; Public Law 89-209, as amended; 20 U.S.C. 951 et seq.

OBJECTIVES: To promote local humanities programming through renewable program grants to humanities councils within each of the 50 states, the District of Columbia and Puerto Rico for the purpose of regranting funds to local nonprofit organizations, institutions and groups. Under the provisions of Public Law 96-496, only one entity in each State may receive assistance as the State humanities group to administer this program.

TYPES OF ASSISTANCE: Project Grants.

USES AND USE RESTRICTIONS: Grants may be used to fund local and statewide humanities projects within the State, subject to guidelines determined by each State humanities council.

ELIGIBILITY REQUIREMENTS:

Applicant Eligibility: Nonprofit citizen councils in the several states which conform to the requirements of 20 U.S.C. 956(f). If the State matches a certain percentage of the Federal grant, the Governor may designate the existing Council as a State agency. The resulting agency becomes an eligible applicant.

Beneficiary Eligibility: Public and private nonprofit organizations, institutions, groups and individuals which apply directly to the State humanities council.

Credentials/Documentation: Submission of a plan and application from the applicant as outlined in 20 U.S.C. 956(f).

APPLICATION AND AWARD PROCESS:

Preapplication Coordination: Preliminary draft of proposal is requested.

Application Procedure: Filing of required plan from applicant and regular application for renewal of State committee funding. This program is subject to the provisions of OMB Circular No. A-110.

Award Procedure: Applications are reviewed by scholars in the humanities, public representatives, and other appropriate individuals. Awards are made by the Chairman of the National Endowment for the Humanities after recommendation by the National Council on the Humanities.

Deadlines: For existing citizen councils, May 1, 1984; for State agencies, September 1, 1984.

Range of Approval/Disapproval Time: Variable: average five months after deadline.

Appeals: Not applicable.

Renewals: Possible after systematic review.

ASSISTANCE CONSIDERATIONS:

Formula and Matching Requirements: Total matching of grant required.

Length and Time Phasing of Assistance: From 12 to 24 months. Funds must be expended during the grant period. Funds are released as required.

POST ASSISTANCE REQUIREMENTS:

Reports: Progress reports are required annually. Reports on project expenditures are required quarterly. Final progress and expenditures reports are due within 90 days after completion or termination of project support by NEH.

Fig. 10.1 (cont.)

Audits: As determined by the Endowment. In accordance with the provisions of Attachment P to Circular A-102, "Uniform Requirements for Grants to State and Local Governments," audits shall be made of organizations carrying out this program at least once every two years. These audits will be made in accordance with the General Accounting Office guidelines, "Standards for Audit of Government Organizations, Programs, Activities and Functions," and additional OMB guidance.

Records: To be retained by the grantee for three years from the date submission of the final expenditures report.

FINANCIAL INFORMATION:

Account Identification: 59-0200-01-503.

Obligations: (Grants) FY 82 $20,329,000; FY 83 est $20,329,000; and FY 84 est $15,990,000.

Range and Average of Financial Assistance: (FY 82) $318,000 to $811,000.

PROGRAM ACCOMPLISHMENTS: A singular achievement of the State Programs has been the establishment, in all 50 states, the District of Columbia and Puerto Rico, of 52 continuing institutions which have succeeded at serving as the link between the humanities and the interests and concerns of the States' citizens. Approximately 30,000 projects, with 10.3 million active participants, reached 200 million persons through the media and well over 30,000 scholars involved as project workers and council members indicate the wide public support for a program initiated to test means of bringing together scholarship in the humanities and the public. In fiscal year 1982, the programs reached over 25 million Americans and involved over 14,000 scholars in the 3,500 regrants it supported. Each State council sets its own guidelines for application categories to respond to the needs and resources in its State.

REGULATIONS, GUIDELINES, AND LITERATURE: 45 CFR 1100 and 1105. A program announcement and guidelines as well as a publication entitled "Overview of Endowment Programs for 1982-83" are available upon request from the National End,owment for the Humanities, Room 409, Washington, DC 20506. Available from the Superintendent of Documents, U.S. Government Printing Office, Washington, DC 20402 are: The Endowment's official publication, "Humanities" by subscription (6 issues annually, $14.00 domestic, $17.25 foreign) and the Endowment's Seventeenth Annual Report - Fiscal Year 1982 ($9.50 domestic, $11.90 foreign).

INFORMATION CONTACTS:

Regional or Local Office: Located in each State. Addresses available from National Endowment for the Humanities.

Headquarters Office: Donald Gibson, Director, Division of State Programs, National Endowment for the Humanities, Room 411, Washington, DC 20506. Telephone: (202) 786-0254.

RELATED PROGRAMS: 45.104, Promotion of the Humanities—Media Humanities Projects; 45.113, Promotion of the Humanities—Program Development; 45.115, Promotion of the Humanities—Youth Grants; 45.125, Promotion of the Humanities—Humanities Projects in Museums and Historical Organizations; 45.127, Promotion of the Humanities—Instruction in Elementary and Secondary Schools; 45.133, Promotion of the Humanities—Humanities, Science, and Technology; 45.151, Promotion of the Humanities—Summer Seminars for Secondary School Teachers.

EXAMPLES OF FUNDED PROJECTS: (1) The Louisiana Committee for the Humanities awarded a grant to Tulane University Law School in New Orleans for "The Civil Code--A Humanistic Appraisal," a major scholary conference and statewide series of community discussion programs which involved scholars from the disciplines of jurisprudence, linguistics, history, and philosophy in an analysis of Louisiana's unique legal system--the only state legal system derived from the Napoleonic Code. "Louisiana's Legal History," a follow-up project, was made possible by a state council grant to the Louisiana State Museum for a conference, interpretive publications and a traveling exhibit for the general public. (2) "History, Ethics, and Politics: A Conference Based on the Work of Hannah Arendt," was sponsored by Empire State College with funds from the New York Council for the Humanities. Arendt was the subject of a major retrospective which took place

in October 1981, six years after her death. Noted political theorists, philosophers, thinkers, and writers, from the United States, Europe, and Israel assessed Arendt's life and work.

CRITERIA FOR SELECTING PROPOSALS: Each state council sets its own guidelines and criteria for assessing proposals, which are widely disseminated within the state. The criteria for state council proposals to NEH are established in The National Foundation on the Arts and the Humanities Act of 1965, as amended, 20 U.S.C. Section 950 and 956 and by the NEH Division of State Programs.

45.130 PROMOTION OF THE HUMANITIES— CHALLENGE GRANTS PROGRAM

FEDERAL AGENCY: NATIONAL ENDOWMENT FOR THE HUMANITIES, NATIONAL FOUNDATION ON THE ARTS AND THE HUMANITIES

AUTHORIZATION: National Foundation on the Arts and Humanities Act of 1965; Public Law 89-209, as amended; 20 U.S.C. 951 et seq. Arts, Humanities and Cultural Affairs Act of 1976; Public Law 94-462.

OBJECTIVES: To support cultural institutions and organizations in order to increase NEH's financial stability and to sustain or improve the quality of humanities programs. Institutions must raise at least three dollars in new or increased donations from nonfederal sources to receive each Federal dollar.

TYPES OF ASSISTANCE: Project Grants.

USES AND USE RESTRICTIONS: Funds may be applied to a variety of institutional needs which an applicant has demonstrated serve both the humanities and an institution's long-term objectives. The major purpose of a Challenge Grant is to support fund-raising for building long-term capital resources. Expenditures of grant funds may include endowments or cash reserves, renovations and repairs, reduction or payment of cumulative debts, equipment purchases, acquisitions, and other costs attributable to humanities programs and activities.

ELIGIBILITY REQUIREMENTS:

Applicant Eligibility: Any nonprofit institution or organization working wholly or in part within the humanities may apply for a Challenge Grant. Such institutions include the following: two-year and four-year colleges; universities, museums, historical societies, research libraries; public libraries; advanced study centers; media organizations; university presses; professional societies; educational, cultural, or community groups. Local, county and State governments are eligible to apply on their own behalf or on behalf of nonprofit institutions, associations or organizations within their jurisdictions. Individuals and public and private elementary and secondary schools are not eligible to apply.

Beneficiary Eligibility: Same as Applicant Eligibility.

Credentials/Documentation: Certification of tax-exempt status is required.

APPLICATION AND AWARD PROCESS:

Preapplication Coordination: None required, but preliminary contact is strongly encouraged.

Application Procedure: Direct application to Challenge Grant Program, NEH. Application instructions and forms provided by Office of Challenge Grants upon receipt of general inquiry; prospective applicants should submit "notice of intent" to apply one month prior to application deadline.

Award Procedure: Applications are reviewed by staff for eligibility and by outside consultants with knowledge of the kinds of applicant institutions, and expertise in administration, financial and fundraising plans and schedules. Awards are made by the Chairman of the National Endowment for the Humanities after recommendation by the National Council on the Humanities.

Deadlines: Once a year. Next deadline June 1, 1983. Contact NEH Office of Challenge Grants for information.

Range of Approval/Disapproval Time: Variable: average six-eight months after deadline.

Appeals: None, but applicant may reapply with revised proposal.

Renewals: Not applicable.

ASSISTANCE CONSIDERATIONS:

Formula and Matching Requirements: Matching by a minimum of three times the grant amount, in new or increased non-Federal contributions.

Length and Time Phasing of Assistance: From one to three years. Funds must be expended during the grant period. Federal funds are released as matching amounts are certified to the Endowment and minimum matching requirements are met.

POST ASSISTANCE REQUIREMENTS:

Reports: Narrative progress reports are required annually; reports on non-Federal contributions, matching funds raised and sources of giving are required annually. Final progress and contributions reports are due within 90 days after completion or termination of grant support by NEH.

Audits: As determined by the Endowment. In accordance with the provisions of Attachment P to Circular A-102, "Uniform Requirements for Grants to State and Local Governments," audits shall be made of organizations carrying out this program at least once every two years. These audits will be made in accordance with the General Accounting Office guidelines, "Standards for Audit of Government Organizations, Programs, Activities and Functions," and additional OMB guidance.

Records: To be retained by the grantee for three years from the date of submission of the final progress and contributions report.

FINANCIAL INFORMATION:

Account Identification: 59-0200-0-1-503.

Obligations: (Direct Payments) FY 82 $20,736,000; FY 83 est $22,064,000; and FY 84 est $16,500,000.

Range and Average of Financial Assistance: $2,000 to $1,000,000 over three years (1.5 million in exceptional instances); $315,000 average.

PROGRAM ACCOMPLISHMENTS: In fiscal year 1982, 213 institutions received grant funds. In fiscal year 1983, approximately 183 institutions will receive grant funds. In fiscal year 1983, 84 awards were made out of a total of 247 applications received.

REGULATIONS, GUIDELINES, AND LITERATURE: 45 CFR 1100 and 1105. A program announcement and guidelines as well as a publication entitled, "Overview of Endowment Programs for 1982-83" are available upon request from the National Endowment for the Humanities, Room 409, Washington, DC 20506. Available from the Superintendent of Documents, U.S. Government Printing Office, Washington, DC 20402 are: The Endowment's official publication, "Humanities" by subscription (6 issues annually, $14.00 domestic, $17.25 foreign) and the Endowment's Seventeenth Annual Report - Fiscal Year 1982 ($9.50 domestic, $11.90 foreign).

INFORMATION CONTACTS:

Regional or Local Office: Not applicable.

Headquarters Office: Thomas S. Kingston, Office of Challenge Grants, Room 429, National Endowment for the Humanities, Washington, DC 20506. Telephone: (202) 786-0361.

RELATED PROGRAMS: None.

EXAMPLES OF FUNDED PROJECTS: (1) An historical society in Illinois is using its Challenge Grant to establish a development office to broaden its membership base in community support as well as business, corporate and foundation support. The society is also utilizing the grant to partially amortize the accumulated liabilities in its pension and endowment funds. (2) A college in Vermont is using its grant support to provide new strengths in the college's humanities disciplines, particularly in the expansion of Language, English Literature, and History programs and the creation of new endowments. New sources of giving from alumni, friends, foundations and corporations have added to the college's traditional pool of supporters to provide continuing support. (3) A state museum was awarded a grant to raise monies for the development of a museum association. The recently established museum on Tennessee history and culture will now be able to hire a public relations director and provide for needed equipment and storage facilities. (4) An historical library and museum in Delaware received a grant for capital improvements, including new storage facilities for archival research collections and energy conservation measures. Funds will also be used for special self-help and out-reach programs, including the increase and consolidation of new sources of financial support, the completion of an operational efficiency study and the expansion of various humanities programs.

CRITERIA FOR SELECTING PROPOSALS: To form decisions about funding, all reviewers of Challenge Grants applications must judge the existing and potential quality of the applicant's programs, needs, management, and fund-raising. In light of the goals of the Challenge Grants Program, reviewers assess each application in accordance with the following six questions: 1. Within the context of the organizations's or institution's mission, audience, and interpretive philosophy, what is the ability to sustain or attain a high level of quality for programs and activities within the humanities? 2. What is the likely long-term of a Challenge Grant upon the quality of the applicant's programs, resources, and services within the humanities? 3. Is there a demonstration of financial and programmatic need for a Challenge Grant in light of the applicant's experience, objectives, and priorities? 4. To what extent does the proposal reflect effective long-range planning about the programs, finances, and management? 5. What is the likely impact of a Challenge Grant upon the applicant's financial stability and capability to use resources more efficiently? 6. What is the probability that the fund-raising plan will prove successful and will develop sources likely to continue contributing beyond the grant period?

45.132 PROMOTION OF THE HUMANITIES— RESEARCH MATERIALS: PUBLICATIONS

FEDERAL AGENCY: NATIONAL ENDOWMENT FOR THE HUMANITIES, NATIONAL FOUNDATION ON THE ARTS AND THE HUMANITIES

AUTHORIZATION: National Foundation on the Arts and Humanities Act of 1965; Public Law 89-209 as amended; 20 U.S.C. 951 et seq.

OBJECTIVES: To ensure through grants to publishing entities the dissemination of works of scholarly distinction that without support could not be published.

TYPES OF ASSISTANCE: Project Grants (Contracts).

USES AND USE RESTRICTIONS: Awards are made to presses to offset deficits incurred in the publication of materials of significance from all fields of the humanities. Although the program was initiated to help ensure the publication of volumes whose preparation had been supported previously by NEH grants, applications will currently be accepted from a press for the support of up to two works per year whose research or preparation was not aided by earlier grants from NEH. Grants are limited to $10,000 per individual volume and no more than $30,000 during a single fiscal year to any publisher. Subventions take into account plant, paper, printing, binding, and overhead costs, but generally exclude royalties paid to authors.

ELIGIBILITY REQUIREMENTS:

Applicant Eligibility: Nonprofit and commercial presses.

Beneficiary Eligibility: Same as Applicant Eligibility.

Credentials/Documentation: For entities of State and local government, costs will be determined in accordance with OMB Circular No. A-87 and OMB Circular A-21 for educational institutions.

APPLICATION AND AWARD PROCESS:

Preapplication Coordination: After individual program guidelines have been received, brief descriptions of proposed projects should be submitted to determine eligibility and competitiveness at least eight weeks prior to formal application. The standard application forms as furnished by the Federal agency and required by OMB Circular No. A-102 must be used for this program.

Application Procedure: Direct application to Research Resources: Publications, Division of Research Programs, Room 319. NEH application instructions provided upon receipt of initial inquiry outlining eligible project. This program is subject to the provisions of OMB Circular No. A-110.

Award Procedure: Applications are reviewed by panels of scholars and publishers. Awards are made by the Chairman of the Endow-

Fig. 10.1 (cont.)

ment upon recommendation by the National Council for the Humanities.

Deadlines: Twice a year, November 1 and May 1. Write to Margot Backus, Program Officer, Publications Program, Division of Research Programs, Room 319, NEH, Washington, DC 20506. Telephone: (202) 786-0204.

Range of Approval/Disapproval Time: Approximately five months.

Appeals: None, but applicant may reapply with a revised proposal.

Renewals: Publishers of multi-volume series may reapply for different volumes, but renewed funding for the same project would only occur for separate volumes of a multi-volume series.

ASSISTANCE CONSIDERATIONS:

Formula and Matching Requirements: Press must support all but deficit for which subsidy is requested.

Length and Time Phasing of Assistance: On the average, 18 months. Funds released as required, and must be expended during grant period.

POST ASSISTANCE REQUIREMENTS:

Reports: Progress reports are required annually if the project extends over 18 months. Reports on project expenditures are required quarterly. Final progress and expenditures reports are due within 90 days after completion or termination of project support by NEH.

Audits: As determined by the Endowment. In accordance with the provisions of Attachment P to Circular A-102, "Uniform Requirements for Grants to State and Local Governments," audits shall be made of organizations carrying out this program at least once every two years. These audits will be made in accordance with the General Accounting Office guidelines, "Standards for Audit of Government Organizations, Programs, Activities and Functions," and additional OMB guidance.

Records: Any and all records and journals required for audit under generally accepted accounting systems should be retained for a period of three years from the date of submission of the final expenditures report.

FINANCIAL INFORMATION:

Account Identification: 59-0200-0-1-503.

Obligations: (Grants) FY 82 $400,000; FY 83 est $400,000; and FY 84 est $400,000.

Range and Average of Financial Assistance: $2,000 to $10,000; $5,000 (per volume).

PROGRAM ACCOMPLISHMENTS: In fiscal year 1982, the program received 135 proposals of which 83 were funded.

REGULATIONS, GUIDELINES, AND LITERATURE: 45 CFR 1100 and 1105. A program announcement and guidelines as well as a publication entitled, "Overview of Endowment Programs for 1982-83" are available upon request from the National Endowment for Humanities, Room 409, Washington, DC 20506. Available from the Superintendent of Documents, U.S. Government Printing Office, Washington, DC 20402 are: The Endowment's Official publication, "Humanities" by subscription (6 issues annually, $14.00 domestic, $18.25 foreign) and the Endowment's Seventeenth Annual Report - Fiscal Year 1982 ($9.50 domestic, $11.90 foreign).

INFORMATION CONTACTS:

Regional or Local Office: None.

Headquarters Office: Jeffrey Field, Assistant Director, Division of Research Programs for Research Resources, Room 319, National Endowment for the Humanities, Washington, DC 20506. Telephone: (202) 786-0204.

RELATED PROGRAMS: 45.145, Promotion of the Humanities—Research Materials/Tools and Reference Works; 45.146, Promotion of the Humanities—Research Materials/Editions; 45.147, Promotion of the Humanities—Research Materials/Translations; 45.140, Promotion of the Humanities—Basic Research; 45.142, Promotion of the Humanities—Fellowships for Independent Study and Research; 45.143, Promotion of the Humanities—Fellowships for College Teachers.

EXAMPLES OF FUNDED PROJECTS: (1) A university press in Maryland received a subvention grant to make possible the publication of a study of the American Revolution and political society

in New York from 1760 to 1790, which was awarded the 1982 Bancroft Prize. (2) A press in California received assistance in the publication of a facsimile edition of the Shakespeare Quartos at the Huntington library. (3) A press in Minnesota was awarded a grant to help publish a study of Scandinavian accentology by a Russian linguist in the United States. (4) A foundation in New York state received a grant to help publish the sketch books of the architect Le Corbusier. (5) A press in Philadelphia was awarded a grant for the publication of a social history of black immigrants in San Francisco at the turn of the century.

CRITERIA FOR SELECTING PROPOSALS: The significance and quality of the finished work; the perceived contribution of the work to knowledge in the humanities; the soundness of the publisher's budget and marketing plan.

45.133 PROMOTION OF THE HUMANITIES— HUMANITIES, SCIENCE, AND TECHNOLOGY

FEDERAL AGENCY: NATIONAL ENDOWMENT FOR THE HUMANITIES, NATIONAL FOUNDATION ON THE ARTS AND THE HUMANITIES

AUTHORIZATION: National Foundation on the Arts and Humanities Act of 1965; Public Law 89-209 as amended; 20 U.S.C. 951 et seq.

OBJECTIVES: To support a limited number of projects which will serve as central references in the sciencevalues field, or as models of scientist-humanist collaboration, and to support Inter-disciplinary Incentive Awards to scientists and humanists involved in humanities projects involving science and technology.

TYPES OF ASSISTANCE: Project Grants (including individual awards).

USES AND USE RESTRICTIONS: Most preliminary inquiries are referred for funding consideration by an appropriate divisional program of the Endowment, or by the Ethics and Values in Science and Technology Program of the National Science Foundation (NSF). (Projects approved through the NSF Program are subsequently considered for joint support through the Endowment Program. Approved Individual Awards are jointly supported by NSF and NEH).

ELIGIBILITY REQUIREMENTS:

Applicant Eligibility: Entities of State and local government, U.S. citizens and residents, U.S. nonprofit organizations, and academic institutions are eligible. Foreign institutions are not eligible and foreign nationals are also ineligible unless affiliated with a U.S. institution or organization, or a resident within the U.S. for 3 consecutive years prior to the time of application.

Beneficiary Eligibility: Same as Applicant Eligibility.

Credentials/Documentation: Costs will be determined in accordance with OMB Circular No. A-87 for entities of State and local government and OMB Circular No. A-21 for educational institutions.

APPLICATION AND AWARD PROCESS:

Preapplication Coordination: Preliminary inquiry to program office before submission of proposal is essential for project grants. The standard application forms as furnished by the Federal agency and required by OMB Circular No. A-102 must be used for this program.

Application Procedure: Application forms will be made available if preliminary inquiry indicates basis for an application. This program is subject to the provisions of OMB Circular No. A-110.

Award Procedure: Applications are reviewed by experts in the subject area and other appropriate individuals. Awards are made by the Chairman of the National Endowment for the Humanities after recommendation by the National Council on the Humanities.

Deadlines: Deadlines for preliminary proposals to be considered for joint NSF/NEH project support are January 2, May 1, and September 1; for formal proposals, deadlines are April 1, August 1, and December 1. The deadline for proposals for NEH funding only is February 1.

Range of Approval/Disapproval Time: Variable: from four to nine months.

Appeals: None, but applicant may reapply with a revised proposal.
Renewals: Applications for renewal of Project Grants are processed as new applications.

ASSISTANCE CONSIDERATIONS:
Formula and Matching Requirements: Significant cost sharing by applicant institution is encouraged for Project Grants.
Length and Time Phasing of Assistance: Funds must be expended during the grant period. Funds are released as required.

POST ASSISTANCE REQUIREMENTS:
Reports: Progress reports are required at least annually but no more frequently than quarterly. Final progress and expenditures reports are due within 90 days after completion or termination of project support by NEH.
Audits: As determined by the Endowment. In accordance with the provisions of Attachment P to Circular A-102, "Uniform Requirements for Grants to State and Local Governments," audits shall be made of organizations carrying out this program at least once every two years. These audits will be made in accordance with the General Accounting Office guidelines, "Standards for Audit of Government Organizations, Programs, Activities and Functions," and additional OMB guidance.
Records: To be retained by the grantee for three years from the date of submission of the final expenditures report.

FINANCIAL INFORMATION:
Account Identification: 59-0200-0-1-503.
Obligations: (Grants) FY 82 $807,000; FY 83 est $850,000; and FY 84 est $500,000.
Range and Average of Financial Assistance: $15,000 to $300,000; $100,000.
PROGRAM ACCOMPLISHMENTS: In fiscal year 1982, the program jointly funded 22 projects through the Ethics and Values in Science and Technology (EVIST) program of NSF. The amount of the NEH contribution to these grants was $807,490. For fiscal year 1983, it is anticipated that there will be approximately $850,000 of such joint funding.
REGULATIONS, GUIDELINES, AND LITERATURE: 45 CFR 1100 and 1105. A program announcement and guidelines as well as a publication entitled "Overview of Endowment Programs for 1982-83" are available upon request from the National Endowment for the Humanities, Room 409, Washington, DC 20506. Available from the Superintendent of Documents, U.S. Government Printing Office, Washington, DC 20402 are: The Endowment's official publication "Humanities" by subscription (6 issues annually, $14.00 domestic, $17.25 foreign) and the Endowment's Seventeenth Annual Report - Fiscal Year 1982 ($9.50 domestic, $11.90 foreign).
INFORMATION CONTACTS:
Regional or Local Office: Not applicable.
Headquarters Office: David E. Wright, Program Officer, Division of Research Programs, National Endowment for the Humanities, Room 319, Washington, DC 20506. Telephone: (202) 786-0207.
RELATED PROGRAMS: 45.116, Promotion of the Humanities—Summer Seminars for College Teachers; 45.121, Promotion of the Humanities—Summer Stipends; 45.124, Promotion of the Humanities—Research Resources—Organization and Improvement Grants; 45.125, Promotion of the Humanities—Humanities Projects in Museums and Historical Organizations; 45.129, Promotion of the Humanities—State Programs; 45.130, Promotion of the Humanities—Challenge Grants Program; 45.132, Promotion of the Humanities—Research Materials: Publications; 45.135, Promotion of the Humanities—Youth Projects; 45.140, Promotion of the Humanities—Basic Research; 45.142, Promotion of the Humanities—Fellowships for Independent Study and Research; 45.143, Promotion of the Humanities—Fellowships for College Teachers; 45.145, Promotion of the Humanities—Research Materials/Tools and Reference Works; 45.146, Promotion of the Humanities—Research Materials/Editions; 45.147, Promotion of the Humanities—Research Materials/Translations; 47.053, Scientific, Technological, and International Affairs.
EXAMPLES OF FUNDED PROJECTS: Five projects previously jointly funded by NEH through the NSF EVIST program are as follows: (1) A college in Kentucky - To prepare a bibliography on

philosophy of technology. (2) A university in Delaware will continue comparative analysis of philosophical accounts of the role of technology in society and will establish related collaborative research efforts in four science-related colleges of the university. (3) An institute of technology in Illinois - To prepare a bibliography of engineering ethics. (4) A university in Massachusetts - To conduct an epistemological study of the controversy over risks and benefits of Recombinant DNA research. (5) A university and a community organization in Washington State will collaborate in scholarly research on the value assumptions of two technical research efforts involved in recent policy decisions and will follow up with public workshops on the role of technical expertise in the formation of public policy.
CRITERIA FOR SELECTING PROPOSALS: In addition to general criteria on significance of subject matter, soundness of project design, and qualifications of personnel, there is particular emphasis on collaboration of scientists, engineers, and physicians with scholars in fields such as history, literature, philosophy, ethics and jurisprudence, in addressing ethical issues related to developments in science, technology and medicine.

45.134 PROMOTION OF THE HUMANITIES— RESEARCH CONFERENCES

FEDERAL AGENCY: NATIONAL ENDOWMENT FOR THE HUMANITIES, NATIONAL FOUNDATION ON THE ARTS AND THE HUMANITIES
AUTHORIZATION: National Foundation on the Arts and Humanities Act of 1965; Public Law 89-209 as amended; 20 U.S.C. 951 et seq.
OBJECTIVES: To support conferences, symposia, and workshops which enable scholars to discuss and advance the current state of research on a particular topic or to consider directions in which research in a given field should move.
TYPES OF ASSISTANCE: Project Grants.
USES AND USE RESTRICTIONS: Grants support the basic costs of symposia, scholarly workshops, or conferences, including released time for principal investigator(s), research/administrative assistance, honoraria, travel, and per diem for invited participants, duplication costs, office supplies, and publicity. Costs of permanent equipment and long-term operating expenses are not allowable; support for post-project, pre-publication costs are acceptable as requests for released time and research/administrative assistance only (see also 45.132, Promotion of the Humanities—Research Publications). The program supports basic research in the humanities that is interdisciplinary, evaluative, interpretive, experimental, comparative, or coordinative. Projects must address research questions or assess research methodologies. Note: This program is differentiated from the Basic Research Program -- 45.140 --in that it encourages and supports conference work, symposia and other workshops which are not included in that program. It seeks thereby to encourage and to support the open discussion and public dissemination of ideas of either a general or specific nature necessary to the understanding and enlargement of one or more disciplines of the humanities.

ELIGIBILITY REQUIREMENTS:
Applicant Eligibility: U.S. citizens and residents, U.S. nonprofit organizations, local governments, and academic institutions are eligible. Foreign institutions or organizations are not eligible, and foreign nationals are also ineligible unless affiliated with a U.S. institution or organization or a resident within the U.S. for 3 consecutive years prior to the time of application.
Beneficiary Eligibility: Same as Applicant Eligibility, except that foreign scholars may have their expenses paid to a conference funded under this program.
Credentials/Documentation: Costs will be determined in accordance with OMB Circular No. A-87 for entities of State and local government and OMB Circular No. A-21 for educational institutions.

amples that follow, nor will they appear in the actual CFDA document.

1. *Federal Agency:* This is the branch of the government administering the program—not much help to you, except as general knowledge or for looking up program and agency in the U.S. Government Manual.

2. *Authorization:* You need this information to fill out some program applications or to look up the testimony and laws creating the funding (for the "hard-core" researcher and grant seeker only).

3. *Objectives:* Good to review these general program objectives to compare to your project. Don't give up if you are off the mark slightly—contact with the funding source may uncover new programs, changes, or hidden agendas.

4. *Types of Assistance:* Good to review and record the general type of support from this source and compare to your project redefinition.

5. *Eligibility Requirements:* Review this section to be sure your organization is designated as a legal recipient. If it's not—find the type that is designated and apply as a consortium or cooperative agreement.

6. *Application and Award Process:* This information should be reviewed and recorded on your Research Worksheet. Don't let the deadline data bother you—if the award cycle has passed you should still contact the agency and position yourself for next year with (a) copies of old application; (b) list of current grantees; (c) a request to be a reviewer.

7. *Assistance Considerations:* Record information on the match you are required to provide. This will be useful in evaluating which funding sources you will apply to as well as assisting you in developing your project planner to see what you can donate or match from your organization.

8. *Financial Information:* This information is useful for seeing what funds the agency program *may* have received. Don't take this as the last word. One entry recently said they had 3 million dollars

for research. When contacted, they had over 30 million dollars to disseminate under this program and similar ones not in CFDA.

9. *Regulations, Guidelines, and Literature:* Record and send for any information you can get on the funder.

10. *Information Contacts:* Record and use to begin the steps outlined in this book on contacting funders. Note name of contact person and phone number. While the person or number may change, you at least have a place to start.

11. *Related Programs:* In some CFDA entries the government may suggest other programs that are similar or related to your area of interest. While these are usually obvious and programs your research may have already uncovered, review them for leads.

12. *Criteria For Selecting Proposals:* While this may appear after related programs or examples of funded projects, your best choice is to review and record but go on to get rules printed in *Federal Register* or get from reviewers.

STEP 3

You will then select the best government funding program (see the Prospect Analysis Form, Chapter 12).

STEP 4

You will contact the federal agency by using the contact person listed under information contacts (#10 above).

The Federal Assistance Programs Retrieval System (Enhanced Version)

The Federal Assistance Program Retrieval System (FAPRS) is a computerized question-answer system that is designed to provide rapid access to federal domestic assistance program information. The system provides information on federal programs that meet the development needs of the applicant and for which the applicant meets basic eligibility criteria. Program information provided by FAPRS is determined from input supplied by the requestor. Input required includes the name of the state, county, city, town, or federally designated Indian tribe for which program information is requested; the population of the city or town; the type of applicant (e.g., state or local governments, federally designated Indian tribes, nonprofit organizations, small businesses, or individuals), the type of assistance under which programs are administered (e.g., grants, loans); and the specific functional categories and subcategories of interest. Based upon the input supplied by the requestor, the output provided by FAPRS consists of: (1) a list of program numbers and titles: (2) the full text of selected programs: or (3) specific sections of the program text.

As originally developed by the Department of Agriculture, FAPRS was designed to aid small, rural, isolated communities unfamiliar with federal assistance programs or unable to locate federal aid programs that have the greatest funding potential. FAPRS has been developed based on the requirements for federal information systems. The following features have been incorporated into the new FAPRS system:

1. Expansion of functional categories and subcategories. As listed in the Functional Index and the catalogue, the enhanced version of FAPRS uses 20 functional categories and 176 subcategories to specify an area of interest.
2. Expansion of the applicant eligibility specification to include twelve government-related and 10 non-government-related applicant types.
3. Specification of the type(s) of assistance desired as one of the search criteria. At present, the catalogue lists up to fifteen types of assistance provided by federal programs.
4. Display of definitions for functional subcategories, applicant types, and types of assistance.
5. Selection of specific sections of catalogue text to be displayed.
6. Formatted display of federal circular coordination requirements for a selected list of programs.

States have designated access points where FAPRS searches may be requested. In addition, bulletins on FAPRS are available from the system to inform users of the addition or deletion of programs, changes to program numbers from one edition of the catalogue to the next, and enhancements and changes to the system. For further information on FAPRS, the location of the nearest state access point, or a list of the time-sharing companies from which interested persons may arrange for direct access to the system, write to the Office of Management and Budget, Budget Review Division, Federal Program Information Branch, Washington, D.C. 20503. Your congressperson will be able to assist you in locating where you can obtain a FAPRS search in your area.

The Federal Register

The *Federal Register* is the newspaper of the federal government. In order for the government to make legal notices on a great variety of federal issues, it must publish notices in the *Federal Register*.

Areas that must be published in the *Federal Register* in the grants area are the creation of new government granting programs and the rules governing both new and old programs. The rules to evaluate the proposal are also printed. The following points will help you in reading the sample entry in Figure 10.2.

1. *Highlights:* this gives you an overview of the contents of today's *Federal Register.* You can skim this and see if you need to read the specific parts for their applicability to your grants area.
2. *Federal Register Purposes and Prices.*
3. *Contents:* this is a detailed accounting of what is in the *Federal Register.*
4. *Reader Aids:* describes services and phone numbers under services. (*Note:* Public Briefings: "The Federal Register and How To Use It." The government sponsors classes around the United States and in Washington D.C. on how to read and understand the *Federal Register.* Call the phone number listed to find the nearest class and plan to attend one.)
5. *CFR Parts Affected during Past Month:* this will help you if you are keeping track of the changes that affect the Code of Federal Regulations.
6. *Reminders:* deadlines of comments; if you want to skim what rules you may want to comment on, this can be a help.

FIGURE 10.2   A sample of *The Federal Register*.

3-27-84
Vol. 49   No. 60
Pages 11615-11798

Tuesday
March 27, 1984

---

① **Selected Subjects**

Air Carriers
Civil Aeronautics Board

Air Pollution Control
Environmental Protection Agency

Authority Delegations (Government Agencies)
Agriculture Department

Aviation Safety
Federal Aviation Administration

Banks, Banking
Federal Reserve System

Cargo Vessels
Customs Service

Electric Utilities
Rural Electrification Administration

Employment
Wage and Hour Division

Energy Conservation
Conservation and Renewable Energy Office

Fisheries
National Oceanic and Atmospheric Administration

Freedom of Information
Justice Department
Peace Corps

Grant Programs—Education
Human Development Services Office

CONTINUED INSIDE

II   **Federal Register** / Vol. 49, No. 60 / Tuesday, March 27, 1984 / Selected Subjects

Selected Subjects

FEDERAL REGISTER Published daily. Monday through Friday. (not published on Saturdays, Sundays, or on official holidays), by the Office of the Federal Register, National Archives and Records Service, General Services Administration, Washington. D.C. 20408, under the Federal Register Act (49 Stat. 500, as amended; 44 U.S.C. Ch. 15) and the regulations of the Administrative Committee of the Federal Register (1 CFR Ch. I). Distribution is made only by the Superintendent of Documents, U.S. Government Printing Office, Washington, D.C. 20402.

The **Federal Register** provides a uniform system for making available to the public regulations and legal notices issued by Federal agencies. These include Presidential proclamations and Executive Orders and Federal agency documents having general applicability and legal effect, documents required to be published by Act of Congress and other Federal agency documents of public interest. Documents are on file for public inspection in the Office of the Federal Register the day before they are published, unless earlier filing is requested by the issuing agency.

The **Federal Register** will be furnished by mail to subscribers for $300.00 per year, or $150.00 for six months, payable in advance. The charge for individual copies is $1.50 for each issue, or $1.50 for each group of pages as actually bound. Remit check or money order, made payable to the Superintendent of Documents, U.S. Government Printing Office, Washington D.C. 20402.

There are no restrictions on the republication of material appearing in the **Federal Register**.

Questions and requests for specific information may be directed to the telephone numbers listed under INFORMATION AND ASSISTANCE in the READER AIDS section of this issue.

Highways and Roads
  Federal Highway Administration

Marketing Agreements
  Agricultural Marketing Service

Mortgage Insurance
  Housing and Urban Development Department

Motor Carriers
  Interstate Commerce Commission

Oil and Gas Reserves
  Land Management Bureau

Radio Broadcasting
  Federal Communications Commission

Surface Mining
  Surface Mining Reclamation and Enforcement Office

Television Broadcasting
  Federal Communications Commission

84   THE "HOW TO" GRANTS MANUAL

Fig. 10.2   (cont.)

Contents

Federal Register

Vol. 49, No. 60

Tuesday, March 27, 1984

Fig. 10.2 (cont.)

Federal Register / Vol. 49, No. 60 / Tuesday, March 27, 1984 / Contents V

Internal Revenue Service
PROPOSED RULES
Income taxes:
11684 DISC income; shareholder taxation; correction

International Development Cooperation Agency
See Agency for International Development.

International Trade Administration
NOTICES
Export privileges, action affecting:
11698 McVey, Charles J., Jr., et al.
11697 Export trade certificates of review: applications

International Trade Commission
NOTICES
11746 Meetings; Sunshine Act (2 documents)

Interstate Commerce Commission
PROPOSED RULES
Motor carriers:
11693 Commercial zones; Houston, Tex.
NOTICES
Railroad operation, acquisition, construction, etc.:
11726 Southern Railway Co. et al.

Justice Department
See also Antitrust Division; National Institute of Justice; Parole Commission.
RULES
11624 Freedom of Information Act; implementation
NOTICES
Pollution control; consent judgments:
11726 Northland Gold Dredging, Ltd.

Labor Department
See also Wage and Hour Division.
NOTICES
Meetings:
11730 Trade Negotiations and Trade Policy Labor Advisory Committee

Land Management Bureau
RULES
Oil and gas leasing:
11636 Mineral leases changing collection process; amendment
NOTICES
Exchange of public lands for private land:
11721 Montana
Management framework plans, etc.
11722 New Mexico
Meetings:
11722 Montrose District Grazing Advisory Board
11723 Phoenix District Advisory Council
Oil and gas leases:
11723 Wyoming
Recreation management restrictions, etc.:
11722 Steens Mountain Recreation Plan, Oreg.
Sale of public lands:
11721 Colorado
11720 South Dakota

Legal Services Corporation
RULES
11638 Grievance opportunity and/or complaint by eligible clients and members of public; withdrawn

Minerals Management Service
NOTICES
Outer Continential Shelf; development operations coordination:
11723 Corpus Christi Oil & Gas Co.

National Credit Union Administration
NOTICES
11730 Agency information collection activities under OMB review

National Highway Traffic Safety Administration
PROPOSED RULES
Motor vehicle safety standards:
11692 Transmission shift lever sequence; termination of rulemaking

National Institute of Justice
NOTICES
Grants, competitive solicitation:
11730 Police and prosecutor coordination; improving evidence gathering

National Oceanic and Atmospheric Administration
RULES
Fishery conservation and management:
11640 Pacific Coast groundfish
11641 Tanner crab off Alaska
PROPOSED RULES
Fishery conservation and management:
11694 Swordfish; Gulf of Mexico Fishery Management Council; hearings; correction
NOTICES
Coastal zone management programs:
11699 California
Fishery conservation and management:
11700 Foreign fishing permit applications
Marine mammal permit applications, etc.:
11699 McHugh, Mark Blane
11700 Moclips Cetological Society
11700 National Zoological Park

National Park Service
NOTICES
Concession contract negotiations:
11724 Bevington, Robert F., Jr.
11723 Ye Olde Sun Shack, Inc.
11724 Yosemite Medical Group
Historic Place National Register; pending nominations:
11724 Alabama et al.

National Science Foundation
NOTICES
Meetings:
11730 Linguistics Advisory Panel
11731 Social and Economic Science Advisory Pan

National Transportation Safety Board
NOTICES
11746 Meetings; Sunshine Act

Nuclear Regulatory Commission
NOTICES
Applications, etc.:
11732 Florida Power Corp. et al.; correction
11732, 11733 Niagara Mohawk Power Corp. (2 documents

Federal Register / Vol. 49, No. 60 / Tuesday, March 27, 1984 / Notices   **11701**

526 S.W. Mill Street, Portland, OR 97201, 503–221–6352

Jim H. Branson, Executive Director, North Pacific Fishery Management Council, 605 W. Forth Avenue, Anchorage, AK 99510, 907–271–4064

Kitty M. Simonds, Executive Director, Western Pacific Fishery Management Council, 1164 Bishop Street, Room 1608, Honolulu, Hawaii 98613, 808–523–1368

For further information contact Shirley Whisted or John D. Kelly (Fees, Permits, and Regulations Division), 202–634–7432.

The Magnuson Act also requires the Secretary of State to publish a notice of receipt of all applications for such permits summarizing the contents of the applications in the Federal Register. The National Marine Fisheries Service, under the authority granted in a memorandum of understanding with the Department of State effective November 29, 1983 issues the notice on behalf of the Secretary of State.

Individual vessel applications for fishing in 1984 have been received between March 22, 1984 and March 22, 1985 from the Government(s) shown below.

Dated: March 23, 1984.

Carmen J. Blondin,
Deputy Assistant Administrator, for Fisheries Resource Management, National Marine Fisheries Service.

Fishery codes and designation of regional councils which review applications for individual fisheries are as follows:

Code	Fishery	Regional council
ABS	Atlantic Billfishes and Sharks.	New England, Mid-Atlantic, South Atlantic, Gulf of Mexico, Caribbean.
BSA	Bering Sea and Aleutian Islands Groundfish	North Pacific
GOA	Gulf of Alaska	North Pacific.
NWA	Northwest Atlantic Ocean.	New England, Mid-Atlantic, South Atlantic, Gulf of Mexico, Caribbean.
SMT	Seamount Groundfish (Pacific Ocean).	Western Pacific
SNA	Snails (Bering Sea)	North Pacific.
WOC	Pacific Groundfish (Washington, Oregon, and California).	Pacific
PBS	Pacific Billfishes and Sharks.	Western Pacific

Activity codes which specify categories of fishing operations applied for are as follows:

Activity Code	Fishing Operations
1	Catching, Processing, and Other Support.
2	Processing and Other Support, Only
3	Other Support Only.

Activity Code	Fishing Operations		
4	"Joint Venture" in Support of U.S. Vessels		

Nation, vessel name, vessel type	Application No.	Fishery	Activity
Government of Japan:			
Akebono Maru No. 2, Medium Stern Trawler.	JA–84–1154	BSA	1
Akebono Maru No. 22, Medium Stern Trawler.	JA–84–0317	BSA	1
Akebono Maru No. 1, Medium Stern Trawler.	JA–84–1153	BSA	1
Akebono Maru No. 3, Medium Stern Trawler.	JA–84–0165	BSA, SMT	1
Kaiyo Maru No. 11, Medium Stern Trawler.	JA–84–0313	BSA	1
Government of the Republic of Korea:			
Dasin No. 52, Large Stern Trawler	KS–84–0037	GOA	1
No. 1 Han Sung, Large Stern Trawler.	KS–84–0106	GOA	1
No. 215 Tae Baek, Medium Stern Trawler.	KS–84–0105	GOA	1
No. 315 Tae Baek, Medium Stern Trawler.	KS–84–0117	GOA	1

Korea

The Government of Korea has applied for fishing permits to engage in joint venture activities with the American partners ALASKA JOINT VENTURE FISHERIES, ALASKA CONTACT LTD., AND DAERIM AMERICAN INC. The application between Korea and the American partner Alaska Joint Venture Fisheries requests the harvest of 1,300 mt of Pacific cod, and 700 mt of other species in the GOA fishery. This joint venture will take place between the months of April–July. The application between Korea and the American partner Alaska Contact Ltd., requests the harvest of 2,000 mt of Pacific cod and 500 mt of other species in the GOA fishery. This joint venture will take place between the months of July–September. The application between Korea and the American partner Daerim American Inc., requests the harvest of 1,500 mt of Pacific cod and 1,000 mt of other species in the GOA fishery. This joint venture will take place between the months of May–December.

Japan

The Government of Japan has applied for fishing permits to engage in joint venture activities with the American partner PETER PAN SEAFOODS, INC. The application requests 4,500 mt of yellowfin sole and 400 mt of other species. This joint venture will take place between the months of April–June and August–September.

[FR Doc. 84-8274 Filed 3-26-84; 8:45 am]
BILLING CODE 3510-22-M

DEPARTMENT OF EDUCATION

Office of Special Education and Rehabilitative Services

Research in Education of the Handicapped

AGENCY: Department of Education.

ACTION: Application notice establishing the closing date for transmittal of new grant applications—Research in Education of the Handicapped Program.

Applications are invited for new Field-Initiated Research projects under the Research in Education of the Handicapped program.

Authorization for this program is contained in sections 641 and 642 of Part E of the Education of the Handicapped Act.

(20 U.S.C. 1441, 1442)

Applications may be submitted by State and local educational agencies institutions of higher education, and other public agencies and nonprofit private organizations.

The purpose of the Research in Education of the Handicapped program is to make awards for research and related activities, and to conduct research, surveys, or demonstrations relating to the education of handicapped children and youth.

On October 26, 1983, the Secretary published (48 FR 49533) an application notice establishing the closing date for transmittal of new grant applications for Field-Initiated Research projects. As in previous years, most of these applications for projects propose to conduct research on problems that can be addressed in a relatively short period (12 to 36 months). Certain research efforts, however, require a longer period. For example, in order to answer some research questions, a longitudinal design is necessary, or a series of studies building on one another may be required. In other instances, new measurement techniques or instruments must be developed or field tested before the principal research activities can begin. In order to provide the sustained support required for those kinds of research projects, the Secretary invites applications for new awards for Field-Initiated Research projects that require support for a 60-month period.

The appropriate study areas for proposed Field-Initiated Research projects are limited only by the purpose of the research program and the need for a 60-month period of support to accomplish the research objectives and activities.

Closing date for transmittal of applications: An application for a grant

Fig. 10.2 (cont.)

must be mailed or hand delivered by May 21, 1984.

Applications delivered by mail:
Applications sent by mail must be addressed to the Department of Education, Application Control Center, Attention: CFDA Number 84.023H, 400 Maryland Avenue, S.W., Washington, D.C. 20202.

An applicant must show proof of mailing consisting of one of the following:

(1) A legibly dated U.S. Postal Service postmark.
(2) A legible mail receipt with the date of mailing stamped by the U.S. Postal Service.
(3) A dated shipping label, invoice, or receipt from a commercial carrier.
(4) Any other proof of mailing acceptable to the U.S. Secretary of Education.

If an application is sent through the U.S. Postal Service, the Secretary does not accept either of the following as proof of mailing: (1) A private metered postmark, or (2) a mail receipt that is not dated by the U.S. Postal Service.

An applicant should note that the U.S. Postal Service does not uniformly provide a dated postmark. Before relying on this method, an applicant should check with its local post office.

An applicant is encouraged to use registered or at least first class mail.

Each late applicant will be notified that its application will not be considered.

Applications delivered by hand:
Hand-delivered applications must be taken to the Department of Education, Application Control Center, Room 5673, Regional Office Building 3, 7th and D Streets, S.W., Washington, D.C.

The Application Control Center will accept hand-delivered applications between 8:00 a.m. and 4:30 p.m. (Washington, D.C. time) daily, except Saturdays, Sundays, and Federal holidays.

An application for a new project that is hand delivered will not be accepted by the Application Control Center after 4:30 p.m. on the closing date.

Available funds: It is estimated that approximately 10 awards will be made for new Field-Initiated Research projects under this program. For fiscal year 1984, the average amount of these awards will be approximately $50,000. This estimate of funding level does not bind the U.S. Department of Education to a specific number of grants or to the amount of any grant, unless that amount is otherwise specified by statute or regulations. Grant approval is for a 60-

month period subject to an annual review of progress and availability of funds.

Application forms: Application forms and program information packages are expected to be ready for mailing by April 6, 1984. These materials may be obtained by writing to the Research Projects Branch, Office of Special Education Programs, U.S. Department of Education, 400 Maryland Avenue, S.W. (Switzer Building, Room 3076), Washington, D.C. 20202.

Applications must be prepared and submitted in accordance with the regulations, instructions, and forms included in the application package. However, the program information is only intended to aid applicants in applying for assistance. Nothing in the program information package is intended to impose any paperwork, application content, reporting, or performance requirements beyond those imposed under the statute and regulations.

The Secretary strongly urges that the narrative portion of the application not exceed twenty (20) pages in length. The Secretary further urges that applicants submit only the information that is requested.

(OMB 1820–0028—Expires 2/28/87)

Applicable regulations: Regulations applicable to this program include the following:

(a) The regulations governing the Research in Education of the Handicapped Program (34 CFR Part 324).
(b) The Education Department General Administrative Regulations (EDGAR) (34 CFR Parts 74, 75, 77, and 78).

FOR FURTHER INFORMATION CONTRACT:
Eileen Lehman, Research Projects Branch, Office of Special Education Programs, U.S. Department of Education, 400 Maryland Avenue, S.W. (Switzer Building, Room 3523), Washington, D.C. 20202. Telephone: (202) 732–1120.

(20 U.S.C. 1441, 1442)

(Catalog of Federal Domestic Assistance Number 84.023; Research in Education of the Handicapped)

Dated: March 22, 1984.

Madeleine Will,
Assistant Secretary, Office of Special Education and Rehabilitative Services.

[FR Doc. 84–8128 Filed 3–26–84; 8:45 am]
BILLING CODE 4000–01–M

DEPARTMENT OF ENERGY

Office of the Secretary

National Petroleum Council, Coordinating Subcommittee of the Committee on the Strategic Petroleum Reserve' Meeting

Notice is hereby given that the Coordinating Subcommittee of the Committee on the Strategic Petroleum Reserve will meet in April 1984. The National Petroleum Council was established to provide advice, information, and recommendations to the Secretary of Energy on matters relating to oil and natural gas or the oil and natural gas industries. The Committee on the Strategic Petroleum Reserve will address various aspects of the Strategic Petroleum Reserve and the long-term availability and movement patterns of tankers worldwide. Its analysis and findings will be based on information and data to be gathered by the various task groups. The time, location, and agenda of the Coordinating Subcommittee meeting follows:

The Coordinating Subcommittee will hold its second meeting on Tuesday, April 3, 1984, starting at 8:00 a.m., in the Monticello Room of the Madison Hotel, 15th and M Streets, NW., Washington, D.C.

The tentative agenda for the Coordinating Subcommittee meeting follows:

1. Opening remarks by the Chairman and Government Co-Chairman.
2. Discuss an organizational structure for the study.
3. Discuss a timetable for completion of the study.
4. Discuss any other matters pertinent to the overall assignment from the Secretary of Energy.

The meeting is open to the public. The Chairman of the Coordinating Subcommittee is empowered to conduct the meeting in a fashion that will, in his judgment facilitate the orderly conduct to business. Any member of the public who wishes to file a written statement with the Coordinating Subcommittee will be permitted to do so, either before or after the meeting. Members of the public who wish to make oral statements should inform Gerald J. Parker, Office of Oil, Gas and Shale Technology, Fossil Energy, 301/353–3032 prior to the meeting and reasonable provision will be made for their appearance on the agenda.

Summary minutes of the meeting will be available for public review at the Freedom of Information Public Reading Room, Room 1E–190, DOE Forrestal

11730   Federal Register / Vol. 49, No. 60 / Tuesday, March 27, 1984 / Notices

Accordingly, none are being filed along with this Competitive Impact Statement.

Dated: —————.

Respectfully submitted.
Kenneth L. Jost, Angela L. Hughes,
Attorneys for the United States. United States Department of Justice. Antitrust Division, Washington, D.C. 20530. (202) 724-6498.

[I R Doc. 84-8123 Filed 3-26-84; 8:45 am]
BILLING CODE 4410-01-M

National Institute of Justice

Solicitation; Improving Evidence Gathering Through Police and Prosecutor Coordination

Police and prosecutor coordination is essential if felony case attrition is to be kept at a minimum. The problem of felony arrests resulting in no conviction has been estimated to be as high as fifty percent. While a certain amount of this attrition is warranted, a portion results from either the poor quality of the arrest cases when they are presented to the prosecutor, or to problems in coordination and cooperation between law enforcement and prosecuting agencies.

To address the problem of felony case attrition the National Institute of Justice announces a competitive research grant program on "Improving Evidence Gathering Through Police and Prosecutor Coordination". Proposals are requested for experimental research designed to reduce the rate of avoidable felony case attrition through improved case preparation and policy coordination between police and prosecutors.

This solicitation requests proposals from organizations desiring either: (1) To develop, implement and assess new methods of improving felony case evidence gathering and preparation or, (2) to evaluate the effects of an already existing program or policy aimed at enhanced felony case evidence gathering and preparation. It is anticipated that three to five awards will be made from the $500,000 planned for this program.

Both the qualifications of the research team and evidence of cooperation of the participant jurisdiction are among the review criteria.

All proposals must be received no later than June 1, 1984.

A copy of the solicitation may be obtained by sending a self addressed *mailing label* to: Announcement Request, Improving Evidence Gathering, National Criminal Justice Reference Service, Box 6000, Rockville, Maryland 20850.

Dated: March 16, 1984.
James K. Stewart,
Director. National Institute of Justice
[FR Doc. 84-8156 Filed 3-26-84. 8:45 am]
BILLING CODE 4410-18-M

DEPARTMENT OF LABOR

Office of the Secretary

The Steering Subcommittee of the Labor Advisory Committee for Trade Negotiations and Trade Policy; Meeting

Pursuant to the provisions of the Federal Advisory Committee Act (Pub. L. 92–463 as amended). notice is hereby given of a meeting of the Steering Subcommittee of the Labor Advisory Committee for Trade Negotiations and Trade Policy.

Date, time and place: April 10, 1984, 9:30 a.m., Rm. S4215 A & B Frances Perkins, Department of Labor Building, 200 Constitution Avenue, NW., Washington, D.C. 20210.

Purpose: To discuss trade negotiations and trade policy of the United States.

This meeting will be closed under the authority of Section 10(d) of the Federal Advisory Committee Act. The Committee will hear and discuss sensitive and confidential matters concerning U.S. trade negotiations and trade policy.

For further information contact: Fernand Lavallee, Acting Executive Secretary, Labor Advisory Committee, Phone: (202) 523–6565, March 20, 1984.

Signed at Washington, D.C. this 20th day of March 1984.
Robert W. Searby,
Deputy Under Secretary, International Affairs.
[FR Doc. 84-8224 Filed 3-26-84; 8:45 am]
BILLING CODE 4510-28-M

NATIONAL CREDIT UNION ADMINISTRATION

Agency Forms Submitted to OMB for Review

The following package is being submitted to the Office of Management and Budget (OMB) for clearance in compliance with the Paperwork Reduction Act (44 CFR Chapter 35). The current valid OMB clearance expires on March 31, 1984.

Subject: 12 CFR 701.31 Nondiscrimination Requirements (3133–0068).

This regulation requires a Federal Credit Union to keep a copy of the property appraisal. It also requires that

a Federal Credit Union using geographic factors in evaluating real estate loan applications must disclose such fact on the appraisal and state its justification.

Respondents: Federal Credit Unions
OMB Desk Officer: Judith McIntosh.
Copies of the above information collection clearance packages can be obtained by calling the National Credit Union Administration. Special Projects Officer, on 202–357–1080.

Written comments and recommendations for listed information collections should be sent directly to the OMB Desk Officer designated above at the following address: OMB Reports Management Branch, New Executive Office Building, Room 3208, Washington. DC 20503. Attn: Judith McIntosh.

Dated: March 19, 1984.
Rosemary Brady,
Secretary of the NCUA Board.
[FR Doc. 84-8162 Filed 3-26-84; 8:45 am]
BILLING CODE 7535-01-M

NATIONAL SCIENCE FOUNDATION

Advisory Panel for Linguistics; Meeting

In accordance with the Federal Advisory Committee Act, Pub. L. 92–463, as amended, the National Science Foundation announces the following meeting:

Name: Advisory Panel for Linguistics.
Date and Time: April 12 and 13, 1984; 9:00 a.m. to 5:00 p.m. each day.
Place: National Science Foundation, 1800 G Street, NW., Room 338, Washington, D.C. 20550.
Type of Meeting: Part Open—Open 4/13— 9:00 a.m. to 11:00 a.m., closed 4/12—9:00 a.m. to 5:00 p.m.. closed 4/13—11:00 a.m. to 5:00 p.m.
Contact Person: Dr. Paul G. Chapin, Program Director, Linguistics Program, Room 320, National Science Foundation, Washington, D.C. 20550, (202) 357–7696.
Summary Minutes: May be obtained from the Contact Person at the above stated address.
Purpose of Meeting: To provide advice and recommendations concerning support for research in linguistics.
Agenda: Open—General discussion of the current status and future plans of the Linguistics Program.
Closed—To review and evaluate research proposals as part of the selection process for awards.
Reason for Closing: The proposals being reviewed include information of a proprietary or confidential nature, including technical information, financial data, such as salaries, and personal information concerning individuals associated with the proposals. These matters are within exemptions (4) and (6) of 5 U.S.C. 552b(c), Government in the Sunshine Act.

Fig. 10.2 (cont.)

Authority To Close Meeting: This determination was made by the Committee Management Officer pursuant to provisions of Section 10(d) of Pub. L. 92–463. The Committee Management Officer was delegated the authority to make such determinations by the Director, NSF, on July 6, 1979.

March 22, 1984.

M. Rebecca Winkler,
Committee Management Coordinator.

[FR Doc. 84–8217 Filed 3–26–84; 8:45 am]
BILLING CODE 7555-01-M

Subpanel on Regulation and Policy Analysis Advisory Panel for Social and Economic Science; Meeting

In accordance with the Federal advisory Committee Act, Pub. L. 92–463, as amended, the National Science Foundation announces the following meeting:

Name: Subpanel or Regulation & Policy Analysis of the Advisory Panel for Social & Economic Science.

Date/Time: April 13, 1984—8:00 a.m. to 6:00 p.m.

Place: National Science Foundation, 1800 G St., NW. (Rm 643) Washington, DC 20550.

Type of Meeting: Closed.

Contact Person: Dr. Laurence C. Rosenberg, Program Director Regulation & Policy Analysis, National Science Foundation, Washington, DC 20550, Room 335, Phone (202) 357–7417.

Purpose of Subpanel: To provide advice and recommendations concerning research in Regulation and Policy Analysis.

Agenda: To review and evaluate research proposals as part of the selection process for awards.

Reason for Closing: The proposals being reviewed include information of a proprietary or confidential nature, including technical information; financial data, such as salaries; and personal information concerning individuals associated with the proposals. These matters are within exemptions (4) and (6) of 5 U.S.C. 552b(c), Government in the Sunshine Act.

Authority To Close Meeting: This determination was made by the Committee Management Officer pursuant to provisions of Section 10(d) of Pub. L. 92–463. The Committee Management Officer was delegated the authority to make such determinations by the Director NSF on July 6, 1979.

M. Rebecca Winkler,
Committee Management Coordinator.

[FR Doc. 84–8216 Filed 3–26–84; 8:45 am]
BILLING CODE 7555-01-M

NUCLEAR REGULATORY COMMISSION

Advisory Committee on Reactor Safeguards; Meeting

In accordance with the purposes of section 29 and 182b. of the Atomic Energy Act (42 U.S.C. 2039, 2232b.), the Advisory Committee on Reactor Safeguards will hold a meeting on April 5–7, 1984, in Room 1046, 1717 H Street NW., Washington, DC. Notice of this meeting was published in the **Federal Register** on March 27, 1984.

The agenda for the subject meeting will be as follows:

Thursday, April 5, 1984

8:30 a.m.–8:45 a.m.: Chairman's Report (Open)—The ACRS Chairman will report briefly to the Committee regarding items of current interest.

8:45 a.m.–12:00 noon: Maintenance Policies and Practices (Open/Closed)—The members will hear and discuss the report of its subcommittee and members of the NRC staff regarding maintenance policies and practices in nuclear power plants.

A portion of this session will be closed to discuss information provided in confidence by a foreign source.

1:00 p.m.–2:00 p.m.: Items for Meeting with NRC Commissioners (Open)—The members will discuss the ACRS position regarding matters to be discussed with the NRC Commissioners including the proposed NRC Safety Research Program for FY 1985, ACRS activities related to QA/QC practices in the nuclear industry, and establishment of an NTSB type board for evaluation of nuclear power plant accidents.

2:00 p.m.–3:30 p.m.: Meeting with NRC Commissioners (Open)—The members will meet with the NRC Commissioners to discuss items noted above.

3:30 p.m.–4:15 p.m.: Implementation of Regulatory Guide 1.97, Instrumentation of Light-Water-Cooled Nuclear Power Plants to Assess Plant and Environs Conditions During and Following an Accident (Open)—The members will hear a briefing regarding the status of implementation of Regulatory Guide 1.97.

4:15 p.m.–5:00 p.m.: Subcommittee Action (Open)—The members will hear and discuss reports of designated Subcommittees regarding the status of assigned activities including provisions for ECCS and decay heat removal.

Friday, April 6, 1984

8:30 a.m.–11:30 a.m.: Ginna Nuclear Power Plant (Open)—The members will hear and discuss reports from its subcommittee, the NRC Staff, and the Licensee regarding the request for a full term operating license for this facility.

Portions of this session will be closed as necessary to discuss Proprietary Material applicable to this matter.

11:30 a.m.–12:30 p.m.: Activities of NRC Regional Offices (Open)—The members will hear and discuss a report from an NRC Regional Director regarding the activities of NRC regional offices.

1:30 p.m.–2:30 p.m.: Severe Accident Policy (Open)—The members will hear a briefing by a representative of the NRC Staff regarding the status of a proposed NRC policy statement regarding consideration of severe nucler power plant accidents in the regulatory process.

2:30 p.m.–3:30 p.m.: Nuclear Power Plant Operating Experience (Open)—The Committee will hear and discuss a proposed NRC Bulletin regarding operation of undervoltage trip devices in nuclear power plant circuit breakers.

3:30 p.m.–4:00 p.m.: Passive Containment System (Open)—The Committee will discuss a proposed ACRS reply to the request for a preapplication review of the passive containment system.

4:00 p.m.–5:00 p.m.: Preparation of ACRS Reports (Open/Closed)—The Committee will discuss proposed ACRS reports/letters regarding items considered during the meeting.

Portions of this session will be closed as necessary to discuss Proprietary Information applicable to the matters being considered and to discuss information involved in an adjudicatory proceeding.

Saturday, April 7, 1984

8:30 a.m.–9:15 a.m.: Appointment of ACRS Members (Closed)—The members will discuss the qualifications of candidates proposed for appointment to the Committee.

This portion of the meeting will be closed to discuss information the release of which would represent an unwarranted invasion of personal privacy.

9:15 a.m.–12:30 p.m.: Preparation of ACRS Reports (Open/Closed)—The Committee will complete preparation of reports/letters regarding items considered during this meeting.

Portions of this session will be closed as necessary to discuss Proprietary Information applicable to the matters being considered and information involved in an adjudicatory proceeding.

Procedures for the conduct of and participation in ACRS meetings were published in the **Federal Register** on September 28, 1983 (48 FR 44291). In accordance with the procedures, oral or written statements may be presented by members of the public; recordings will be permitted only during those portions of the meeting when a transcript is being kept, and questions may be asked only by members of the Committee, its consultants, and Staff. Persons desiring

i

Reader Aids

Federal Register

Vol. 49, No. 60

Tuesday, March 27, 1984

INFORMATION AND ASSISTANCE

SUBSCRIPTIONS AND ORDERS

Subscriptions (public)	202–783–3238
Problems with subscriptions	275–3054
Subscriptions (Federal agencies)	523–5240
Single copies, back copies of FR	783–3238
Magnetic tapes of FR, CFR volumes	275–2867
Public laws (Slip laws)	275–3030

PUBLICATIONS AND SERVICES

Daily Federal Register

General information, index, and finding aids	523–5227
Public inspection desk	523–5215
Corrections	523–5237
Document drafting information	523–5237
Legal staff	523–4534
Machine readable documents, specifications	523–3408

Code of Federal Regulations

General information, index, and finding aids	523–5227
Printing schedules and pricing information	523–3419

Laws

Indexes	523–5282
Law numbers and dates	523–5282
	523–5266

Presidential Documents

Executive orders and proclamations	523–5230
Public Papers of the President	523–5230
Weekly Compilation of Presidential Documents	523–5230
United States Government Manual	523–5230

Other Services

Library	523–4986
Privacy Act Compilation	523–4534
TDD for the deaf	523–5229

FEDERAL REGISTER PAGES AND DATES, MARCH

7553–7794	1
7795–7980	2
7981–8226	5
8227–8416	6
8417–8580	7
8581–8886	8
8887–9162	9
9163–9406	12
9407–9558	13
9559–9706	14
9707–9858	15
9859–10072	16
10073–10246	19
10247–10530	20
10531–10650	21
10651–10918	22
10919–11134	23
11135–11614	26
11615–11798	27

CFR PARTS AFFECTED DURING MARCH

At the end of each month, the Office of the Federal Register publishes separately a list of CFR Sections Affected (LSA), which lists parts and sections affected by documents published since the revision date of each title.

1 CFR

Proposed Rules:
Ch. III	9738, 9904, 10935

3 CFR

Executive Orders:
12467	8229
12468	11139

Proclamations:
4940 (Amended by Proc. 5164)	10535
5155	8227
5156	8231
5157	8417
5158	8887
5159	9163
5160	10073
5161	10075
5162	10531
5163	10533
5164	10535
5165	10651
5166	10919
5167	11135
5168	11137
5169	11615

4 CFR

101	8889
102	8889
103	8889
104	8889
105	8889

5 CFR

110	7553
737	9808

7 CFR

2	10539, 11617
56	10540
58	10077
59	10540
70	10540
180	8233
400	7795, 8419, 9407
413	9407
422	8581
432	10541
631	11141
660	11145
726	9707
760	8905
907	8234, 9408, 10247, 11145
910	7796, 8906, 9859, 10541, 10921
911	11618
915	7553, 11618
984	10653
985	10654, 10655
989	10082

1 CFR

1033	10656
1205	8419
1729	11619
1794	9544, 10083

Proposed Rules:
29	10265
210	9426, 10125
220	9426, 10125
319	8619
431	8620
916	10270
917	10270
979	9427
991	9740, 11185
1036	7571
1434	9740
1476	9906
1700	8933
1736	8933
1942	9190
1964	9192
1965	9192

8 CFR

204	8420
238	8581, 9559

9 CFR

73	10528, 10921
81	7978, 8582
91	9408
92	9708
201	7796, 8235
327	11146
381	9409

Proposed Rules:
94	9214

10 CFR

2	7981, 8583, 9352
30	9352
40	9352
50	7981, 8422, 9352, 9711, 10657
51	9352, 10922
61	9352
70	9352
72	9352
110	9352
140	11146
430	11764

Proposed Rules:
35	8621
50	8445
110	7572
430	10071

11 CFR

114	7981

12 CFR

5	7981

Fig. 10.2   (cont.)

REMINDERS

The "reminders" below identify documents that appeared in issues of a <u>Federal Register</u> 15 days or more ago. Inclusion or exclusion from this list has no legal significance.
DEADLINES FOR COMMENTS ON PROPOSED RULES FOR THE WEEK OF MAY 31 THROUGH JUNE 6, 1981

> AGRICULTURE DEPARTMENT
>
> Animal and Plant Health Inspection Service--
> 19817 4-1-81/ Change in desease status of the Channel Islands and Great Britain (England, Scotland, Wales, and Isle of Man). because of foot-and-mouth-desease; comments by 6-1-81
>
> Federal Grain Inspection Service--
> 19699 3-31-81/ U.S. standards for rough rice, brown rice for processing and milled rice; comments by 6-1-81
>
> Food Safety and Quality Service--
> 25097 5-5-81/ U.S. standards for grades of canned ripe olives; comments by 6-4-81
>
> Rural Electrification Administration--
> 19500 3-31-81/ Revision of REA Bulletin 80-11, "Reports of Progress of Construction and Engineering Services"; comments by 8-1-81
>
> 19500 3-3-81/ Revision of REA Specification DT-5C:PE-9, "Wood Poles, Stubs, and Anchor Logs and the Preservative Treatment of These Materials"; comments by 6-1-81
>
> CIVIL AERONAUTICS BOARD
>
> 20563 4-6-81/ Liberalization of rules for indirect cargo air carriers; comments by 6-5-81
>
> DEFENSE DEPARTMENT
>
> Office of the Secretary--
> 20564 5-4-81/ Implementation of the Civilian Health and Medical Program of the Uniform Services; comments by 6-3-81
>
> EDUCATION DEPARTMENT
>
> 19000 3-27-81/ Review of regulations and interpretations; comments by 5-31-81
>
> ENERGY DEPARTMENT
>
> 25302 5-6-81/ Procurement regulations; comments by 6-5-81
>
> Economic Regulatory Administration--
> 25315 5-6-81/ Tertiary incentive program in the Crude oil price regulations; comments by 6-5-81
>
> Federal Energy Regulatory Commission--
> 25643, 5-8-81/High-cost natural gas produced from tight formations; price; Colorado
> 25644 (2 documents); comments by 6-3-81
>
> 17023 3-17-81/ Revision of Commission Rules of Practices; comments by 6-1-81
>
> ENVIRONMENTAL PROTECTION AGENCY
>
> 24596 5-1-81/ Air pollution; stack height emission limitation control additional technical information; comments by 6-1-81

Other Publications

Another publication that will help you locate information on government sources is the *U.S. Government Manual* (see Fig. 10.3).

If you are an experienced grant seeker, you may wish to become involved in the government contracts marketplace, and in this case will utilize the *Commerce Business Daily* (Fig. 10.4). For the purposes of this book, however, only the grants area is treated in depth—the contracts business requires a special effort on your part.

1976/1977 United States

GOVERNMENT MANUAL

Revised May 1, 1976

Office of the Federal Register
National Archives and Records Service

General Services
Administration

FOREWORD

The United States Government Manual is the official handbook of the
Federal Government. It describes the purposes and programs of most
Government agencies and lists top personnel. Briefer statements are
included for the quasi-official agencies and certain international
organizations.

The department and agency descriptions emphasize activities, not interna
agency structure. More detailed organizational information may be
found in statements which each agency is required to publish in the
Federal Register. Persons interested in these statements should consult
the indexes to the daily Federal Register, write directly to the agency,
or write to the Office of the Federal Register.

EDUCATION DIVISION
Office of the Assistant Secretary for Education
400 Maryland Avenue SW., Washington, D.C. 20202
Phone, 202-245-8430

Assistant Secretary for Education . . . . Virginia Y. Trotter
    Special Assistant . . . . Becky L. Schergens
    Executive Assistant . . . . John J. Stephens III
    Director of Administration . . . . Charles E. Hansen
Deputy Assistant Secretary for Education . . . . Robert P. Hanrahan
Deputy Assistant Secretary for Education
    (Policy Development) . . . . Philip E. Austin
Deputy Assistant Secretary for Education
    (Policy Communication) . . . . Becky L. Schergens,
        Acting
Director, Fund for the Improvement of
    Postsecondary Education . . . . Virginia B. Smith
Administrator, National Center for Education
    Statistics . . . . Marie D. Eldridge

Office of Education
400 Maryland Avenue SW., Washington, D.C. 20202
Phone, 202-245-8795

Commissioner of Education · · · · · · · · · · · · · · · · · · T. H. Bell
    Assistant to the Commissioner . . . . Howard A. Matthews
    Special Assistant to the Commissioner . . . . Robert R. Weatherford
    Special Assistant to the Commissioner for
      Regional Liaison . . . . William E. McLaughlin
    Ombudsman to State Educational Agencies . . . . Elam K. Hertzler
    Nonpublic Educational Services . . . . Dwight R. Crum
    Director, Officer of External Relations . . . . Harry Gardner
    Director, Special Projects . . . . Jim Moore

FIGURE 10.3.   A sample of *U.S. Government Manual*.

94

FIGURE 10.4.   A sample of *Commerce Business Daily*.

FRIDAY, NOVEMBER 4, 1983
Issue No. PSA-8069

A daily list of U.S. Government procurement invitations, contract awards, subcontracting leads, sales of surplus property and foreign business opportunities

---

U.S. GOVERNMENT PROCUREMENTS

Services

A Experimental, Developmental, Test and Research Work (research includes both basic and applied research)

Defense Supply Service-Washington, Room 1D245, The Pentagon, Washington DC 20310 Attn: U Joiner
★ A -- IMPLICATIONS OF INDEPENDENT EUROPEAN BALANCE ASSESSMENTS, PART II. Negotiations, based on an unsolicited proposal, are currently being conducted with C&L Associates, Potomac MD. For info only. See note 46.
★ A -- DISTRIBUTED C3 PROGRAM. Negotiations are being conducted on a sole-source basis with Science Applications, Inc, 1710 Goodridge Dr, PO Box 1303, McLean, VA 22102. See note 46.
★ A -- EUROPEAN VIEWS ON SOVIET MILITARY POWER AND STRATEGY AGAINST NATO. Defense Supply Service-Washington contemplates negotiating a contract with Harold Rosenbaum Associates, Inc, 111 S Bedford St, Burlington MA 01803. (304)

NASA, Goddard Space Flight Center (GSFC), Greenbelt Rd, Greenbelt MD 20771, Attn: Gina Komp, Code 284.1
A -- EXTENSION OF INTEGRATION AND TEST (I&T) AND FIELD SUPPORT FOR THE LANDSAT D' MISSION. NASA/GSFC will issue Request for Proposal (RFP)5-65177/360 to Fairchild Space Co, Germantown MD. All interested persons are invited to identify their interest and capability to respond to such requirement within 30 days after publication of this notice. (304)

Goddard Space Flight Center (GSFC), Greenbelt Rd, Greenbelt MD 20771 Attn: Wilfred Colon, Code 289.
A -- DESIGN, FABRICATE, TEST AND DELIVER 100 SECOND-GENERATION EMERGENCY LOCATOR TRANSMITTERS (ELT'S). RFP5-48130-259. Offerors must develop and provide an ELT designed to minimize false alarms and to turn on in the event of an airplane crash; the ELT must be light enough to be installed in the tail of a general aviation airplane, and strong enough to survive a crash in operating condition. A selected contractor shall fabricate 100 second-generation ELT's to the conceptual design selected at award. Request for RFP packages must be in writing and must be received within 10 working days after the publication of this synopsis. (304)

NASA Goddard Space Flight Center (GFSC), Attn: Cathy Cavey, Code 284.1, Greenbelt Rd, Greenbelt MD 20771
A -- FLEXIBLE SPACECRAFT DYNAMICS (FSD) ENHANCEMENT FOR OPEN SPACECRAFT.Request for Proposal 5-17900/355 issued to AVCO Corporation, Wilmington MA 01887. Interested persons are invited to identify their interest and capability to respond to such requirement, or to submit proposals in response to such notice, within thirty days from the date of this publication. (304)

Contracting Officer, Naval Research Lab, Washington DC 20375
A -- SYNCHROTRON RADIATION PROGRAM. Scope increase. Negotiations are being conducted on a sole source basis with Sachs/Freeman Associates, Inc, Bowie MD 20715 for an increase in scope. See note 46. (304)

Contracting Officer, Naval Research Lab, Washington DC 20375, Code 1232.RC
★ A -- FLARE TEST PROGRAM of research to perform measurements and analysis of flare properties in support of countermeasures programs. Anticipate negotiations with Raven Inc, Springfield VA 22150. See note 46. (304)

Defense Supply Service-Washington, Rm 1D245, The Pentagon, Washington DC 20310 Attn: Mrs Edna Clark
★ A -- A RESEARCH STUDY ENTITLED, "JOINT OPERATION PLANNING AND EXECUTION SYSTEM"(JOPES). Negotiations are being conducted on a sole source basis with Systems Research and Applications Corp, 2425 Wilson Blvd, Suite 245, Arlington VA 22201. See note 46. (304)

Headquarters Ballistic Missile Office, Air Force Systems Command (AFSC), Norton AFB, CA 92409 Attn: G P Newman, PMS-3, 714/382-4873.
A -- SMALL ICBM WEAPONS SYSTEM DEFINITION. RFP F04704-83-R-001 for the definition of weapons system requirements/configuration for a small, mobile single-warhead missile will be issued to the Boeing Co, 808 E Mill St, Suite 201, San Bernardino CA; Martin Marietta Aerospace, 164 Hospitality Ln, Suite 10, San Bernardino CA 92408; General Dynamics Corp, 1881 Commerce Center East, Suite 213, San Bernardino CA 92408; Lockheed Missiles & Space Co, 1918 S Business Center Dr, Suite 215, San Bernardino CA 92408; and McDonnell Douglas Inc, 5301 Bolsa Ave, Huntington Beach CA 92647, approx 21 Oct 1983. This is for info purposes only.
A -- SMALL ICBM BOOSTER CONCEPTS AND TECHNOLOGIES DEFINITION. RFP F04704-83-R-002 for the definition of booster concepts and technologies for a small, mobile single warhead missile will be issued to Hercules Inc, 1908 S Business Center Dr, Suite 205, San Bernardino CA 92408; Aerojet Strategic Propulsion Co, PO Box 15690C, Sacramento CA 95813; Morton Thiokol Inc, PO Box 524, Brigham City UT 84032; United Technologies, PO Box 50015, San Jose CA 95150; and Atlantic Research, 8558 W Jackman, Suite 110, Lancaster CA 93535, approx 21 Oct 1983. This is for info purposes only. (304)

NASA-Ames Research Center, M/S 241-1, Brian G Bowman, 415/965-5813, Moffett Field CA 94035
A -- CONTROLLED ECOLOGICAL LIFE SUPPORT SYSTEM (CELSS) PROGRAM PLANNING SUPPORT-conceptual design. Negotiations are to be conducted with Boeing Aerospace Company, Seattle WA on their unsolicited proposal. Contemplated proposal issue date 11/03/83. Contemplated proposal return date 11/23/83. See note 22. RFP2-31192(BGB). (304)

NASA-Ames Research Center, M/S 241-1, William A. McKenna, 415/965-5786, Moffett Field CA 94035
A -- EMS HELICOPTER STUDY NASA Ames plans to award contracts approx $50,000 each to four helicopter manufacturers, Bell Helicopter, Boeing-Vertol, Hughes, and Sikorsky to study helicopter emergency medical service applications and equipment. The following subjects will be addressed: Missions requirements; potential market, benefits assessment; and identification of technologies ready, or nearly ready for development which are judged to be useful for EMS applications. The technologies to be examined will emphasize precision guidance, all weather capability, low altitude performance, internal and external noise reduction, enhanced low speed/hover performance, vibration reduction, contingency power, and advanced transmissions. This program could result in development assistance for selected technologies. Contemplated proposal issue date 11/07/83. Contemplated proposal return date 12/07/83. See note 22. RFP2-31403(WAM). (305)

Contracting Officer, Naval Weapons Support Center, Crane IN 47522 Attn: Purchase Services Branch 812/854-1826
A -- DEVELOP DEMIL PROCESSING TECHNOLOGY FOR PLASTIC BONDED EXPLOSIVES (PBX) of interest to the Navy. This study will allow for DEMIL Process Development for PBXN-3, PBXN-5 and PBXN-6. RFQ N00164-84-Q-3111, closing date 15 Dec 1983. (305)

Corvallis Environmental Research Laboratory, 200 SW 35th St, Corvallis OR 97333
A -- COOPERATIVE RESEARCH IN THE GENERAL AREA OF THE EFFECTS OF HAZARDOUS WASTE-SITE CONTAMINANTS ON SOIL AND AQUATIC MICROBIAL PROCESSES. Preference will be given to preproposals identifying both field and laboratory research studies capable of defining the impact of Hazardous Waste disposal upon microbial

functions including, soil respiration, carbon and nitrogen cycling. Interested applicants eligible to receive Federal Assistance under the Resource Conservation and Recovery Act, Public Law 94-580, Section 8001 are invited to submit a preproposal that includes a brief statement of work to be performed and the applicant's qualifications. Only state and local governments, nonprofit institutions of higher education, individuals or nonprofit research organizations are eligible to receive federal assistance under this section of the act. Recipients of EPA assistance are required to cost share a minimum of 5% of the total project costs. Total funding for this research is approx $90,000 for two years. Preproposals are to be received NLT Dec 15, 1983 and are to be forwarded to William E. Miller at address above. Preproposal applicants selected will be asked to attend a workshop held at Corvallis OR Jan 17-19, 1984. Following the workship, the participants will be requested to submit proposals for conduct of the microbial research. An EPA project officer prior to award of the research agreement. (305)

HQ Space Div (AFSC) (PMG), PO Box 92960, Worldway Postal Center, Los Angeles CA 90009
A -- TECHNICAL SERVICES SUPPORTING GPS USER CHARGES IMPLEMENTATION INTERFACE CONTROL WORKING GROUP Contractor will identify interface requirements; develop and review interface control documents, specs, and prime item development specs; plan/schedule activities; and provide technical interface control Potential sources must have the following capabilities and meet requirements as listed: a) A comprehensive involvement in the User Charges development process. b) Continuity of personnel involved with the above process. c) A thorough technical and literature data base on User Charges issues & techniques. d) Classified storage, processing, and handling. e) Immediate availability. Only known source Analytical Systems Engineering Corp, 1725 Jefferson Davis Hwy, Arlington VA 22202. Charles R Willett, PCO, 213/643-2814. See notes 22, 44 & 99. (305)

Ballistic Missile Defense Systems Command, Contracts Office, BMDSC-CRR, Attn: Lester Young, 205/895-4420, PO Box 1500, Huntsville AL 35807
★ A -- "OVERLAY TECHNOLOGY UTILITY ASSESSMENT." A nine month R&D effort to be performed for the Ballistic Missile Defense Systems Command, Huntsville AL, RFQ DASG60-84-Q-0007. Negotiations will be conducted with Spectra Research Systems, 1811 Quail St, Newport Beach CA 92660. See notes 22, 46. (305)

Office of Naval Research, 800 N. Quincy St, Arlington VA 22217
★ A -- CONTINUE THE DEVELOPMENT OF NEW TECHNIQUES FOR SEAWATER SAMPLING ON A FINE SPACE AND TIME GRID. Negotiations are to be conducted with Northeastern Research Foundation, Bidelow Lab for Ocean Sciences, McKown Point, West Boothbay Harbor ME 04575. See note 46. Contract Negotiator J Adams 202/696-4510.
★ A -- PERFORM A SERIES OF EXPERIMENTS TO MEASURE THE SPATIOTEMPORAL PATTERNS OF HUMAN BRAIN ELECTRICAL PATTERNS. Negotiations are to be conducted with the EEG Systems Laboratory, 1855 Folsom St, San Francisco CA 94103. See note 46. Contract Negotiator R Engebretson 202/696-4513.
★ A -- CONDUCT A SERIES OF EXPERIMENTS WHOSE RESULTS QUANTIFY ASPECTS OF A THEORY OF DIAGNOSTIC INFERENCE. Negotiations are to be conducted with National Opinion Research Center, 6080 S. Ellis, Chicago IL 60637. See note 46. Contract Negotiator R Engebretson 202/696-4513. (305)

Eastern Space and missile Center (AFSC), Contracts Division/PMPC, Patrick AFB, FL 32925 Attn: Karen Riendeau 305/494-7091
★ A -- DISCRIMINATION RESEARCH. Negotiations are to be conducted with S-Cubed, La Jolla CA. See notes 40 & 46. (305)

Content

(Cont.)

Fig. 10.4 (cont.)

Harry Diamond Laboratories, Contracts Branch (Vint Hill), Mrs Payne 703/347-6227, Vint Hill Farms Station, Warrenton VA 22186

★ A -- **FY84 ENGINEERING MANAGEMENT, LOGISTICAL AND OTHER TECHNICAL SUPPORT TO U.S.A. SIGNALS WARFARE LABORATORY,** VHFS, Warrenton VA. Quest Research Corp/Engineering Resources Inc, McLean VA. See note 46.

U.S. Department of Energy, San Francisco Operations Office, 1333 Broadway, Oakland, CA 94612

★ A -- **THIN FILM MATERIALS RESEARCH FOR LOW COST SOLAR COLLECTORS.** The Department of Energy has selected Acurex Corp, 555 Clude Ave, Mountain View CA 94039 to negotiate a contract in support of a project entitled above. Sol DE-RA03-83SF11922. (305)

Contracts Branch, Harry Diamond Laboratories, Adelphi, MD 20783, Attn J Petro, DELND-PR-CA 202/394-1606

★ A -- **TECHINCAL SERVICE AND SOFTWARE IN SUPPORT OF THE BETA TEST BEDS;** mod to existing contract DAAG39-78-C-0055. Negotiations to be conducted with TRW Inc, Redondo Beach, CA 90278. RFP DAAK21-84-R-9014. See note 46.

★ A -- **EVALUATION AND REVIEW OF SOVIET TEXT "HELICOPTERS CALCULATION OF INTEGRAL AERODYNAMIC CHARACTERISTICS AND FLIGHT MECHANICS DATA."** Negotiations are being conducted with International Technical Assoc, LTD of Upper Darby PA, see ntoe 46. (305)

Department of Transportation, FHA, Office of Contracts and Procurement, Washington DC 20590

A -- **AMENDMENT-"APPLICATION OF FIBER COMPOSITE CABLES FOR BRIDGES".** RFPDTFH61-84-R-0021. The government will be receptive to joint industry-government sponsorship of research on this topic, and cost sharing of expenses to the level of available government funds. (305)

Mr. Douglas W. Frye, Contracting Officer for Division of Lung Diseases, National Heart, Lung and Blood Institute, 5333 Westbard Av, Rm 654, Bethesda MD 20205, 301/496-7334

A -- **EARLY INTERVENTION FOR CHRONIC OBSTRUCTIVE PULMONARY DISEASE.** The Division of Lung Diseases, National Heart, Lung and Blood Institute, is soliciting proposals from clinical centers who are willing to cooperate in a controlled clinical trial. The objectives of the trial are: 1. To determine the effects on rate of decline in pulmonary function of Special Care, compared with referral to Usual Care, in a population of smokers identified as having mild abnormalities in pulmonary function. Special Care includes presentation to the smoker of his mild abnormality in pulmonary function, smoking cessation counseling, the administration of bronchodilators to those with hyperreactive airways, and diligent follow-up. In Usual Care, the subject is referred to his usual source of medical care and given results of his pulmonary function tests. 2. To determine the additive effect on rate of decline in pulmonary function of the administration of bronchodilators to the subsample of smokers who have hyperreactive airways as well as mile decrements in pulmonary function. Epidemiological studies consistently indicate that smoking is the overwhelming risk factor for accelerated decline in pulmonary function and subsequent development of COPD. Moreover, epidemiological studies also indicate that after cessation of smoking, the rate of decline in pulmonary function decreases to a more normal rate of decline. Another risk factor for accelerated decline in pulmonary function is the presence of hyperreactive airways, yet it is not clear where the mere presence of hyperreactive airways, or the fact that the airways were reacting to various agents over a long period time, is the factor which contributes to accelerated decline. It is possible that if the hyperreactive airway is kep non-reactive by pharmacological means over a period of years, the expected abnormal decline may be lessened. This effect may be enhanced by the cessation of cigarette smoking. Although the evidence is strong that smoking and hyperreactive airways are risk factors for COPD, it has not yet been demonstrated that removal of risk factors at a stage of mild dysfunction will effectively modify the course of COPD. It is for this purpose that the present clinical trial is being developed. The RFP is to establish a collaborative program among several clinical centers to obtain sufficient numbers of smokers with mild decrements in pulmonary function for a randomized, controlled study. Smokers will be screened for level of pulmonary function. Those with mild dystunction, as defined by the study protocol, will be randomized into two study groups, a Special intervention group and a Usual Care group. The study will be conducted in three phases: Phase I will be the development of the collaborative protocol (1 year), Phase II (6 years) will be the subject recruitment, intervention, continued monitoring, and follow-up for five years; Phase III (1 year), will be data analysis. Participating centers will be expected to 1) cooperate with other clinical centers and the Data and Coordinating Center to establish common protocols and procedures for data collection and analysis 2) recruit 650 study subjects who are smokers and who have mild decrements in pulmonary function, half of whom have hyperreactive airways, and who meet other selection criteria, 3) conduct a baseline assessment of each subject, 4) administer the intervention outlined in the developed protocol, which shall include a smoking cessation intervention and the administration of bronchodilators to those with hyperreacitve airways, and 5) follow each patient for 5 years, monioring pulmonary function and encouraging continued non-smoking. It is anticipated that RFP NHLBI-84-11 will be issued o/a 15 Nov 1983. Letters of intent to submit a proposal will be due on 16 Dec 1983. Proposals are due 8 Mar 1984. Copies of the RFP may be obtained by either written or telephone requests. (305)

The **Commerce Business Daily** (USPS 966-360) is published daily, except Saturdays, Sundays and holidays, for $160 a year (1st Class mailing) or $81 a year (2nd Class mailing) by the U S Government Printing Office, Washington, DC 20402. Second Class postage paid at Washington, DC, and additional mailing offices. POSTMASTER: Send address changes to Superintendent of Documents, U S Government Printing Office, Washington, DC 20402, with entire mailing label from last issue received.

The Secretary of Commerce has determined that the publication of this periodical is necessary in the transaction of the public business required by law of this Department. Use of funds for printing this periodical has been approved by the Director of the Office of Management and Budget through 31 July 1985.

Division of Lung Diseases, National Heart, Lung and Blood Institute, National Institutes of Health, Westwood Bldg, Rm 654, Bethesda MD 20205

a -- **COORDINATING CENTER FOR COLLABORATIVE CLINICAL TRIAL ON HIGH FREQUENCY VENTILATION IN PREMATURE INFANTS.** Establishment of a coordinating center to collaborate with clinical centers to evaluate whether high frequency ventilation is superior to standard mechanical ventilation in providing ventilatory support for premature infants. A randomized, controlled, clinical trial in three phases is planned involving 1,000 premature infants. Phase I will involve development of a common study protocol and a manual of operations (8 months). During Phase II, (24 Months), infants will be entered into the study, treated, and followed for 12 months. Phase III will involve data analyses (6 months). The coordinating center will be responsible for : 1) assisting in preparing a common study protocol, reporting forms, and manual of operations; 2) standardizing, printing, and distributing the study of protocol, reporting forms, and manual of operations; 3) collection, processing, storing, and analyzing data collected from the participating clinical centers; 4) preparing and distributing periodic technical and statistical reports to the participating clinical centers; 5) assisting in coordinating and managing regular meetings of the steering committee; and 6) providing regular assessments of the quality of clinical data. The professional staff at the proposed coordinating center must have previous experience in directing a coordinating center for large-scale collaborative cardiovascular or pulmonary clinical trial and in collecting, managing and analyzing data from multiple clinical sites, and must have adequate data processing facilities to assure ready access to data and preparation of up-to-date reports. It is anticipated that RFP NHLBI-84-6 will be available o/a Oct 31, 1983. Copies of the RFP may be obtained by either written or telephone requests addressed to Douglas Frye, 301/496-7334. Letters of intent to submit a proposal will be due Dec 16, 1983. Request for copies of the RFP should include three non-franked, self-addressed labels. It is currently anticipated that proposals will be due on Feb 28, 1984. (305)

Office of Naval Research, 800 N. Quincy St, Arlington VA 22217

★ A -- **RESEARCH ON APPENDAGE EFFORTS ON PROPELLER INFLOW.** Negs are to be conducted with Science Applications, Inc, 1710 Goodridge Dr, PO Box 1303, McLean VA 22102. See note 46. Contract Negotiator M Murphy 202/696-4510

★ A -- **RESEARCH ON HIGH FREQUENCY RADAR.** Negs are to be conducted with SRI International, 333 Ravenswood Av, Menlo Park CA 94025. See note 46. Contract Negotiator B Rothenberg 202/696-4513.

★ A -- **COMMUNICATIONS OF HIGH POWER GAAS WINDOW LASER ARRAY.** Negs are to be conducted with Ortel Corp, 2015 W Chestnut, Alhambra CA 91803. See note 46. Contract Negotiator B Rothenburg 202/696-4513.

★ A -- **CONTINUED DEMONSTRATION OF TWO-STAGE OPERATION BY INTEGRATING QUASI-OPTICAL CAVITY INTO THE UNIVERSITY OF CALIFORNIA,** Santa Barbara FEL facility. Negs are to be conducted with KMS Fusion, Inc., 3621 S State Rd, Ann Arbor MI 48106. See note 46. Contract Negotiator J Christensen 202/696-4513.

★ A -- **RESEARCH ON SEMICONDUCTOR IMPURITIES.** Negs are to be conducted with IBM Corp, Thomas J. Watson Research Center, PO Box 218, Yorktown Heights NY 10598. See note 46. Contract Negotiator B Rothenberg 202/696-4513. (305)

U.S. Dept of Energy, 550 Second St, Idaho Falls, ID 83401

A -- **NOTICE OF PROGRAM INTEREST (NPI): ADVANCED COMPONENT RESEARCH AND DEVELOPMENT FOR INDUSTRIAL HEAT PUMPS.** The Department of Energy (DOE) Office of Industrial Programs seeks novel concepts for heat pump components and working fluids that will lead to significant improvements to advanced state-of-the-art, open or closed, rankine cycle heat pump systems for industrial application. Concepts are sought which will significantly improve temperature boost, efficiency, reliability, operational flexibility and/or economic viability of industrial heat pumps. Any industrial application for the heat pump is permissible, provided that broad application and significant nationwide energy savings can be achieved. Concepts relating to space heating heat pumps are not desired. Heat pump delivery temperatures must be in the 300°F to 500°F range. The specific heat pump system to which the innovative concept will be appled must be defined and expected improvements described and quantified. Proposed work on development of whole heat pump systems as opposed to components will not be considered. Examples of areas of interest are, but are not limited to: 1) Heat exchanger advancements involving more cost-effective heat transfer (eg, heat transfer enhancement, fouling reduction, cost and size reduction); 2) compressor advancements; 3) regenerative components (ie, those which recover energy otherwise lost); 4) both internal and external control system advancements; 5) advanced working fluids with compatible lubricants, seals and bearings. Those interested in responding to this NPI should request reports that describe two, advanced state-of-the-art, open and closed ranking cycle heat pump systems developed for DOE. Proposed concepts must provide significant system improvement over existing systems such as described in these reports. Requests should be addressed to above, Attn: R N Chappell. The DOE brochure "Guide for Submission of Unsolicited Proposals," dtd Jun 1983, will be sent to you with the reports. Tech questions may also be addressed to Mr Chappell in writing or by calling 208/526-0085. Proposed projects having more than one phase will be considered. All R&D phases from conceptual design thru proof-of-concept are permissible. Detailed schedule and cost info are required for Phase I, and est costs and a schedule are required for later phases. Selection will be based upon all phases; however, funding is presently available only for the first phase. Cost sharing commensurate with the degree of risk is desired from all proposers. Responses to this NPI will be evaluated by personnel of the federal government and DOE operating contractors. The DOE funding available for this NPI is $500,000. An effort will be made to fund as many proposals as possible within the available resources and commensurate with the program objectives. DOE reserves the right to support or not support any or all proposals and assumes no responsibility for any costs associated with their preparation and submission. The expiration date for this NPI is 90 days from date of publication. NPI DE-NP07-831D12492". (305)

Defense Supply Service-Washington, Rm 1D245, The Pentagon, Washington DC 20310, Attn: Mrs Meekins

★ A -- **ARMY/ACE TRANSCRIPT SYSTEM (AARTS).** Negotiations are being conducted on a sole source basis with the American Council on Education, Washington, DC. See note 46. (305)

H Expert and Consultant Services

U.S. Army Aviation Research and Development Command, Attn: DRDAV-PDS, (CPT Charles L Buttram, Commercial No. 314/263-1243), 4300 Goodfellow Blvd, St Louis, MO 63120

★ H -- **ENGINEERING SERVICES TO UPGRADE THE AC ELECTRICAL POWER ON THE OV-1D MOHAWK ACFT** to be compatible with the Joint Surveillance Target Attack Radar System (STARS). The U.S. Army Aviation Research and Development Command will negotiate a contract with Grumman Aerospace Corp, Stuart, FL. See note 46. (304)

Defense Logistics Agency, Defense Property Dsposal Service, Federal Center, Battle Creek, MI 49016

❶ H -- **SURVEILLANCE OF ELECTRONIC SCRAP**-#555,000 destination unknown. IFB DLA-200-84-B-0305. BOD o/a 16 Dec 1983. Surveillance, assay and process analysis service for a government contract which requires the recovery of all precious metals from electronic scrap and their conversion to an assayable bar. See note 42.

❶ H -- **SURVEILLANCE OF ELECTRONIC SCRAP**-#425,000 destination unknown. IFB DLA-200-84-B-0307. BOD o/a 16 Dec 1983. Surveillance, assay and process analysis service for a government contract which requires the recovery of all precious metals from electronic scrap and their conversion to an assayable bar. See note 42. (305)

ASD/YPKSA, Attn: Capt Dennis A Seal, Wright-Patterson AFB OH 45433, Tel 513/255-6846

H -- **PRODUCTION BASE ANALYSIS (PBA).** Conduct an industrial responsiveness assessment for the F-16 acft production program to include identification of production acceleration constraints, and identification of peacetime program cost reduction opportunities. It requires cooperative planning and analysis between government and industry. The purpose of this synopsis is to determine whether a competitive sol may be issued. The successful contractor will be required to establish/document lead-time and rate capacity baselines; compute total peacetime demand rates (production and logistics support) for F-16 worldwide operational support; conduct production rate capacity analyses; conduct sensitivity analyses for varying levels of demand rates; and identify critical bottle necks, capabilities, and opportunities for improving peacetime acquisition management. The successful contractor is required to have a detailed knowledge of F-16 component lead times, supplier capacities, prime-supplier business terms, coproduction/dual allocation plans, potential alternate sources, and integrated production installation schedules. The original PBA was a seven month effort with General Dynamics Corp. Prospective contractors are invited to state their interest and capability to perform this follow-on effort. Inquires pertaining to this acquisition should be directed to address above. See note 22. (305)

Contracting Office, Headquarters, U.S. Army Support Command, HI, Fort Shafter, HI 96858, Dale A Peck, Contracting Officer, 808/438-1686

❶ H -- **DATA PROCESSING SERVICES**—Convert approx 220,000 lines of 63-card column transactions to government-supplied 9-track tapes. Source documents and blank 9-track tapes will be delivered to and picked up at the vendor's site by government personnel. Source documents will be delivered bi-weekly in single batches of approx 2,115 lines and vendor will have conversion to 9-track tape accomplished and ready for pickup when next batch is delivered. Interested offerors should submit their responses NLT 30 calendar days from the date of this notice to Mrs Dale A Peck at the address given above. (305)

Immigration and Naturalization Service (ROPMP) 311 N Stemmons Freeway Dallas TX 75207 Attn: Linda Fabac Contract Specialist 214/767-6090

H -- **SIMULTANEOUS AND CONSECUTIVE INTERPRETER SERVICE** for the Miami FL District Office for the period 1/1/84 through 12/30/84—A copy of this sol is available for review at INS Central Office (Contracting & Procurement) Rm LL100 425 I St NW Washington DC 20536—IFB DLS-12-84 bid opening o/a 12/21/83. (305)

Ms Jeri Ligon, Dept of the Treasury, Bureau of Government Financial Operations, Procurement Branch, Treasury Annex 1, Rm 39, Washington, DC 20226

H -- **STATE-OF-THE-ART COLLECTION AND PAYMENT MECHANISM SYSTEMS**—The Bureau of Government Financial Operations has a requirement to establish an indefinite delivery-indefinite qty (fixed-rate) task order type contact for technical and managerial assistance in establishing efficient state-of-the-art collection and payment mechanisms systems. The anticipated contract will be for one year with options for an additional two years. RFP-BGFO-84-11 will be issued o/a Nov 28, 1983. Closing date is tentatively scheduled for Dec 28, 1983. Requests shall be addressed to he attention of Ms Jeri Ligon at the address noted above and must be in writing. For further info contact Ms Ligon at 202/566-8474.

H -- **ENHANCING THE GOVERNMENT-WIDE ACCOUNTING SYSTEMS.** The Bureau of Government Financial Operations has a requirement to establish an indefinite delivery-indefinite qty (fixed-rate) task order type contract for technical and managerial assistance in enhancing the government-wide accounting systems. The anticipated contract will be for one year with an option for one additional year. RFP BGFO 84-14 will be issued o/a Nov 28, 1983. Closing date is tentatively scheduled for Dec 28, 1983. Requests shall be addressed to the attention of Ms Jeri Ligon at the address noted above and must be in writing. For further info contact Ms Ligon at 202/566-8474. (305)

U.S. Dept of Energy, Attn: Document Control Specialist, PO Box 2500, Washington, DC 20013

H -- **PATENT SERVICES INCLUDING PATENT APPLICATION PREPARATION, PROSECUTION, AND PAYMENT OF ANNUITIES IN FRANCE.** All requests for this sol

CHAPTER 11

Characteristics of Government Grants

Many nonprofit agencies exhibit great fear and trepidation over concerns about strings attached to federal monies. While some of these fears are warranted, they are the concern of organizations that don't have adequate fiscal accountability. The restrictions governing usage of federal funds are understandable and in most cases reasonable. Yes, there are instances of disallowed expenditures many years after the grant has terminated, but they are avoidable and most people remember the exception rather than the rule. There are 25 billion dollars in federal grant funds and not everyone will have their expenditures disallowed.

The use of the Federal Grants-Requirements Worksheet (pp. 99–100) will help you comply with federal details.

Another important factor with federal funds is *time*. See Figure 11.1 for several considerations involved in this area.

Raising Matching Funds

One of the usual characteristics of a federal grant is the requirement for matching funds (also known as cost sharing). An

FIGURE 11.1. The time factor in federal funding.

Developing federal funds through the grants mechanism takes considerable lead time to generate. State funds have the same cycle constraints.

° You develop a proposal idea and redefine your project and start a search.

° You find through research that a federal program accepts proposals twice a year -- sometimes only once a year. In these cases your lead time may be more than one year.

Idea Generation Redefinition	Source & Deadline Research	Pre-proposal Contract	Deadline Date & Submit	Peer and Staff Review	Answer on Grant	1 year for generation of funds from grant proposal
			(months)			
1	3	5	7	9	12	

Meanwhile the federal bureaucracy has had a similar time constraint.

Draft Announcement in Federal Register	Announcement Comments	Publish Comments	Publish Final Grant Rules or Interim Rules	Publish Guidelines	Due Date	Review	Award Hardly Possible in 12 months from start of process
			(months)				
1	3	5	7	9	10	11	12

The federal and state bureaucracies have to have six months to one year to get their mechanism to follow prescribed rules and produce applications. They do extremely well to get funds out of the system in twelve months of the federal year. Remember, federal year starts October 1 and ends September 30.

The federal system will not respond to your _funding_ needs. They do have funds that can be used to fund unsolicited proposals. These monies are reserved _funds_ or leftover funds (funds given back by inconsiderate grantees who didn't develop an accurate cash flow). If you know enough to inquire about the use of these funds, the federal bureaucrats may respond to a unique project that meets a need of the category or type of area they deal with. You may not always be successful, however, the program director will at least be aware that you know how to "play the game."

FEDERAL GRANTS -- REQUIREMENTS WORKSHEET

Project Title _____

Funding Sources _____

____ Periodic Progress Reports (see Project Planner)

____ Final Completion Reports   Date Due: _____

      Individual Responsible: _____

      Delivered to Whom: _____

____ OMB Circulars Applicable -- List Them: _____

      In Grants Library: _____ Ordered and Received: _____

____ Rules on Continuation of Funding -- How Many Years: _____

      Is there a progression in awards (first consulting grant, then

demonstration, then evaluation, etc.)? If so, what is best progression?

_____

_____

____ Cost Sharing Requirement -- How Much Matching Funds Do You Have To

      Contribute

      _____ % -- $_____

____ Rules Governing Materials Produced on

      Grants:

      Copyrights:

      Patents:

____ On-site Visits by Feds.

                Announced Yes____   No____

____ Review OMB and FMC guidelines governing procedures requirements and

      rules for this grant. (Find rules listed in CFDA Appendix.) This

      is not an impossible task to accommodate.

                                                        (Cont.)

FEDERAL GRANTS -- REQUIREMENTS WORKSHEET (Cont.)

_____   Can We Provide Human Subjects Review?

Do We Need A Committee?

These are just a few eye-opening concerns to be raised at this point

in our search for federal funds. These concerns are only a few of the many

assurances you will be required to sign. This page is meant to get you

thinking. Federal funds do have their "strings."

---

organization can be asked to supply either cash, services, or facilities to match a percentage of the grant.

The worksheet on Sources of Matching Funds (p. 101) can help you plan a successful matching-funds campaign, even before you begin to approach federal agencies; it contains several standard methods for cost sharing and provides you with an evaluation system for each method.

Federal Grants-Management Circulars

Perhaps the most imposing characteristics of federal grants are the highly regulated, detailed rules about grant management: allowable costs, indirect cost rates, accounting requirements, and the like.

Before getting involved in government grants, you and/or your accounting department should review the appropriate grants management circulars.

The Office of Management and Budget produces OMB circulars that outline uniform standards for financial dealings with government granting agencies. These circulars are described in Table 11.1 and Figure 11.2.

The circulars can be ordered free from the Office of Management and Budget, 17th and Pennsylvania Avenue, N.W., Washington, D.C. 20503, or directly at your federal regional office.

SOURCES OF MATCHING FUNDS

Project Title: _____

TYPE	HOW IS THIS APPLICABLE TO THE PROJECT	LIST SUGGESTIONS THAT CAN BE USED	HOW MUCH MONEY COULD BE ATTRIBUTED TO THIS METHOD
In-kind contributions, donated services, space, equipment			
If training is involved, how much more will trainees be paid after training is completed			
Fund Raising Techniques			
Direct Mail			
Dance			
Raffles			
Wills & Bequest			
Sales – Products			
Can you donate indirect costs?			
Matching Grants – can you get a grant to match this grant? Example – Community Foundation to match federal or state grant			

TABLE 11.1. A Brief Description of the Major OMB Circulars

Name	What It Does	Areas Covered	Special Ramifications
OMB Circular A-21	Defines cost principles for federal research and development grants to educational institutions	Cost definition, allowable costs, unallowable costs	Long and complex circulars; wide range of allowable costs
OMB Circular A-95	Designates a procedure of review by local government before dispursing Federal funds	Any grant area covered is listed in *CFDA* by program number	Get on the local committee or develop a "friend" who is on it; call your county planning department for information
OMB Circular A-102	Sets administrative standards for federal agencies in management of grants to state and local governments	Application forms, grant payments, eligibility, matching share, financial management system, property management procurement standards	Although different federal agencies may set their own guidelines, they are usually in harmony with the standard set down in this circular

OMB Circular A-110	Set administrative standards for federal agencies in the management of grants to nonprofit organizations	Application forms, grant payment, matching shares, procurement standards	No federal agency may set more rigid standards than those outlined in the circular, exceptions to this rule are allowed when grantee has weak financial history
OMB Circular A-111	Sets out guidelines for joint funding of grant programs		Tells how to get funding from more than one agency for your project
Federal Management Circular 74-4	Establishes principles and standards for determining costs applicable to grants and contracts to state and local government	Outlines what costs are allowable under grants and contracts	Tells what rules apply to lease and rental of equipment, etc.

Note: You don't have to be an expert on OMB circulars; these government publications were researched to provide information for matrixes for regulations on purchase/lease applicability.

FIGURE 11.2.   A description of OMB circulars.
Appendix I: Programs Requiring Circular Coordination

This appendix lists programs requiring Circular coordination. The Circulars represented are OMB Circular No. A-87; OMB Circular No. A-102; Environmental Impact Statement; OMB Circular A-110; and OMB Circular No. A-111.

A-87

OMB Circular No. A-87 establishes principles and standards for determining costs applicable to grants and contracts with State and local governments. They are designed to provide the basis for a uniform approach to the problem of determining costs and to promote efficiency and better relationships between grantees and the Federal Government.

When State and local governments are recipients, the following programs listed in the Catalog of Federal Domestic Assistance are subject to the provision of A-87, except where restricted or prohibited by law.

Included also in the list are programs falling under the purview of A-87 because the Federal grantor agencies have elected to use the A-87 standards for recipients and programs not otherwise covered by the circular.

A-102

OMB Circular No. A-102 establishes uniform administrative standards for the administration of grants and contracts to State and local governments.

When State and local governments are recipients, the following programs listed in the Catalog of Federal Domestic Assistance are subject to the provisions of OMB Circular No. A-102.

Included also in the list are programs falling under the purview of OMB Circular No. A-102 because the Federal grantor agencies have elected to use the OMB Circular No. A-102 standards for recipients and programs not otherwise covered by the circular.

Environmental Impact Statement

Specific programs listed in the Catalog of Federal Domestic Assistance have been determined to have a significant effect on the environment and require an environmental assessment or an Environmental Impact Statement (EIS) under Section 102(2)(C) of the National Environmental Policy Act of 1969 (Public Law 90-190; 42 U.S.C. 4332(2)(C), and Executive Order 11514 (34 FR 4247) of March 4, 1970, (Significant effects include actions that may have both beneficial and detrimental effects.)

In the early stages of project application, and in all cases prior to agency decisions concerning major action, the applicant should be advised by the Federal agency from which assistance is being sought that he will be required to submit environmental impact information (to be submitted under agency guidelines) in connection with the proposed project for an environmental assessment (to be made by the Federal agency), or an Environmental Impact Statement (to be supplied by the Federal agency) concerning the proposed project.

Although the list below is not inclusive, it contains programs normally requiring either an environmental assessment or an Environmental Impact Statement.

For EIS coordination requirements, refer to the Preapplication Coordination section of each program description.

On October 1, 1982, the Federal Assistance Award Data System (FAADS) replaced Treasury Circular 1082 (TC 1082) as the means of notifying the states of Federal assistance awards.

A-110

OMB Circular No. A-110 sets forth administrative requirements for the administration of grants and other agreements to include money or property in lieu of money; does not include technical assistance programs providing services, loans, loan guarantees, insurance, or direct payments to individuals. Reference to this circular appears in the Application Procedure section of programs that apply.

Applicants are public and private institutions of higher education, hospitals, and other quasi-public and private nonprofit organizations.

A-111

OMB Circular No. A-111 establishes policies and procedures to be followed in the joint funding of related programs of Federal assistance pursuant to the Joint Funding Simplification Act of 1974. Under one application, applicants may apply for resources available from more than one Federal agency, program, or appropriation, including assistance from State sources. Programs identified as suitable for joint funding are identified in the Uses and Use Restrictions section of the programs. For programs that are not identified as suitable for joint funding, the applicant may consult the headquarters or field office of the appropriate agency for further information on statutory or other restrictions involved.

Applicants are State and local governments, Indian tribal bodies and private nonprofit organizations acting separately or jointly in seeking assistance with respect to a single project.

PROGRAM DESCRIPTION

Program Description	A-111			A-87	A-102	EIS	A-110
DEPARTMENT OF AGRICULTURE							
10.001 Agricultural Research—Basic and Applied Research						X	
10.156 Federal-State Marketing Improvement Program				X	X		
10.200 Grants for Agricultural Research, Special Research Grants						X	
10.202 Cooperative Forestry Research						X	
10.203 Payments to Agricultural Experiment Stations Under Hatch Act						X	
10.205 Payments to 1890 Land-Grant Colleges and Tuskegee Institute						X	
10.206 Grants for Agricultural Research—Competitive Research Grants						X	
10.207 Animal Health and Disease Research						X	
10.208 Alcohol Fuels Research						X	
10.209 1890 Research Facilities						X	
10.405 Farm Labor Housing Loans and Grants				X	X	X	X
10.411 Rural Housing Site Loans					X		
10.414 Resource Conservation and Development Loans				X	X		
10.415 Rural Rental Housing Loans					X		
10.418 Water and Waste Disposal Systems for Rural Communities				X	X		X
10.419 Watershed Protection and Flood Prevention Loans				X	X		
10.420 Rural Self-Help Housing Technical Assistance				X	X	X	
10.421 Indian Tribes and Tribal Corporation Loans				X			
10.422 Business and Industrial Loans				X	X		
10.423 Community Facilities Loans				X	X		
10.475 Cooperative Agreements with States for Intrastate Meat and Poultry Inspection				X	X		X
10.500 Cooperative Extension Service						X	
10.550 Food Distribution				X	X		
10.553 School Breakfast Program				X	X	X	
10.555 National School Lunch Program				X	X	X	
10.556 Special Milk Program for Children					X	X	
10.557 Special Supplemental Food Program for Women, Infants, and Children				X	X		
10.558 Child Care Food Program				X	X	X	
10.559 Summer Food Service Program for Children				X	X	X	
10.560 State Administrative Expenses for Child Nutrition				X			
10.561 State Administrative Matching Grants for Food Stamp Program				X	X		
10.564 Nutrition Education and Training Program				X	X		
10.565 Commodity Supplemental Food Program				X			
10.567 Food Distribution Program Commodities in Lieu of Food Stamps (Indian Reservations)				X	X		
10.652 Forestry Research				X	X	X	X
10.664 Cooperative Forestry Assistance				X	X	X	X
10.669 Accelerated Cooperative Assistance for Forest Programs on Certain Lands Adjacent to the Boundary Waters Canoe Area				X	X		
10.850 Rural Electrification Loans and Loan Guarantees					X		
10.851 Rural Telephone Loans and Loan Guarantees					X		
10.852 Rural Telephone Bank Loans					X		
10.901 Resource Conservation and Development				X	X	X	
10.904 Watershed Protection and Flood Prevention				X	X	X	
10.909 Resource Appraisal and Program Development				X	X		
DEPARTMENT OF COMMERCE							
11.108 International Trade Promotion					X		
11.300 Economic Development—Grants for Public Works and Development Facilities	X			X	X	X	X
11.301 Economic Development—Business Development Assistance	X			X	X		X
11.302 Economic Development—Support for Planning Organizations	X			X	X		X
11.303 Economic Development—Technical Assistance	X			X	X	X	X
11.304 Economic Development—Public Works Impact Projects	X			X	X	X	X
11.305 Economic Development—State and Local Economic Development Planning				X	X		X

CHAPTER 12

How to Contact Government Funding Sources

The importance of pre-proposal contact with government funding sources cannot be overemphasized. In a study of 10,000 federal proposals, the only variable that was statistically significant in separating the funded and rejected proposals was *pre-proposal contact with the funding source.*

It is estimated that chances for success go up 300 percent when contact with the funding source before the proposal is written. Up to this point in our book, we have not discussed the writing of the proposal; instead we have discussed the organization of the funding effort or project. You cannot write a proposal accurately until you know about the funding source. Who will read your application? What should you say? What should you avoid saying?

Contact is encouraged by letter (see sample on p. 111), phone, and when possible, in person. One way to force yourself to follow this systematic approach to funding sources is to set up a schedule of preproposal contact as follows:

SAMPLE LETTER TO A FEDERAL AGENCY

(for mailing list and past grantees)

Date:

Name
Title
Address

Dear _____:

Our organization is interested in carrying out a project under
your program title _____. The project will
deal with meeting the needs in the area of _____.

Please add me to your mailing list to receive the necessary
application forms, program guidelines and any existing priorities
statements or information that you feel would be helpful to me.
Please include a list of last year's grant recipients under this
program.

If my project is ineligible under your current guidelines or
there are no funds available, could you please refer me to a more
appropriate agency?

I have enclosed a self-addressed stamped envelope for your
convenience in returning the list of successful grantees. Thank
you for your cooperation and assistance in this matter.

Sincerely,

Name
Title
Phone Number

Note to the Letter Writer: You will receive the agency's publications as a
result of this letter (see, e.g., Fig. 12.1).

- *Week 1:* Write to two funding sources.

- *Week 2:* Write to two more funding sources.

- *Week 3:* Call the first two funding sources from Week 1 and
  ask for appointments.

- *Week 4:* Call the second two funding sources from Week 2
  and ask for appointments.

- *Week 5:* Follow up on appointments from phone conversations.

The worksheets in this chapter will help you organize your approach. Follow these suggestions and your chances of winning a grant and developing a positive relationship with the funding source will increase.

First, evaluate each funding source by utilizing the federal grants Prospect Analysis Form (pp. 109–110). Then move on to contacting those sources with the highest probability of funding your proposal.

Prospect Analysis Form

This worksheet will help you draw conclusions from your interviews and grant research. Use it to determine how well matched your project is with the funding agencies you have investigated. Fill out one analysis form for each prospective grant source.

Evaluate each of the criteria on the basis of the information you have gathered. Circle a number in the "Match" column corresponding to the amount of similarity between what you have and what they want. Multiply this figure by the "Weight" of each criterion and place that number in the "Total" column, then add up the totals and interpret your score. A higher score means a higher probability of winning grant support from a funding source.

The top or highest score will become the first funding source you will approach by personal contact.

Questions for Past Grantees

You have requested a list of previous grantees by letter (see sample on (p. 107) and enclosed a self-addressed stamped envelope for their convenience. You may have to request the list again by phoning the funding source. (It is wise to keep a checklist of requested materials, and a summary sheet of each contact with the funding source—see pp. 113 and 114.) Let the funding source know that you are aware that you are entitled to a list under the "Sunshine Law" (or Freedom of Information

PROSPECT ANALYSIS FORM

Fill out this sheet if you are within the funder's:

° geographic scope of giving (has this funding source given in your

geographic vicinity?)

° type of funding (does funding source buy what you have to sell -- bricks

and mortar, equipment?)

° restrictions (do they give to your type of organization, 501 C-3 Tax

Exempt?)

CRITERION	MATCH	WEIGHT	TOTAL
A. Your staff, expertise advocates -- will they appeal to this funding source	0 1 2 3 4 5	X2	
B. Interest Area -- how important is the need in this area to the funding source -- have they given to the need you represent	0 1 2 3 4 5	X2	
C. Financial Giving Patterns -- average grant size -- can they afford you	0 1 2 3 4 5	X1	
D. Contact/Friends -- can you link yourself to funding source	0 1 2 3 4 5	X3	
	TOTAL SCORE		

(*Cont.*)

Act). If all else fails, you may ask your congressperson to get the list for you. By law, federal bureaucrats have to respond to a congressperson's request. He or she *will* get the list! Once your list is in hand:
1. Select a grantee that is not in close proximity to you.
2. Call grantee and tell them where you got their name.

PROSPECT ANALYSIS FORM (Cont.)

0 = NO MATCH BETWEEN YOUR PROJECT AND FUNDING SOURCE

1 = POOR MATCH

2 = FAIR MATCH

3 = GOOD MATCH

4 = EXCELLENT MATCH

5 = PERFECT MATCH

Interpreting Your Score

Below 20:   buy a lottery ticket

20-25:   borderline

25-40:   good matches

Adapted from "Matching Your Proposal With Foundations Not All Luck," by

Robert F. Semple, in Fund Raising Management, September-October 1971, pp.

29-32.

---

3. Ask to speak to the director or person who worked on the proposal. (They will generally feel flattered you called.)
4. Prioritize or select from the following list of questions, or ask
   any of your own that will assist you in learning about the funding source.

   • Did you call or go see the funding source before writing the
     proposal?

   • Whom did you find most helpful on funding source staff?

   • How did you use your advocates or congresspeople?

   • Did you utilize a review by the funding source before sub-
     mission?

   • Did you use consultants to help you on the proposal?

SAMPLE LETTER TO A GOVERNMENT AGENCY

(for appointment)

Date:

Name
Title
Address

Dear _____:

     My research on your funding program _____ indicates
that the research/project that we have developed in _____
would be appropriate for funding by your agency.

     I will be in ___(city)___ on ___(date)___ and would appreciate
10 minutes to discuss the project. Your insights, knowledge, and
information on any grants that have been funded which utilized a
similar approach would be invaluable. [You may list benefits here,
such as: a great savings in time as I explore the grant possibilities
in this area.]

     I will call to confirm the possibility of a brief meeting to
discuss this important area.

                              Sincerely,

                              Name
                              Title
                              Phone Number

Note to the Letter Writer: You will not get a response back from
this letter. Its intent is to show protocol and that you mean
business.

- Was there a hidden agenda to the program's guidelines?

- When did you begin the process of developing your application—contacting the funding source?

- What materials did you find the most helpful in developing your proposal?

- Did the funding source come to see you (site visit) before the proposals were awarded? After awarded? Who came

bulletin

Vol. 9 No. 4   December 1981

NATIONAL
SCIENCE
FOUNDATION
WASHINGTON, D. C. 20550

NSF Announcements for December

This issue of the *NSF Bulletin* contains information on agency programs, deadlines, meetings, publications, and sources for more detailed information. Publications listed in this *Bulletin* may be obtained on the Publications Order Form. The area code of all telephone numbers listed is 202, unless otherwise indicated. The address of the National Science Foundation is 1800 G St., N.W., Washington, D.C. 20550.

Collection of Data on Race and/or Ethnic Origin of Principal Investigators and Project Directors

The NSF Authorization and Science and Technology Equal Opportunities Act (Dec. 12, 1980), Part B, requires the collection and reporting of certain statistical data regarding women and minorities in science and technology. In partial response to the Act, NSF has been authorized by the Office of Management and Budget to amend the NSF grant application process to include the collection of race and/or ethnic information on principal investigators (PIs) and project directors (PDs). Gender information has been collected since Jan. 1981. Providing such information to NSF is voluntary; refusal will in no way affect consideration of an application.

Race and/or ethnic and gender information concerning PIs and PDs will be maintained in a secure system of records under requirements of the Privacy Act of 1974. Information from this system will be used for aggregate statistical purposes only, and will not identify individuals.

To provide NSF with the information it needs for this important task, PIs and PDs are requested to complete NSF Form 1153, and attach a single copy to the face page of the signature copy of the application. This form may be reproduced locally for distribution to potential PIs and PDs.

Upon receipt and assignment of the application by NSF, Form 1153 will be detached from the application. It will *not* be duplicated, will *not* be made available to the NSF program officer, and will *not* be a part of the review process. Data will be confidential. For further information and a copy of NSF Form 1153, request NSF Important Notice No. 88 on the Publications Order Form.

Alan T. Waterman Award Nominations

The deadline for receipt of nominations for the 1982 Alan T. Waterman Award is Dec. 31, 1981. The Award, presented annually to an outstanding young scientist, mathematician or engineer, will be announced and presented in May 1982. For further information and/or a copy of the guidelines for submission, contact Mrs. Lois Hamaty, Office of Planning and Resources Management (357-7512).

Awards for Ethics and Values in Science and Technology

NSF and the National Endowment for the Humanities announce the availability of guidelines for the Interdisciplinary Incentive Awards and Sustained Development Awards programs, administered by NSF's Ethics and Values in Science and Technology (EVIST) program. The objective is to develop among individuals and institutions a greater capacity to analyze issues in the field of ethics and values in science and technology. Closing date for the submission of applications is Feb. 1, 1982, with awards announced in June 1982. Brochures on the two programs may be ordered on the Publications Order Form: SE 81-62A for the Interdisciplinary Incentive Awards; and SE 81-62B for the Sustained Development Awards. For further information, contact Dr. Rachelle Hollander, EVIST (357-7552).

NSF International Travel Grants

NSF's International Travel Grant (ITG) program has been discontinued as of Oct. 1, 1981. A separate ITG program and budget no longer exists. However, proposals for NSF support of travel to international scientific meetings held abroad may be submitted to the NSF unit with responsibility for the area of scientific interest.

New Investigators in Research in Information Science

The deadline for new investigators to submit proposals for Special Research Initiation Awards in Information Science is Feb. 3, 1982.

The program announcement, *Research in Information Science and Technology*, defines the program goals: to increase understanding of the properties and structures of information and information transfer, and to contribute to the store of scientific and technical knowledge which can be applied in the design of information systems.

Copies of the announcement, NSF 81-34, may be requested on the Publications Order Form, or by contacting the Division of Information Science and Technology (357-9569).

The *NSF Bulletin* is issued monthly (except July and August) to disseminate information on NSF programs, policies, and activities. Use of funds for printing this periodical has been approved by the Director of the Office of Management and Budget through Sept. 30, 1981. Editor Barbara Tulty, Public Information Branch

FIGURE 12.1.   A sample of National Science Foundation *Bulletin*.

CHECKLIST OF MATERIALS FROM PUBLIC FUNDING SOURCES

Directions: Check those materials sent for. Put the date requested in column A and the date received in column B.

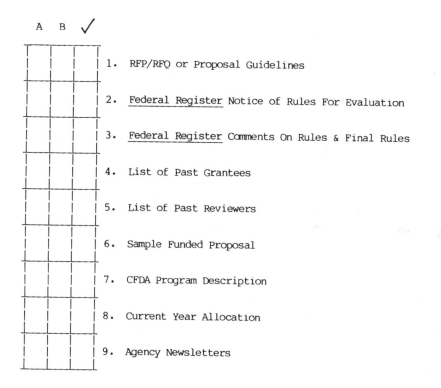

A B ✓

1. RFP/RFQ or Proposal Guidelines

2. <u>Federal Register</u> Notice of Rules For Evaluation

3. <u>Federal Register</u> Comments On Rules & Final Rules

4. List of Past Grantees

5. List of Past Reviewers

6. Sample Funded Proposal

7. CFDA Program Description

8. Current Year Allocation

9. Agency Newsletters

on the visit? What did they wear? How old were they? Would you characterize them as conservative, moderate, liberal? Did anything in the process surprise you?

- How close was your initial budget to the awarded amount? (You can check honesty here by taking a look at their proposal when you visit the funding source. The Freedom of Information Act allows you to see any proposal funded by government money.)

- Who on the funding source's staff negotiated the budget?

- What would you do differently next time?

PUBLIC FUNDING SOURCE CONTACT

SUMMARY SHEET

Project Title: _____

This sheet should be added to each time you contact a public funding source:

AGENCY NAME: _____

PROGRAM OFFICER: _____

Contacted on (date): _____

By Whom: _____

Contacted by: LETTER _____   PHONE _____

              PERSONAL CONTACT _____

Staff or Advocates Present: _____

DISCUSSED: _____

_____

_____

_____

_____

RESULTS: _____

_____

_____

_____

_____

Questions for Past Reviewers

You have requested a list of reviewers (see sample on p. 115) Under the Sunshine Law, you *can* demand one, but don't. Tell the funding source you are concerned about the make-up or background of their reviewers. If they are reluctant to give names, try to get general information on the reviewers, their

<u>SAMPLE LETTER TO A FEDERAL AGENCY</u>

(for a list of reviewers)

Date:

Name
Title
Address

Dear _____:

    I am presently developing a proposal under your _____
program. I would find it very helpful to have a list of last year's
reviewers. Such a list would assist me in developing my approach
and the appropriate writing style. Please advise me if the make-up
or background of the review committee will change significantly in
the next grant year.

    My proposal is based upon the level, expertise and diversity of
the reviewers. Information on the composition of the review committee
will be used to prepare a quality proposal based upon the reviewers'
background.

    I have enclosed a self-addressed stamped envelope for your
convenience in responding to this request. I will utilize the
materials you send and I thank you for your consideration in
providing them.

                    Sincerely,

                    Name
                    Title
                    Phone Number

<u>Note to the Letter Writer</u>: You want a list of last year's reviewers
so you can write a proposal based on their expertise, reading level,
biases, etc. Once you have the list, you can contact the reviewers
themselves to discuss the points they look for when reviewing proposals. (See "Questions for Past Reviewers.")

---

selection process, and the process of reviewing and allocating
points to a proposal.

    You can utilize your congressperson or his or her administra-
tive assistant to procure your list. If you use this method, ask your

congressperson not to use your name in describing who wants the material.

When you get the list, examine it for bias and make-up (where they are from, background, etc.), call a reviewer and explain that you understand that he or she was a reviewer for_____program. Then ask:

- How did you get to be a reviewer?

- Did you review proposals at a funding source location or at home?

- What training or instruction did the funding sources give you?

- Did you follow a point system? What and how?

- What were you told to look for?

- How would you write a proposal differently now that you have been a reviewer?

- What were the most common mistakes that you saw?

- Did you meet other reviewers?

- How many proposals were you given to read?

- How much time did you have to read them?

- How did the funding source handle discrepancies in point assignments?

- What did the funding source wear, say, and do during the review process?

- Did you know about a staff review to follow your review?

Using the Phone with Federal and State Funding Sources

Calling public funding sources on the phone is best described as an experience in itself. The informational contact you develop from your research seldom yield the correct name and phone number of the best individual to handle your request. Ask who else could help you or where the person listed in your research has moved to. There is usually a person in your congressperson's office assigned to help people in your district with grants. These techniques should enable you to locate the office that administers the funds for the program your research has uncovered.

The best approach is to go see the funding source. If this is the approach you choose, use the techniques outlined in "Making an Appointment with a Public Funding Source Official."

If you cannot go to visit the funding source, you will want to gather the same information over the phone that you would if you were face to face with the funding source. Although it is harder to "read" what the funding source is really saying through voice inflection as opposed to watching the nonverbal behavior visible in personal contact, you need to uncover his or her hidden agenda so that you can meet the needs of the funding source and increase your chances of success.

Review the suggestions under "Questions to Ask a Program Officer," below.

Making an Appointment with a Public Funding Source Official

The objective of seeking an appointment is to get an interview with a decision maker in the program.

- Step 1: Call and ask for the program officer or information contact.

- Step 2: Get the secretary's name and ask when his or her boss can be reached. (Some federal employees are on flextime or come in and leave at odd hours to cope with the D.C. traffic.)

- Step 3: Call back; try person-to-person, and if that fails, ask the secretary for help.

An alternative plan might involve any of the following:
a. Try to get an advocate to set up your appointment.
b. Try getting congressional help with appointment.

c. Try going in "cold" early in the week to get an appointment for later in the week. They prefer to get you out of the way *now!*

- Step 4: Ask the secretary if anyone else can answer technical questions on the program. You may get an appointment with a screen (they're better than talking to yourself).

- Step 5: When you get to the program person on the phone, introduce yourself and give a brief (ten words) description of your organization. Say:
  a. The need for _____ in our area is extreme.
  b. We are uniquely suited to deal with the problem, the research, etc.
  c. You understand that their programs deal with these needs and you would like to make an appointment to talk to them about their program priorities and your approaches.

  When you get an appointment, stop and hang up. If no appointment is possible, refer to "Questions to Ask a Program Officer." Tell them you have some questions; can you set up a ten-minute call or would they prefer to answer your questions now? (*Note:* fill in any information you get—names, phone numbers, etc.—on the research sheet.)

The Visit and Questions to Ask

PRE-PROPOSAL CONTACT WITH PUBLIC FUNDING OFFICIALS

This initial meeting is vital to getting the input you need to prepare a proposal that is tailored to the funding source (see p. 119). This visit will allow you to review and update any information you have.

The object of such a visit is to find out as much as possible about the funding source and how they perceive their role in the awarding of these grants. With your newly acquired information you can produce a proposal that reflects a sensitivity to their needs

TAILORING WORKSHEET

A. From your background on the funding source, what approach to meeting the needs would be preferred by them? How will you tailor your approach?

_____

_____

B. How many points has the funding source assigned to each of the following grant components?

POINTS

_____ THE TITLE: _____

_____

_____ THE NEEDS: _____

_____

_____ THE OBJECTIVES: _____

_____

_____ THE METHODOLOGY: _____

_____

_____ THE BUDGET: _____

_____

_____ THE EVALUATION: _____

_____

_____ OTHER: _____

_____

_____ TOTAL POINTS: _____

_____

These points will determine importance and time appropriated to each section of the proposal.

and their perception of their mission. In *A Theory of Cognitive Dissonance,* Festinger states that the more different we are perceived to be from what the funding source expects, the greater the problems with communication, agreement, and acceptance. We want the funder to *love us,* so we need to produce less dissonance and more agreement by looking and talking as the funder "thinks" we should. Dress is critical. If you don't know the funding source's expectations on dress, play it safe and read *Dress for Success* by John T. Molloy (New York: Warner Books, 1976).

PLAN FOR YOUR VISIT

In a personal visit, two people are better than one. An advocate or graduate of your program has more credibility than a paid staff member. Try to match up age, interests, and other characteristics of your people with funding executive (see p. 121). Before the visit, it will be helpful to role-play your presentation with your team member and to decide who will take responsibility for the various parts of the presentation.

WHAT TO TAKE

1. Materials that help demonstrate the *need.*
2. Your Proposal Development Workbook (Swiss Cheese Book).
3. Audio-visual aids—short filmstrip, videotape, film-loop, slide presentation, pictures, cassette tape, or the like—that document the need. Visual aids should be short (three to five minutes long). Avoid talking about your methods and solution. Be sure you can work machines with ease and replace bulbs, etc. Bring extension cords, three-prong to two-prong plug adapter, and whatever other peripheral equipment you will need.
4. Information on your organization that you can leave, but *never leave a proposal.*

QUESTIONS TO ASK A PROGRAM OFFICER

Check over these questions you will ask:

• Do you agree that the need addressed by our project is important?

FUNDING SOURCE STAFF PROFILE

Before each visit to a funding source, review this sheet to be sure you are taking the correct materials, advocates, and staff.

AGENCY DIRECTOR: _____

PROGRAM DIRECTOR: _____

CONTACT PERSON YOU WORK WITH: _____

_____

PROFILE: Birthdate: _____ Title: _____

_____

Education: College _____

              Postgraduate _____

Work Experience: _____

Military Service: _____

Service Clubs: _____

Religious Affiliations: _____

Interests/Hobbies: _____

Publications: _____

_____

_____

- Your average award in this area last year was *X* dollars; do you expect that to change?

- How will successful grantees from last year affect people putting in new or first applications? Will last year's grantees be in competition with me or have their funds been set aside? If so, how much is left for new awards?

- Are there any unannounced programs or unsolicited proposal funds in your agency to fund an important project like ours?

- What is the most common mistake or flaw in proposals you receive?

- Are there any areas you would like to see addressed in a proposal that may have been overlooked by the other grantees or applicants?

- We have developed several approaches to this needs area. You may know whether or not one of our approaches has been tried. Could you review our concept paper and give us any guidance?

- Would you review or critique our proposal if we got it to you early?

- Would you recommend a previously funded proposal for us to read for format and style? (Remember—you are entitled to read funded proposal, but be cool!)

- What changes do you expect in types or number of awards this year (fewer new awards versus continuing awards, etc.)?

- Is there a relationship between the type of grant programs and awards? Is there a progression (consultant grant—demonstration—evaluation)?

- The guidelines call for _____ copies of the proposal. Could you use more? If I provided all copies, may I bind them in an inexpensive binder? What type do you prefer?

- Will I create any problems by using tabs or dividers in my proposal?

CHAPTER 13

The Project Planner

How To Control the Proposal-Preparation Process

The Project Planner (see pp. 124–125) is arranged in the order in which you approach each phase of the proposal-preparation process. You must take each part separately and control the process or it can overwhelm even experienced grant seekers.

The end result is a proposal that is tailored to the funding source by using the information you have obtained and recorded on the preceding worksheets.

The *order* that a typical proposal follows when it is to be read *is not* the same order used to construct the proposal.

The "How To" Grants Manual is designed in a step-by-step process that follows the sequence involved in proposal preparation. The sequence that most proposal outlines follow is misleading to the beginning grant writer. The order of the parts of the proposal and the sequence designated by the funder have been designed for accuracy and understanding while reading the proposal, and are *counterproductive when applied to the writing of the proposal.*

PROJECT PLANNER™

PROJECT TITLE: _____

A. List Project objectives or outcomes A. B. B. List Methods to accomplish each objective as A-1, A-2, A-3 ... B-1, B-2 ...	MONTH		TIME	PROJECT PERSONNEL	PERSONNEL COSTS		
	BEGIN	END			SALARIES & WAGES	FRINGE BENEFITS	TOTAL
	C / D		E	F	G	H	I

TOTAL DIRECT COSTS OR COSTS REQUESTED FROM FUNDER ▶

MATCHING FUNDS, IN-KIND CONTRIBUTIONS, OR DONATED COSTS ▶

TOTAL COSTS ▶

Sheet _____ of _____

Proposal Developed for _____

PROJECT DIRECTOR: _____ Proposed starting date _____ Proposal Year _____

CONSULTANTS • CONTRACT SERVICES			NON-PERSONNEL RESOURCES NEEDED SUPPLIES • EQUIPMENT • MATERIALS				SUB-TOTAL COST FOR ACTIVITY	MILESTONES PROGRESS INDICATORS	
TIME	COST/WEEK	TOTAL	ITEM	COST/ITEM	QUANTITY	TOT. COST	TOTAL I. L. P	ITEM	DATE
J	K	L	M	N	O	P	Q	R	S

T   ◄ % OF TOTAL

◄

100%   ◄

Typical Proposal Sequence	Project Planner Sequence	
		Page
A. Cover Letter	1. Needs Statement	000
B. Title Page	2. Objectives	000
C. Summary	3. Methods	000
D. Introduction	4. Evaluation	000
E. Problem/Need	5. Future Funding	000
F. Objectives	6. Dissemination	000
G. Methods	7. Budget	000
H. Evaluation	8. Title Page	000
I. Future Funding	9. Summary	000
J. Dissemination	10. Attachments	000
K. Budget	11. Cover Letter	000
L. Attachments		

The Project Planner can be used to develop a variety of proposals and projects. Each part of the process has the corresponding page numbers and the forms and worksheets that will help the beginning grant seeker to write the section, while the veteran may use the forms as a checklist to insure that he or she has included all he or she can under each section.

Needs Statement

Most grant seekers feel very strongly about the need for their project or research. Too many grant seekers assume that the funding source shares the same feelings of concern and the urgency of addressing the need as soon as possible. This wishful thinking is rarely correct. The funding source has to choose from among many interesting proposals, and you must *create* the feeling of *immediacy* or *urgency* so that the funding source cannot put you off until next year.

Record any of the following types of data that can demonstrate the need. Keep the data in this section of your Proposal Development Workbook (Swiss Cheese Book). Later, when you write a tailored proposal to each funding source, you can select the data that you think will be best used to convince the particular funding source of the need. Why document the need? The documented

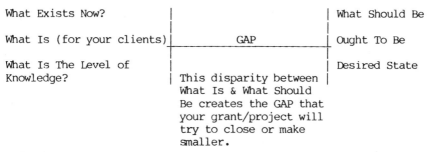

FIGURE 13.1

existence of a problem or need that is viewed by the funding source as a state of affairs that could be better, improved, or different, is the reason they give away their money. Funding sources are "*buying*" a better state of affairs. From pure research to model or demonstration projects, the funding source is supporting a change or improvement in what exists now. This can be represented by the diagram in Figure 13.1.

The urgency is created by how well you document the need and make the funding source feel that the movement toward the desired state cannot wait any longer. Since not all proposals can be funded, reality says that some will have to wait. Those that do not get funded did not do as good a job at:

- documenting a real need (perceived as important)
- demonstrating what ought to be (for clients)
- creating the urgent need to close the gap

DOCUMENTING WHAT IS

1. Review the section on "Ways to Perform Needs Surveys" to assess whether any of these will help document the need.
2. Use statistics from articles and research: e.g., 70 percent of children have . . .
3. Use quotes from leaders or experts in the field: Dr. Flockmeister said—
4. Use case statements: e.g., John Quek, a typical client who lives in a . . .
5. Describe national need and reduce it to a local number that

is more understandable: e.g., 90 percent of the elderly
have . . . This means that at the West Side Senior Center, 215
elderly . . .

6. State need in terms of one person: e.g., the average veteran has
   had . . .

7. Use statements of community people: police, politicians,
   clergy, and others.

To establish what "Ought To Be," proven statistics may be difficult or impossible to find. The use of experts' statements and
quotes to document what ought to be is much more credible than
your opinion. (*Note:* You do not put your opinion in the needs
statement. You are demonstrating your knowledge of the field;
you have surveyed the literature; you know the situation.)

The needs section is written to be motivating. One way to motivate a funding source is to use their own studies, surveys, or statistics. The same basic proposal can be tailored to two different
funding sources by quoting different studies that appeal to their
own view of the need. You can "appear" at the end of the needs
statement as the logical choice to attack the gap and move
toward reducing the problem. If the proposal format required
by the funding source does not have a section that deals with
your capability, the best place to put in your credentials is at the
end of the needs statement.

HERE IS A COMPELLING NEED ⟶ Here is the "right" organiza-
                                    tion to fund to reduce the gap.

This transition from the need to your credibility can come
from a simple sentence that states: It is the mission of our organization to address this need. For example, you develop a gap between what is and what ought to be. This is the basis for need and
urgency to move to close the gap.

After the case is made for the need in a factual way, you add
that:

- It is the mission of our institution to deal with this problem.

- Your unique qualities make you best suited for the job. You
  have the staff or facilities for this project to work or use
  your "sameness" to others: "Our project will serve as a
  model to the many other similar agencies that face this

dilemma each day." (This results in a multiple effect from funding this project; the results potentially have effect on many.)

• The needs are here and now; each day they go unmet and the problem grows.

Objectives

The objectives are measurable steps you will take to narrow or close the gap created in the needs statement (see Figure 13.2).

When you have accomplished Objectives A and B, you will move toward closing the gap. You will have less gap left than you had before.

Objectives follow the needs statement since you cannot write the objectives unless you document the need and what is to be reduced.

Since the accomplishment or attainment of each objective will close the gap, you must write objectives that are measurable and can be evaluated for the degree to which they have been attained, and thus, the amount of the gap that has been closed.

Note for researchers: The search or review of relevant research in the field is analagous to "what is" and what ought to be. The objective of a research proposal is different from a model project in that you seek to disprove the null hypothesis. When this is ac-

FIGURE 13.2

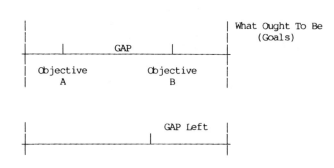

complished at a level of statistical significance, it acts to close the gap on what knowledge we have that is predictable and proven.

There has been increasing pressure by various groups (Proxmire's Golden Fleece Awards, "Reaganism") to make all researchers relate their research in a practical way to what (exactly) can be done with it. Philosophical arguments aside, there are conservative elements that want a component of research grants to deal with such issues as dissemination of results and how the findings can be used by the general public.

WRITING OBJECTIVES

Objectives tell the grant seeker and funding source "what it is" that will be accomplished at the end of the grant—how much or how little change will occur or what will be different at the end of this expenditure of funds from what was there before.

The *methods* tell *how* you will accomplish this change. The objective tells what will be accomplished and *how much* will be accomplished. Objectives state the measurable end for which you will be held accountable.

Methods state the means to that end. The first rule-of-thumb is: If there is only one way to accomplish the objective, you have probably written a method. Accomplishing the objective involves a good choice of methods or activities. For example, one seminar participant stated his objective as: "To build a visitors' center for our museum." Ask yourself how many ways you can build a visitors' center. (Yes, you can build it below ground or above, two stories or three.) Building the visitors' center is not the objective; it is a method—*how you will do it* ("it" being the actual objective).

When asked why he wanted to build a visitors' center, his response was: "To understand the relationship between the museum buildings so visitors can more effectively use the museum." The *"what"* that this man wanted to accomplish could be done in a variety of ways (*methods*). The visitors' center is a means to an end—effective utilization of the museum. Why go through all of this? Because the reason a funding source will give you money relates to helping people use and appreciate the museum, not to the bricks and mortar of a visitors' center. The bricks and mortar do not lend themselves to the kind of measurement that the issue of effective utilization does.

A TECHNIQUE FOR WRITING OBJECTIVES

Step 1: Determine result areas. Result areas are the key places you will look at to see improvements or changes in the client population. Examples include "Health of people over 65 years of age in St. Louis"; "Better-educated minority students"; or "More efficient use of our museum."

Step 2: Determine measurement indicators. Measurement indicators are quantifiable parts of your result area. By measuring your performance with these indicators, you are able to see how well you are doing. Examples include: "Number of hospital readmissions of people over 65 years old"; "Scores on standardized tests"; or "Number of people who understand relationship of museum buildings." Brainstorm a number of measurement indicators for each result area, then select the one that reflects your intent and is the least difficult to deal with.

Step 3: Determine performance standards. Performance standards answer the question, "How much [or how little] of the measurement indicators do we need to consider ourselves successful?" (closing the gap). Using our above examples, we might determine the following performance standards: "10 percent drop in hospital readmissions"; "Scores rising from 80th to 90th percentile on the Flockmeister reading scale"; or "50 percent reduction in direction giving by staff."

Step 4: Determine the time frame. The time frame is the amount of time in which you want to reach your performance standards. It's *your* deadline. You might decide you want to see a 10 percent drop in hospital readmissions within six or eighteen months. Usually, this time frame is determined for you by the funding source. Most grants are for twelve months. Use months one through twelve, instead of January, February, etc., because you seldom get to start the grant when you expect to.

Step 5: Determine cost frame. This is the amount of money that represents the cost of the methods or activities you have selected as your approach to meet this objective. The cost estimate is obtained from the planning document you will fill out next. You may leave this blank until you complete your project planner and then come back and fill it in. *Remember:* a funding source could take the number of clients to benefit and divide the amount requested to complete this objective. The end result could be embarrassing.

Step 6: Write the objectives. This step combines the data you have generated in the previous five steps. The standard format for an objective is: "To [action verb and statement reflecting your *measurement indicator*] by [*performance standard*] by [*deadline*] at a cost of no more than [*cost frame*]." The example concerning reading scores could look like this: "To increase the reading scores of freshmen at Flockmann University minority skills program by 20% on the Flockmann reading scale in 12 months at a cost of $50,000."

Step 7: Evaluate the objective. Review your objective and answer the question: "Does this objective reflect the amount of change we want in the result area?" If your answer is "yes," you probably have a workable objective. If not, the chances are that your measurement indicator is wrong or your performance standards are too low. Go back to those steps and repeat the process.

When writing program objectives, you should go through the same seven steps. Again, remember to emphasize end results, not tasks or methods. Do not say what you are going to do; instead, try to emphasize the ultimate benefit of your program's work.

Methods

The methods, or activities, section is the detailed description of what you will actually do to accomplish or meet the objectives. The methods tell:

- What you will have to do.
- Who will be needed.
- How long they will work.
- The materials and equipment you will need.

These are all a function of what you set out to accomplish. The best order to proceed in is to develop your methods to meet the objectives. Rather than inflating your budget or price for this project, add several methods that would insure the meeting of your objectives. When you negotiate the final award, you will gain much more credibility with the funding source by eliminating methods, instead of lowering the price for the same amount of work.

The methods section will:

- *describe program activities* in detail: How do they fulfill objectives?

- describe the *sequence, flow, and interrelationship* of activities.

- describe planned *staffing of program:* Who is responsible for what?

- describe the *client population* and method of determining client selection.

- present a *reasonable scope of activities* that can be accomplished within the stated time frame and with the resources of your agency.

It should also:

- make reference to the cost/benefit ratio of your project.

- state specific time frames.

- include a discussion of risk (why your success is probable).

- describe the uniqueness of your methods and overall project design.

- assign responsibility to specific individuals for each part of the project.

The Project Planner will provide a form that will insure that your methods section reflects a well-conceived and well-laid-out plan for the accomplishment of your objectives.

Project Planner

The Project Planner we present here is the result of ten years of work with grant and contract preparation. Use these explanations as you look at the form on pp. 124–125.

1. List your objectives or tasks under A. Give them what they want; some contracts may require tasks or enabling objectives.

2. Under B, list the method necessary to meet the objective. These are the tasks you have decided upon and are *your approach* to meeting the need. (Note that this newest form of the Project Planner has combined what were two columns: A and B. This was done to promote more efficient utilization of space. State your Objective A, B, C, ... and list your method as A-1, A-2, A-3 ... B-1, B-2. ...)

3. In Column C/D, place the date you will begin and end each activity.

4. In Column E designate the number of person-weeks (you can use hours or months) needed to accomplish that task.

5. Column F is used for designating the key personnel that will use measurable or significant amounts of time on this activity and the accomplishment of this objective. The designation of key personnel is critical for developing the job description for each individual. If you list the activities for which the key personnel are responsible and the minimum qualifications or background required, you will have a rough job description. Call a placement agency to get an estimate of the salary needed to fill the position. The number of weeks or months will determine full- or part-time classification. (*Note:* This provides the opportunity to look at how many hours of work you are providing in a given time span. If you have your key personnel working more than 160 hours per month, it may be necessary to adjust the number of weeks in Column E to fit a more reasonable time frame. You may have to reschedule activities or shift responsibility to another staff member.)

6. *Personnel costs:* special care should be placed on analyzing staff who will be donated from your organization. This may be a

requirement for your grant (refer back to the section on matching funds). You may want to use this donated contribution to show your good faith and appear as a better investment to the funding source. (*Note:* Put an asterisk by each person you donate to the project. Be sure to include your donation of fringes, as well as wages. As you complete the remaining columns, put an asterisk by anything else you donate.)

7. *Consultants and contract services:* these three columns are for the individuals and services that are most cost-efficiently supplied by individuals who are not in your normal employ. They may be experts at a skill you need that does not warrant your training a staff member or hiring an additional staff person for (evaluation, computers, commercial art, etc.). There are no fringes paid to consultants and contract services.

8. *Nonpersonnel resources needed:* this is where you list the components that are necessary to complete each activity and achieve your objective. Many a grant seeker has gone wrong by underestimating the materials and supplies necessary for success-ful completion of the project. Most grant seekers lose out on the many donated or matching items because they did not sit down and ask themselves, "What do I need to have to complete this ac-tivity?" Notice in the sample that travel, supplies, and telephone communication have been donated.

9. This column can be completed in two ways:

- Each activity can be subtotaled.

- You may wish to subtotal several activities into the subtotal for objectives.

10. *Milestones:* Column R is necessary to record what the funding source will receive as indicators of your working toward the accomplishment of your objectives. Column S lists the date on which the funding source will receive the milestone or progress indicator.

11. *Indirect costs:* federal grants contain a concept that is crit-ically important and poorly understood by *most* grant seekers and *everyone not connected* with grants. The concept involves repaying the recipient of a federal grant for costs that are difficult to break

down individually, but are indirectly attributable to performing the federal grant. These costs include such things as:

- the heat and lights for those individuals on the grant:
- the cost for upkeep on the building:
- the maintenance staff: or
- the payroll department.

Indirect costs are calculated by using a formula that is provided by the Federal Regional Controller's Office. It is expressed as a percentage of the total amount requested from the funding source (represented by the Total in Column Q), or as a percentage of the people on the grant (represented by Total of Column I).

Evaluation

Federal and state funding sources place a much heavier emphasize on evaluation than most private sources do. While there are many books written on evaluation, the best advice on how to handle it is to get an expert. I suggest seeking out a qualified individual at a college or university who has experience in dealing with this area. College professors generally enjoy the involvement and the extra pay. Professors also lead you to a storehouse of inexpensive labor—undergraduate and graduate students. A graduate student in statistics can help you deal with the problem of quantifying your results inexpensively, while he or she gathers valuable insight and experience.

Writing your objectives properly makes the process of evaluation much simpler. Using the sections in this chapter on how to write objectives (pp. 130–132) will provide you with a valuable resource for developing objectives that can be measured. Many grant seekers proceed smoothly with objectives that deal with cognitive areas or areas that provide for results that can be easily qualified. The problems start when they move into the area known as the *affective domain*—values, feelings, and appreciation are difficult to measure.

If you use the form for writing objectives and ask yourself: "What will these people do differently after the grant that they don't do now?," you will help keep yourself on the road to evaluation that will pass the federal and state tests. For example, a grant to increase appreciation for opera could be measured by seeing how many of the subjects attend an inexpensive performance after the free ones are completed.

Future Funding

Most funding sources are buying a piece of the future. It is in their best interest to see the project live on. This way, they are able to take credit for it and its benefits over a greater length of time. Many of us grant seekers begin to show our "tunnel vision" by forgetting the funding sources' needs concerning the future and neglect to plan to keep their investment alive by outlining a future finance plan.

You will continue the project through:

- Service fees
- Membership fees
- Other granting agencies (United Way)
- Big-gift campaigns aimed at wealthy individuals
- Starting an endowment program
- Getting other grants
- Starting a direct-mail campaign
- Other fund-raising mechanisms

Include the cost of one or more of these activities in your expenses and budget for them in the grant. You are not automatically considered an ingrate for doing this, but rather you may come across as a good executor of the funding source's estate. You are planning for continuation.

Dissemination

In addition to the good that will come from meeting the objectives and closing the gap established in the needs statement, much good can come from letting others know what you and the funding source have accomplished in this grant.

The funding source may pay for your dissemination of the results of the grant through one or more of the following mechanisms. Request funds for:

- A final report mailed to others in your field

- A quarterly journal mailed to others

- A newsletter mailed to others in your field

- Sponsoring a seminar or conference on the topic

- Attending a national (try international) conference to deliver results of the project (Many government funding officials cannot travel to conferences, but they can fund you to go and disseminate the results.)

- Production of a film or slide/tape presentation on the project

This type of thinking is viewed by most funding sources as positive and creative. They want their name up in lights too.

The end result is that others in your field will know your name. They will call you to enter consortiums, and other funding sources will ask you to apply for funding.

The Budget

While the budget may produce trauma for most unorganized grant seekers, you can see that the project planner has all the information you need to forecast your financial needs accurately. The Project Planner is not the budget; it is the analysis of what will have to be done and the estimated costs and time frame for each activity.

In most government proposal formats the budget area is not in close proximity to the methodology. Government funders do not understand why you want to talk about your methods when they talk about money. As you know, the budget is a result of what you plan to do. If you cut or reduce the money requested, you have to cut the methods. If you must cut so many methods that you can no longer be sure of accomplishing the objective, consider refusing the funds or reducing the amount of change (reduction of the need) outlined in the objective when you are asked to negotiate the amount of your award.

Draw the public funding source back into your Project Planner so that you both understand what will be missing as a result of a 10 percent budget cut.

The sample budget in Table 13.1 is provided for your review. The format may change, but the information you will need usually lies in your project planner. (If you are required to provide a quarterly cash forecast, list your activities/methods on the Proposed Time Frame and Cash Forecast (p. 142), and place the estimated cost in the far-right column. Total the costs by the quarter and you will develop your cash forecast.)

Title Page

The title of your proposal is very important. It is often hastily conceived as the proposal is "flying" out of the typewriter. *The title of a proposal gets read first,* and sometimes it is the last part that is read. The effect of the title on encouraging the reviewer or staff reader to continue to read the proposal is not known. What must a title do to insure that your proposal gets attention?

The proposal title must:

- Be descriptive of your project.

- Express the end result of the project, not the methods.

- Describe benefits to clients.

- Be short and easy to remember.

T A B L E 13.1.   A Sample Project Budget

Project Name: Nutrition Education for Disadvantaged Mothers through Tele Conferencing.	Expenditure Total	Donated/ In-kind	Requested from This Source
	$60,157	*$29,956*	*$30,201*
I. *PERSONNEL*			
A. *Salaries, Wages*			
Project Director @ $1,200/mo × 12 mos × 50% time	7,200	7,200	
Administrative Assistant @ $800/mo × 12 mos × 100% time	9,600		9,600
Secretary @ $800/mo × 12 mos × 100% time	9,600		9,600
Volunteer Time @ $3.50 × 10 mos × 400 hours	14,000	14,000	
B. *Fringe Benefits*			
Unemployment Insurance (3.6% of first $6,000 of each salary)	648	216	432
FICA (6.65% of first 22,900 of each employee salary)	1,756	479	1,277
Health Insurance ($30/mo per employee × 12 mos) Workmen's Compensation (1% of	1,080	360	720
salaries paid—$26,400)	264	72	192
C. *Consultants/Contracted Service*			
Copy Editor ($80/day × 5)	400		400
PR Advisor ($100/day × 10)	1,000		1,000
Accounting Services ($100/ day × 12)	1,200	1,200	
Legal Services ($125/day × 6)	750	750	
Personnel Subtotal	*$47,498*	*$24,277*	*$23,221*
II. *NONPERSONNEL*			
A. *Space Costs*			
Rent (.50 square feet × 400 square feet office × 12 mos)	2,400	2,400	
Utilities ($30/mo × 12 mos)	360	360	
B. *Equipment*			
Desk ($175 × 1)	175		175
Typewriters (3 @ rental rate of $50/mo × 12 mos)	1,800		1,800
Office chairs (3 × $50/ea)	150		150

T A B L E 13.1. (Cont.)

PROJECT NAME: NUTRITION EDUCATION FOR DISADVANTAGED MOTHERS THROUGH TELE CONFERENCING.	EXPEN-DITURE TOTAL	DONATED/ IN-KIND	REQUESTED FROM THIS SOURCE
	$60,157	$29,956	$30,201
Slide Projectors (2 @ $150/each)	300	300	
File Cabinets (3 @ $95/ea)	285	285	
C. *Supplies (Consumables)* 3 employees × $85/ each/year	255	255	
D. *Travel*			
Local Project Director ($.20 mile × 500 miles/mo × 12 mos)	1,200		1,200
Administrative Asst. ($.20/mile × 750 miles/mo × 12)	1,800		1,800
Out-Of-Time Project Director to American Institute of Nutrition Conference 12/3–5/81 in St. Louis (1 round trip economy @ $275) Per Diem—$75/day × 3	275		275
E. *Telephone* Installation ($15 + $4/line × 3 lines)	27	27	
Monthly Charges ($7/line × 3 lines × 12 mos)	252	252	
Long Distance ($40/mo × 12)	480		480
F. *Other Nonpersonnel Costs* Printing (25,000 brochures × $35/Thousand)	875		875
Postage ($125/mo × 12 mos)	1,500	1,500	
Insurance ($25/mo × 12 mos)	300	300	
Personnel Subtotal:	$12,659	$ 5,679	$ 6,980
Personnel Subtotal:	$47,498	$24,277	$23,221
Project Total:	$60,157	$29,956	$30,201
Percentage:	100%	49.8%	50.2%

PROPOSED TIME FRAME
and CASH FORECAST

For _____ Proposal

Methods	1	2	3	4	5	6	7	8	9	10	11	12	Cost/ Method

Quarterly Cash Forecast for Project					Total Cost Requested from Funder
	1	2	3	4	

The best titles are the "newspaper-type" titles that are descriptive and to the point, for example, "Women Stabbed at Hilton Hotel."

Titles that try to entice the reader by giving only part of the story seldom work. Remember, the reader usually has a pile of grant proposals that are crying out to be read. The same newspaper title, rewritten to "entice" a reader, may turn out to be: "Bloody End in Hotel Lobby while Hundreds Watch." Although some grant seekers have told me that an enticing title got their proposal read, I believe they are in the minority.

Titles can vary in length. Ask funding officials what they prefer. Since you have a list of titles used by past grantees, examine it for clues that may give you an idea of what the funding source wants. Some federal programs have rules on the number of characters or spaces that a title may use. Check the rules.

Titles can be up to ten to thirteen words. The best person to write or select the title may not be you. Have friends read the proposal and ask them what to call it.

Since you have written the proposal, you develop "tunnel vision" and attribute more meaning to the words than a person reading the title for the first time. One good technique is to read your title to other people who know little or nothing about your proposal and then ask them what they think the proposal is about, based on the title.

You must be careful not to assume that the funding source is familiar with references you may make to biblical characters or Greek gods in your proposal title. Calling your solar energy project, "Apollo's Flame," is not a good idea if the reviewer does not know who Apollo is or fails to make the connection.

Acronyms should be used only if the funding source has a preference for them. Trying to develop a title that describes the benefits of your project is difficult enough without adding the additional task of attempting to use specific words to develop an acronym.

The key to checking out your title is to look at the titles of past grants and ask the funding source what they prefer.

TITLE PAGE

Most federal forms and many state granting programs have standard formats for the title page. The key to the title page is to design it like a well-addressed envelope. Insure its delivery to the correct place by including all required information and more. Remember, you are dealing with a bureaucracy, a grants-logging office, a mail dissemination and delivery service, and relogging as your proposal gets to the final destination. You must be sure that the title page allows for anyone to pick it up and:

- Know what program you are applying to.
- See a clear address for the office that will handle the program.
- See the federal contact person.
- Know your return address, phone number, and contact person.

The Summary (or Abstract)

The summary (or abstract) is written after the proposal is completed. It is a summary of each part of the proposal, not a repetition of what you have written. The summary should:

- Summarize the objectives, not list them.
- Summarize the approach, not list methods.
- Summarize the evaluation, not detail every pre-post test.

The summary or abstract is the most important part of the proposal after the title, because the summary is the next most often read part of the proposal. If the summary is not succinct and motivating, you have lost the reader, which you cannot afford to do. Make an outline of each of the preceding sections. Using the points or evaluation system printed or discussed with funding sources or past grantees or reviewers, you may evaluate the space and time spent on developing your abstract to fit the funding source. Show them that they will find what they want in this proposal.

Many forms have explicit directions on the summary and even designate the space and number of words or characters you can use. Some federal forms ask you to underline a certain number of key words or phrases—*do it!*

Attachments (Appendix)

This section can provide the "winning edge" when your proposal is compared to a competitor's for final analysis. Throughout the proposal-development process, collect the materials that will make up the attachments and set them aside. Your task is to present materials in the attachments that will back up your proposal. The funding source may skim over the attachments or look to them for:

- Studies/research and tables or graphs.
- Vitae of key personnel.
- Minutes of Advisory Committee Meetings.
- List of board members.
- Credibility builders—auditor's report/statement.
- Letters of recommendation/endorsement.
- Copy of your tax-exempt designation by the IRS.
- Pictures, architect's drawings.
- Copies of your agency publications.
- List of other funding sources you will approach for funding.

For the appropriate *length* of your attachments section, check funding source rules. Guidelines may state that the attachments can be up to twice as long as the proposal.

Also check funding source rules for the appropriate appendix format. Provide a separate Contents page. Many grant writers number the pages sequentially with the proposal to provide ease in referral to the attachments.

Cover Letter

The cover letter is the last part of the proposal to be written, although it may be the first one read by the funding source. The purpose of the cover letter is to provide the funding source with a reintroduction to you. You may want to remind the funding source of your contact with them and the changes you have made in your proposal on the basis of their input. (You want to remind them that you did what they said: "I did what you told me to do—now fund it!")

If you have had contact with a particular individual on the funding organization's staff and you remind them of it, be sure to note it on *one* of the funding official's or your contact person's copy. Telling *everyone* who reads the proposal that you received special attention is not a good idea.

In public funding, the cover letter is seldom read unless they know you and it is written to a contact person at the funding agency.

If you include a cover letter on each copy of the proposal, it must:

- be short (half a page),
- be motivating,
- say something different, and
- show dramatic need or uniqueness.

In today's world of board-member liability insurance, you may want to use the cover letter to show board commitment. Have the president of the board sign, along with your top-ranking administrator. (It is acceptable to have two signatures on the cover letter.)

Writing Your Federal/State Proposal

WRITING TIPS

- Follow the guidelines exactly (even when they seem senseless).
- Fill in all the blanks.
- Doublecheck all computations.

- Repeat anything they ask for (do not refer them back to what you consider a similar question and answer).

WRITING STYLE

Your writing style must reflect what the funding source wants and what the reviewers will be looking for. Since you have contacted a past reviewer, you know his or her level of expertise and familiarity with your proposal area. You also know the amount of time that a proposal reviewer spends with a proposal. The proposal must be readable and skimmable. Follow these suggestions:

- Begin each section with a strong motivating "lead" sentence.

- Use an active voice and describe emotions and feelings.

- Cite dialogue.

- Use humor (in a nonoffensive way).

- Ask the funding source a question and answer it.

In developing your writing style and preparing your proposal, be sure to check on the aspects of the proposal that follow.

VOCABULARY

Do you use the words they expect? (Your research has given you insight into vocabulary.) Shorter words are generally better than long, complex words.

STYLE

To produce an easily skimmable proposal:

- Use short sentences (no more than two commas).

- Use contractions.

- Use short paragraphs (from five to seven lines).

VISUAL ATTRACTIVENESS

To enhance the "skimmability" of the project, use:

- Underlining.

- Bullets (lower case "o," filled in, "●").
- Use different **type** faces.
- Change margins and s p a c i n g .
- Use **BOLD HEADINGS.**
- Use pictures.
- Use charts and graphs.
- Use *Handwriting* .

CHAPTER 14

Checklist for Government Proposal Preparation

CHECKLIST FOR GOVERNMENT PROPOSAL PREPARATION

_____ Read guidelines again; many have a forms checklist that must be signed and included.

_____ Have you checked the submission date for postmark and/or receipt by funding source?

_____ Correct address and logging center.

_____ Have you included all sections that will be given points by the reviewers?

_____ Check required assurances:

     _____ A-95 Review   _____ Other

     _____ Protection of Human Subjects   _____

     _____ Equal Employment   _____

_____ Check all purchases for equipment:

      _____ Is purchase allowable?

      _____ Can you lease with option to buy?

      _____ Rent?

      _____ Any forms or sign off's for purchases over $ _____

_____ Required number of copies.

_____ Signatures of appropriate officials.

_____ Matching or cost sharing rules.

_____ Indirect costs used appropriately.

Additional Comments: _____

_____

_____

_____

_____

_____

CHAPTER 15

Submission

WHAT TO DO AND WHAT NOT
TO DO

Submission of grants to public funding sources requires a very different and more complex procedure from submissions to private funding sources. Because you are dealing with public funds, the procedure for submission and the deadline dates must comply with public-information laws and give equal voice and opportunity to everyone.

Government officials cannot give you any leeway on deadlines. (*Note:* at the federal level, any change in the deadline date must be announced in the *Federal Register* thirty days before the change.) *Deadlines are exactly that.*

The normal submission procedure is to have a federal proposal stamped in at the post office by a post office employee. Most federal proposals also have a grants-logging center in Washington that can receive the proposal. *Call the funding source regardless of whether you are submitting your proposal by mail or in person,* just to be sure your grant made the trip from the logging center or post office to the correct federal office.

Most public agencies will refuse to talk to you when you have an application under consideration. There are other actions you can take:

1. Send your abstract or summary to your congressperson. Do not ask him or her to contact the government agency; simply state that you have applied and would like any help he or she can offer. State that you know that any assistance he or she could give would be *informal;* you do not want letters to funding officials.
2. Call any "friends" you found in your linkages and webbing and ask them to put in a good word where possible.

Proposal Review

PUBLIC FUNDING SOURCES

The best way to critique your proposal is to use a proposal review committee. The committee may be comprised of your peers, or better yet, individuals whose backgrounds are similar to those of the review committee members. Give your committee as much information as you can concerning the review process, especially the actual length of time spent by the reviewers reading the proposal.

The reviewers can get the proposal in advance and bring it to a review session after careful analysis with the points criteria.

If the funding source reviewers get the proposal to work on for only thirty minutes, pass the proposal out at your review session, ask your reviewers to spend thirty minutes for review, give them the points criteria and let them go to work. (Why spend more time than will be used at the actual review session?)

After they distribute the criteria points, ask them to list the points. Discuss what they think is positive concerning the proposal and what needs improvement.

Some federal programs utilize a review process whereby the reviewers receive, evaluate, and return the proposals by mail. This type of committee may never meet as a group. Many funding sources use a system like this to avoid the reviewers' travel expenses.

CHAPTER 16

Dealing with the Decision of Public Funding Sources

You will receive a response to your proposal in several months. The response will be one of the following:

- Accepted.

- Accepted with budget modifications. (Let's talk about the budget.)

- Approved but not funded. Supportable but not fundable.

- Rejected.

Accepted

If your proposal is accepted, observe the following procedure:
1. Send them a warm personal thank-you letter.
2. Request a critique of your proposal to learn what the funding source liked. Include a mailing label or stamped, self-addressed envelope.

3. Ask the funding source to visit you or arrange for you to visit them.
4. Request any completion forms and learn what records you need to keep.
5. Ask the funding source what the common problems with grants like yours are and how to avoid them.

Accepted with Budget Modifications

Should your proposal receive this response, do the following:
1. Send them a warm personal thank-you letter.
2. Call funding source (they may call you) and refer the funding source to your project planner to negotiate the budget items.
3. Take out some of the methods.
4. Drop the accomplishment of an objective.
5. Be prepared to turn down the funds before you enter into an agreement that will cause you to lose credibility later.

Approved But Not Funded

Observe the following guidelines if your proposal is approved but not offered funding by this source:
1. Send them a warm personal thank-you letter.
2. Call the funding source and ask them how far your proposal was from the funding cut-off point.
3. Ask what you could have done better.
4. Request the reviewers' comments.
5. Try to get additional appropriations.
6. Ask them if they may have discretionary money left over (for unsolicited proposals).

Rejected

If your proposal is rejected, take the following actions:
1. Send them a warm personal thank-you letter.

2. Request the reviewers' comments (enclose self-addressed stamped envelope for their convenience).
3. Ask the funding official for his or her suggestions.
4. Ask if the proposal could be funded as a pilot project, needs assessment, or in some other way.
5. Are there any ways the funding source would assist you in getting ready for the next submission?
6. Should you bother? What are your chances for another try? What would you have to change?
7. Could you become a reviewer to learn and become more familiar with the review process?

CHAPTER 17

Follow-up with Government Funding Sources

The object of follow-up is to make yourself appear as an asset to the funding source and not as a pest. Send the funding source:

- notes on special articles or books in your area;

- an invitation for them to visit you;

- a request for them to review an article you're writing;

- an invitation for one of their representatives to speak at a conference or seminar;

- an invitation to speak at a special grant conference; or

- a request for information about what you could do to impact legislation affecting their funding levels or decisions affecting their allocations.

By remaining on their mailing list and reviewing the *Federal Register*, you will have knowledge of the next opportunity with this funding source.

Do not wait until next year's deadline to begin thinking about your application; start right after the decision. The aggressive grant seeker does not shelve the project for eleven months. The best way to get to know what's going on is to visit the funding source personally. Keep in touch. Watch for meetings announced in the *Federal Register*. Testify at committee hearings that have impact on the agency and its funding level. Send the agency blind carbon copies of your efforts to impact legislation for them (and yourself). Use your association memberships and legislative committees to write and push for changes that benefit the particular agency.

Developing Continued Grant Support

The key to success is to continue the steps that have brought you to this point. If you have put into place the concepts presented in this manual, you have a system that alerts you to changes in program rules, deadlines, and the like, through the mailing lists and personal contacts and webbing linkages you have established.

Although the public funding officials may change, they seem to reappear again and again. This systematic approach to recording research on funding sources and officials will prove its usefulness time and time again.

Once in place, you can keep the funding source on your mailing list and make repeat contacts. By maintaining your relationship, whether you have received funding or not, you demonstrate to the funding source that you plan to be around for a while and that you will not forget them as soon as you receive a check.

One of the best outgrowths of your grants efforts can be your grants library. If you invite others to use your grants resources and demonstrate your systematic grant-seeking abilities, you will be invited into consortiums and end up in other people's proposals.

PART THREE

Private Funding Sources

CHAPTER 18

The Difference between Private and Public Funding

While public funding is characterized by many forms, rules, restrictions and bureaucrats, the opposite is true of the private funding marketplace. Many grant seekers see this lack of restriction as a great advantage and want to apply to the private sector to avoid government restrictions. Private funding sources are sensitive to this issue and some require that you must show why you have not been able to get government funding.

There is good reason for this:

- Foundations give away 3.46 billion dollars each year in the United States. (The federal government grants approximately $25 billion.)

- Foundations account for 5.3 percent of the total of 64.9 billion dollars given away to nonprofits by private philanthropy.

- There were only 32,165 grants for more than $5,000 in the entire United States last year given by 465 grant-making foundations.

- The average grant by a foundation with over $20 million in assets is $20,000.

- The average by all the rest is $1,700.

- The top 10 percent of the foundations have 90 percent of the assets.

Private funding sources view themselves and their role in the philanthropic market very differently from public funding sources. They can give their funds to anyone they please and they do not relate well to pressure. Influence from linkages or webbing contacts can be very helpful and should be used whenever possible.

In addition to having few standard forms, guidelines, and financial requirements, private funding sources are not prone to site visits. Only a handful use professional reviewers. Most have the proposal read by board members, since only approximately 1,000 of the 21,967 foundations have half- to full-time directors.

While the government has an abundance of public information, the foundations require more research. Try to engage volunteer and staff support to develop the research and worksheets that follow in this section.

Note: Remember the vast difference in the total amount of grants: $25 billion, compared to the $3.46 billion that the foundations have to work with. Accurate research is necessary to be successful in the private marketplace. Visit your local college or university for assistance. Many upper-division undergraduate and graduate courses require a practical knowledge of the grants marketplace. Offer a student an internship or scholarship to assist you in your research. It's better than doing it yourself.

CHAPTER 19

How to Record Research and Information

Research Worksheet

Another key to successful grant seeking is gathering complete and accurate information on each funding source you approach. The Corporate and Foundation Research Form (pp. 164–165) will help you to do this. Fill in one worksheet for each granting agency you research; try to fill in as much of the form as possible, but remember, even a partially completed worksheet will help you make a more intelligent decision on whether you should solicit grant support from a funding source. If you do apply, it will serve as a guide to solicitation strategy and proposal development.

Try to enlist the help of volunteers to ferret out this information. (*Note:* The use of data-processing equipment for storing this information has been very successful for many of Bauer Associates' clients.)

CORPORATE AND FOUNDATION RESEARCH FORM

Source & Date

1. Name of Corp./Fdn.: _____

   Address: _____

   _____

   Phone: _____

2. Contacts: _____

   (title) _____

   _____

3. Areas of Interest:

   _____   _____

   _____   _____

   _____   _____

   _____   _____

4. Eligibility Requirements/Restrictions:

   Activities: _____

   _____

   _____

   Organizations: _____

   _____

   Geographic: _____

   _____

5. Policy:

   Guidelines Available?   Sent for: _____

                           Received: _____

   Committee Members/Board of Directors

   _____   _____

   _____   _____

CORPORATE AND FOUNDATION RESEARCH FORM (Cont.)

Source & Date

6. Financial Information: Fiscal Year, 19___

    <u>Corporations</u>:   Asset Base   _____

    Net Earnings Before Taxes   _____

    Total Contributions   _____

    Contributions as % NEBT   _____

    <u>Foundations</u>:   Asset Base   _____

    Total Contributions   _____

    BOTH: High Grant   _____

                Low Grant   _____

                Average Range   _____

                Number of Proposals
                Received   _____

                Number of Proposals
                Funded   _____
                                                       (amount)

7. Sample Grants in 19___

    _____ $ _____

    _____ $ _____

    _____ $ _____

    _____ $ _____

    _____ $ _____

8. Application Process:

    Deadlines:

    Application Form? Sent for: _____

                           Received: _____

    Send letter included:

    Phone inquiry required:

    Submit full proposal:

    Other:

    _____
    RESEACHER: DATE:

    SOURCES:

Funding-Executive Research Worksheet

In addition to the research you conduct on grant-making organizations, you should also uncover and record as much data as possible on the decision makers in those organizations. The following worksheet is designed to help you do this.

<u>FUNDING EXECUTIVE RESEARCH WORKSHEET</u>

<u>Source & Date</u>

1. Funding Source Name: _____

2. Name of Contributions Officer: _____

3. Title: _____ Birthdate: _____

4. Business Address: _____

5. Home Address: _____

6. Education: Secondary: _____

              College: _____

              Post-Graduate: _____

7. Military Service: _____

8. Clubs/Affiliations: _____

9. Corporate Board Memberships: _____

10. Business History (Promotions, other firms, etc.)

11. Religious Affiliation: _____

12. Other Philanthropic Activities of Note: _____

13. Newspaper/Magazine Clippings Attached:

    Yes: _____ No: _____

14. Contacts in Our Organization: _____

15. Recent Articles/Publications: _____

16. Awards/Honors: _____

You can find information on private funding officials in books such as *Trustees of Wealth, Dun & Bradstreet's Directory of Corporate Managements* and *Who's Who* publications. You should also check periodical indexes, libraries, and newspapers.

The data you record here can help you in two ways:

1. It can help you determine, in advance, likely preferences and biases you will encounter at an in-person grant interview.
2. It makes it easier to locate "linkages" between your organization and a funding source.

Note: You do not have to have this information in order to consider a source for a proposal, but it helps. Each step you include will increase your chances of success.

CHAPTER 20

Foundation Funding Source Research Tools

This chapter contains sample entries from selected grants' research tools commonly used in the foundation and corporate grant areas (see pp. 169, 170, 171). The samples have been changed slightly to assist you in understanding the way the research is indexed and what an entry looks like.

To make research on foundations easier for prospective grant seekers, the foundations formed the Foundation Center. National in scope, with cooperating regional libraries, the Foundation Center provides the best possible sources of free information about foundations (who and what they fund).

Locate the Foundation Center's nearest library on the accompanying list (pp. 172–174) and visit it. The national collections have many more resources than mentioned here. The Foundation Center will be happy to sell you a membership program where you become an "associate" for $200.00 and receive:

- Toll-free telephone reference service (10 free calls or $2^{1}/_{2}$ hours of information/month).

THE FOUNDATION DIRECTORY

THE FLORA FLUBOCKER FOUNDATION
20 Money Place
New York, NY 10005 (212) 234-1234
Incorporated in 1952 in New York.

Donor(s): Members of Flubocker Family

Purpose and Activities: Special emphasis
on education for the developmentally
disabled, health care for the aged, and
research on eye diseases. No grants to
individuals. Report published annually.

Financial Data: (yr. ended 12/31/80):
Assets, $27,137,892 (m); gifts received
$8,396,000; expenditures, $936,152;
including $756,300 for 32 grants
(high: $37,000; low: $1,500)

Officers: Melvin J. Flubocker, Pres.
Mary J. Flubocker, Sylvia Skim, Vice
President; Jonathan S. Bills, Treas.

Trustees: Orving Flood, Laurel Lisez
Maxwell Litesky, Luch Maddox, William
Martin, C. Pape, A. Rankin, Anna Slide,
Arthur Flubocker, M. Stillwater, IV.

Write: Mary J. Flubocker, Vice President

Grant Application Information: Board
meets quarterly. IRS Employment
Identification No.: 410896132

THE FOUNDATION DIRECTORY
(Edition 7), Columbia
University Press, 136
South Broadway, Irvington, NY 10533

The Foundation Directory,
Edition 9, is the best
place to find general
data on the largest
private foundations. It
includes the following
information on 4,000
foundations with assets
of over $1 million, or
that made over $100,000
in grants:
  ° Name & Address
  ° Donors
  ° Financial Data
    (including assets,
    number of grants, &
    size of high & low
    grants)
  ° Officers & Trustees
The Directory is indexed by:
  ° Field of Interest
  ° Foundations by State &
    City
  ° Donors, Trustees &
    Administrators
  ° Foundations in
    alphabetical order

A supplement to the
Foundation Directory will
be published in mid-year.
It will include updated
addresses, indexes of
grant-making foundations
and other bibliographical
data.

- Computerized foundation files (one free printout in the category of your choice and additional printouts for $12 each or $4 on microfiche).

- Copy services (associates can get copies of foundation profiles from Source Book Profiles and other information such as foundation assets, officers, etc. for $.90 for the first page and $.45 for each additional page).

THE FOUNDATION GRANTS INDEX

THE FLUBOCKER FOUNDATION

$30,000 to ZAP UNIVERSITY, Ithaca, NY.
1976. For center to rehabilitate
developmentally disabled in Ithaca area.
SD: 1/20/79   (3147)

$8,000 to HARLEM HOSPITAL, New York, NY.
1976. For general support.
SD: 1/20/79   (3149)

$8,500 to COMMUNITY DEVELOPMENT LEAGUE
1976. For programs to find employment
for the developmentally disabled.
SD: 1/20/79   (3150)

$10,000 to SUNY AT BAYSHORE, Bayshore, NY.
1976. For research into development
disabilities. SD: 1/20/79   (3151)

$10,750 to YENTALTA EYE CLINIC. For
research on retina detachment. 1976.
SD: 1/20/79   (3152)

$5,000 to ZOLA CENTER. General operating
expenses. SD: 1/20/79   (3153)

(This is a hypothetical entry)

THE FOUNDATION GRANTS INDEX

Foundation Center
888 7th Avenue
New York, New York

The Foundation Grants Index
is a good place to turn
when you begin searching
for a foundation's
"granting pattern." It
includes listings of grants
over $5,000, some given by
foundations not large
enough to be listed in
The Foundation Directory.

The Foundation Grants Index
lists grants by state and
foundation. It also
indexes them by:
  ° recipients
  ° key words & phrases
  ° subject categories
  ° foundation names

The information you gather
here, along with that you
find in foundation annual
reports and IRS returns,
will give you a good idea
of whether you project fits
into the funding priorities
of a foundation.

You can buy a copy of this
valuable tool from the
Foundation Center, or find
it (along with The
Foundation Directory) in
Foundation Center Regional
Collections.

IRS Forms—990-PF and 990-AR Returns

Foundations are required to submit income tax returns. These returns are public record and can be purchased from the Internal Revenue Service for a minimal fee. They are available for the entire United States at the national Foundation Center and on a geographically limited basis at the regional libraries. You can use them in the library on a "no charge" basis.

IRS returns are good sources to utilize since the source books

THE ANNUAL REGISTER OF GRANTS SUPPORT

R. SAFE FOUNDATION
333 Third Avenue
New York 10010 (212) 949-8990

Incorporated in 1907 in New York.
Donor(s): Mrs. Russel Safe.
Purpose and Activities: "The
Improvement of social and living
conditions in the United States."
Conducts research under the direction
of the staff or in close collaboration
with other institutions. Supports
research relevant to public policy
issues; participates in the planning
of each cooperative venture, publishes
many resulting manuscripts, and usually
continues its interest into at least
the early stages of practical
utilization of the findings. Interests
include culture, citizenship,
institutions, human resources, and
New York City. Grants ordinarily not
made for the support of independent
ongoing activities of other
institutions or to individuals.
Report published annually.

Financial Data (yr. ended 9/30/80):
Assets, $52,777,000 (M); expenditures,
$2,152,000, including $617,000 for 28
grants (high: $79,300; low $3,000)
and $554,700 for 4 programs.

Officers: Marshall A. Robinson,*
President; Arnold R. Shore, Vice
President; Warren H. Bacon,*
Secretary; Loren D. Ross, Treasurer.

Trustees:* Herna Hill Kay, Chair;
Thomas C. Edwards, Jr. Vice-Chair;
Robert McCormick Adams, Guido
Calabresi, William D. Carey, Earl F.
Cheit, Carl Kaysen, Frederick
Mosteller, John S. Reed, Oscar W.
Ruebhausen, Madelon Talley.

Write: Marshall A. Robinson,
President.
Grant Application Information: initial
approach by letter; submit 1 copy of
proposal; board meets 3 times a year
in November or December, March, and
June.
EMPLOYER IDENTIFICATION NO.: 12136234

The Annual Register of Grants Support
includes information on all kinds of
granting programs: foundations,
government, and corporate. Entries
are arranged by field, and are cross-
indexed.

Valuable features of entries in the
Register include:

° information of how grants are
  made
° the ratio of applications to
  grants awarded
° application procedures and
  deadlines

Because it covers so many kinds of
granting programs, The Annual
Register of Grants Support is a good
place to begin your grant research.

No data source, however, can tell
you all you need to know about a
funding source. It's always a good
idea to check as many grant research
tools as possible.

The Annual Register of Grants Support,
Marquis Who's Who, 4300 W. 62nd
Street, Indianapolis, IN 46206

previously mentioned receive their information on a voluntary
basis and it is always at least one year old. It is estimated that about
80 percent of the grants for more than $5,000 are reported vol-
untarily. In order to find the other 20 percent of grants
awarded, you must search out the foundation by looking them
up through their income tax return.

You will notice that many foundation research books give the

The Foundation Center

The Foundation Center has a nationwide network of reference collections for free public use. The collections fall within four basic categories. The reference libraries operated by the Center offer the widest variety of user services and the most comprehensive collections of foundation materials, including all Center publications; books, services and periodicals on philanthropy; and foundation annual reports, newsletters and press clippings. 1) The New York and Washington, D.C. libraries contain the IRS returns for all currently active private foundations in the U.S. 2) The Cleveland and San Francisco field offices contain IRS records for those foundations in the midwestern and western states, respectively. 3) Cooperating collections contain IRS records for those foundations within their own state, and a

complete collection of Foundation Center publications. 4) Local affiliate collections (★) provide a core collection of Center publications for free public use.

Some reference collections (•) are operated by foundations or area associations of foundations. They are often able to offer special materials or provide extra services, such as seminars or orientations for users, because of their close relationship to the local philanthropic community. All other collections are operated by cooperating libraries or other nonprofit agencies. Many are located within public institutions and all are open to the public during a regular schedule of hours.

Please telephone individual libraries for more information about their holdings or hours. To check on new locations call toll-free 800-424-9836 for current information.

Where to Go for Information on Foundation Funding
Reference Collections Operated by The Foundation Center

The Foundation Center
888 Seventh Avenue
New York, NY 10106
212-975-1120

The Foundation Center
1001 Connecticut Avenue
NW
Washington, DC 20036
202-331-1400

The Foundation Center
Kent H. Smith Library
739 National City Bank Bldg.
629 Euclid
Cleveland, OH 44114
216-861-1933

The Foundation Center
312 Sutter Street
San Francisco, CA 94108
415-397-0902

Cooperating Collections

ALABAMA
Birmingham Public
    Library
2020 Park Place
Birmingham 35203
205-254-2541

Auburn University at
    Montgomery Library
Montgomery 36193
205-279-9110

ALASKA
University of Alaska,
    Anchorage Library
3211 Providence Drive
Anchorage 99504
907-263-1848

ARIZONA
Phoenix Public Library
Social Sciences Subject
    Department
12 East McDowell Road
Phoenix 85004
602-262-4782

Tucson Public Library
Main Library
200 South Sixth Avenue
Tucson 85701
602-791-4393

ARKANSAS
Westark Community
    College Library
Grand Avenue at
    Waldron Road
Fort Smith 72913
501-785-4241

Little Rock Public Library
Reference Department
700 Louisiana Street
Little Rock 72201
501-370-5950

CALIFORNIA
• California Community
    Foundation
    Funding Information
    Center
    1151 West Sixth Street
    Los Angeles 90017
    213-413-4719

★ Riverside Public Library
    3581 7th Street
    Riverside 92502
    714-787-7201

★ California State Library
    Reference Services,
    Room 309
    914 Capitol Mall
    Sacramento 95814
    916-322-0369

San Diego Public Library
820 E Street
San Diego 92101
619-236-5565

★• San Diego Community
    Foundation
    625 Broadway, Suite 1105
    San Diego 92101
    619-239-8815

★ Orange County
    Community
    Development Council
    1440 East First Street,
    4th floor
    Santa Ana 92701
    714-547-6801

Santa Barbara Public
    Library
    Reference Section
    40 East Anapamu
    P.O. Box 1019
    Santa Barbara 93102
    805-962-7653

★ Central Sierra Arts Council
    19411 Village Drive
    Sonora 95370
    209-532-2787

★ North Coast
    Opportunities, Inc.
    101 West Church Street
    Ukiah 95482
    707-462-1954

COLORADO
★ Pikes Peak Library District
    20 North Cascade Avenue
    Colorado Springs 80901
    303-473-2080

Denver Public Library
Sociology Division
1357 Broadway
Denver 80203
303-571-2190

CONNECTICUT
Hartford Public Library
Reference Department
500 Main Street
Hartford 06103
203-525-9121

★ D.A.T.A.
    81 Saltonstall Avenue
    New Haven 06513
    203-776-0797

DELAWARE
Hugh Morris Library
University of Delaware
Newark 19711
302-738-2965

FLORIDA
Jacksonville Public Library
Business, Science, and
    Industry Department
122 North Ocean Street
Jacksonville 32202
904-633-3926

Miami-Dade Public Library
Florida Collection
One Biscayne Boulevard
Miami 33132
305-579-5001

★ Orlando Public Library
    10 North Rosalind
    Orlando 32801
    305-425-4694

★ Leon County Public
    Library
    Community Funding
    Resources Center
    1940 North Monroe Street
    Tallahassee 32303
    904-487-2665

★ Selby Public Library
    1001 Boulevard of the Arts
    Sarasota 33577
    813-366-7303

GEORGIA
Atlanta Public Library
1 Margaret Mitchell
    Square at Forsyth and
    Carnegie Way
Atlanta 30303
404-688-4636

HAWAII
Thomas Hale Hamilton
    Library
General Reference
University of Hawaii
2550 The Mall
Honolulu 96822
808-948-7214

HAWAII

Thomas Hale Hamilton
Library
General Reference
University of Hawaii
2550 The Mall
Honolulu 96822
808-948-7214

• ★ Community Resource
Center
The Hawaiian Foundation
Financial Plaza of the
Pacific
111 South King Street
Honolulu 96813
808-525-8548

IDAHO

Caldwell Public Library
1010 Dearborn Street
Caldwell 83605
208-459-3242

ILLINOIS

★ Belleville Public Library
121 E. Washington Street
Belleville 62220
618-234-0441

• Donors Forum of Chicago
208 South LaSalle Street
Chicago 60604
312-726-4882

★ DuPage Township
300 Briarcliff Road
Bolingbrook 60439
312-759-1317

Sangamon State University
Library
Shepherd Road
Springfield 62708
217-786-6633

INDIANA

★ Allen County Public
Library
900 Webster Street
Fort Wayne 46802
219-424-7241

★ Indiana University
Northwest Library
3400 Broadway
Gary 46408
219-980-6580

Indianapolis-Marion
County Public Library
40 East St. Clair Street
Indianapolis 46204
317-269-1733

IOWA

Public Library of Des
Moines
100 Locust Street
Des Moines 50308
515-283-4259

KANSAS

Topeka Public Library
Adult Services Department
1515 West Tenth Street
Topeka 66604
913-233-2040

★ Wichita Public Library
223 South Main
Wichita 67202
316-262-0611

★ **KENTUCKY**
Western Kentucky
University
Division of Library Services
Helm-Cravens Library
Bowling Green 42101
502-745-3951

• ★ The Louisville
Foundation, Inc.
623 West Main Street
Louisville 40202
502-585-4649

Louisville Free Public
Library
Fourth and York Streets
Louisville 40203
502-584-4154

LOUISIANA

East Baton Rouge Parish
Library
Centroplex Library
120 St. Louis Street
Baton Rouge 70802
504-344-5291

New Orleans Public
Library
Business and Science
Division
219 Loyola Avenue
New Orleans 70140
504-524-7382 ext. 33

★ Shreve Memorial Library
424 Texas Street
Shreveport 71101
318-226-5894

MAINE

University of Southern
Maine
Center for Research and
Advanced Study
246 Deering Avenue
Portland 04102
207-780-4411

MARYLAND

Enoch Pratt Free Library
Social Science and History
Department
400 Cathedral Street
Baltimore 21201
301-396-5320

MASSACHUSETTS

• Associated Grantmakers of
Massachusetts
294 Washington Street
Suite 501
Boston 02108
617-426-2608

Boston Public Library
Copley Square
Boston 02117
617-536-5400

★ Walpole Public Library
Walcott Avenue at Union
Street
East Walpole 02032
617-668-0232

★ Western Massachusetts
Funding Resource Center
Campaign for Human
Development
Chancery Annex,
73 Chestnut Street
Springfield 01103
413-732-3175 ext. 67

★ Grants Resource Center
Worcester Public Library
Salem Square
Worcester 01608
617-799-1655

MICHIGAN

Alpena County Library
211 North First Avenue
Alpena 49707
517-356-6188

Henry Ford Centennial
Library
16301 Michigan Avenue
Dearborn 48126
313-943-2337

Purdy Library
Wayne State University
Detroit 48202
313-577-4040

Michigan State University
Libraries
Reference Library
East Lansing 48824
517-353-8816

★ Farmington Community
Library
32737 West 12 Mile Road
Farmington Hills 48018
313-553-0300

University of Michigan-
Flint Library
Reference Department
Flint 48503
313-762-3408

Grand Rapids Public
Library
Sociology and Education
Dept.
Library Plaza
Grand Rapids 49503
616-456-4411

Michigan Technological
University Library
Highway U.S. 41
Houghton 49931
906-487-2507

MINNESOTA

★ Duluth Public Library
520 Superior Street
Duluth 55802
218-723-3802

Minneapolis Public Library
Sociology Department
300 Nicollet Mall
Minneapolis 55401
612-372-6555

★ Saint Paul Public Library
90 West Fourth Street
Saint Paul 55102
612-292-6311

MISSISSIPPI

Jackson Metropolitan
Library
301 North State Street
Jackson 39201
601-944-1120

MISSOURI

• Clearinghouse for Mid-
continent Foundations
Univ. of Missouri, Kansas
City
Law School, Suite 1-300
52nd Street and Oak
Kansas City 64113
816-276-1176

Kansas City Public Library
311 East 12th Street
Kansas City 64106
616-221-2685

• Metropolitan Association
for Philanthropy, Inc.
5585 Pershing Avenue
Suite 150
St. Louis 63112
314-361-3900

Springfield-Greene County
Library
397 East Central Street
Springfield 65801
417-866-4636

MONTANA

Eastern Montana College
Library
Reference Department
Billings 59101
406-657-2262

★ Montana State Library
Reference Department
1515 E. 6th Avenue
Helena 59620
406-449-3004

NEBRASKA

W. Dale Clark Library
Social Sciences
Department
215 South 15th Street
Omaha 68102
402-444-4822

NEVADA

Clark County Library
1401 East Flamingo Road
Las Vegas 89109
702-733-7810

Washoe County Library
301 South Center Street
Reno 89505
702-785-4190

NEW HAMPSHIRE

• The New Hampshire
Charitable Fund
One South Street
Concord 03301
603-225-6641

★ Littleton Public Library
109 Main Street
Littleton 03561
603-444-5741

NEW JERSEY

★ The Support Center
17 Academy St., Suite 1101
Newark 07102
201-643-5774

New Jersey State Library
Government Reference Unit
185 West State Street
P.O. Box 1898
Trenton 08625
609-292-6220

NEW MEXICO

• ★ Albuquerque Community
Foundation
6400 Uptown Boulevard,
N.E., Suite 500-W
Albuquerque 87110
505-883-6240

New Mexico State Library
325 Don Gaspar Street
Santa Fe 87503
505-827-3824

NEW YORK

New York State Library
Cultural Education Center
Humanities Section
Empire State Plaza
Albany 12230
518-474-7645

Buffalo and Erie County
Public Library
Lafayette Square
Buffalo 14203
716-856-7525

Levittown Public Library
Reference Department
One Bluegrass Lane
Levittown 11756
516-731-5728

Plattsburgh Public Library
Reference Department
15 Oak Street
Plattsburgh 12901
518-563-0921

★ Adriance Memorial Library
93 Memorial Street
Poughkeepsie 12601
914-485-3445

Rochester Public Library
Business and Social
  Sciences Division
115 South Avenue
Rochester 14604
716-428-7328

Onondaga County Public
  Library
335 Montgomery Street
Syracuse 13202
315-473-4491

★ White Plains Public Library
100 Martine Avenue
White Plains 10601
914-682-4488

NORTH CAROLINA
North Carolina State
  Library
109 East Jones Street
Raleigh 27611
919-733-3270

● The Winston-Salem
  Foundation
229 First Union National
  Bank Building
Winston-Salem 27101
919-725-2382

NORTH DAKOTA
★ Western Dakota Grants
  Resource Center
Bismarck Junior College
  Library
Bismarck 58501
701-224-5450

The Library
North Dakota State
  University
Fargo 58105
701-237-8876

OHIO
Public Library of
  Cincinnati and Hamilton
  County
Education Department
800 Vine Street
Cincinnati 45202
513-369-6940

★ Ohio Dept. of Economic
  and Community Development
  Office of Grants Assistance
30 East Broad Street,
  24th floor
Columbus 43215
614-466-6652

Toledo-Lucas County
  Public Library
Social Science Department
325 Michigan Street
Toledo 43624
419-255-7055 ext. 221

OKLAHOMA
Oklahoma City University
  Library
NW 23rd at North
  Blackwelder
Oklahoma City 73106
405-521-5072

★ The Support Center
1117 North Shartel, Suite 909
Oklahoma City 73103
405-236-8133

Tulsa City-County Library
  System
400 Civic Center
Tulsa 74103
918-592-7944

OREGON
Library Association of
  Portland
Education and Documents
801 S.W. Tenth Avenue
Portland 97205
503-223-7201

PENNSYLVANIA
★ Northhampton County
  Area Community
  College
  Learning Resources Center
3835 Green Pond Road
Bethlehem 18017
215-865-5358

★ Erie County Public Library
3 South Perry Square
Erie 16501
814-452-2333 ext. 54

★ Dauphin County Library
  System
  Central Library
101 Walnut Street
Harrisburg 17101
717-234-4961

★ Lancaster Public Library
125 North Duke Street
Lancaster 17602
717-394-2651

The Free Library of
  Philadelphia
Logan Square
Philadelphia 19103
215-686-5423

Hillman Library
University of Pittsburgh
Pittsburgh 15260
412-624-4528

RHODE ISLAND
Providence Public Library
Reference Department
150 Empire Street
Providence 02903
401-521-7722

SOUTH CAROLINA
★ Charleston County Public
  Library
404 King Street
Charleston 29403
803-723-1645

South Carolina State
  Library
Reader Services
  Department
1500 Senate Street
Columbia 29211
803-758-3181

SOUTH DAKOTA
South Dakota State Library
State Library Building
322 South Fort Street
Pierre 57501
605-773-3131

TENNESSEE
Knoxville-Knox County
  Public Library
500 West Church Avenue
Knoxville 37902
615-523-0781

Memphis Public Library
1850 Peabody Avenue
Memphis 38104
901-528-2957

★ Public Library of Nashville
  and Davidson County
8th Avenue, North and
  Union Street
Nashville 37203
615-244-4700

TEXAS
● The Hogg Foundation for
  Mental Health
The University of Texas
Austin 78712
512-471-5041

Corpus Christi State
  University Library
6300 Ocean Drive
Corpus Christi 78412
512-991-6810

Dallas Public Library
Grants Information Service
1515 Young Street
Dallas 75201
214-749-4100

● El Paso Community
  Foundation
El Paso National Bank
  Building, Suite 1616
El Paso 79901
915-533-4020

★ Funding Information
  Center
Texas Christian University
  Library
Ft. Worth 76129
817-921-7000 ext. 6130

Houston Public Library
Bibliographic &
  Information Center
500 McKinney Avenue
Houston 77002
713-224-5441 ext. 265

Funding Information
  Library
1120 Milam Building
115 E. Travis Street
San Antonio 78205
512-227-4333

UTAH
Salt Lake City Public
  Library
Business and Science
  Dept.
209 East Fifth South
Salt Lake City 84111
801-363-5733

VERMONT
State of Vermont Depart-
  ment of Libraries
Reference Services Unit
111 State Street
Montpelier 05602
802-828-3261

VIRGINIA
Grants Resources Library
Hampton City Hall
9th Floor
22 Lincoln Street
Hampton 23669
804-272-6496

Richmond Public Library
Business, Science, &
  Technology Department
101 East Franklin Street
Richmond 23219
804-780-8223

WASHINGTON
Seattle Public Library
1000 Fourth Avenue
Seattle 98104
206-625-4881

Spokane Public Library
Funding Information
  Center
West 906 Main Avenue
Spokane 99201
509-838-3361

WEST VIRGINIA
Kanawha County Public
  Library
123 Capitol Street
Charleston 25301
304-343-4646

WISCONSIN
Marquette University
  Memorial Library
1415 West Wisconsin
  Avenue
Milwaukee 53233
414-224-1515

WYOMING
Laramie County
  Community College
  Library
1400 East College Drive
Cheyenne 82001
307-634-5853

CANADA
● Canadian Centre for
  Philanthropy
185 Bay Street, Suite 504
Toronto, Ontario M5J 1K6
416-364-4875

ENGLAND
★ Charities Aid Foundation
12 Crane Court
Fleet Street
London EC4A 2JJ
1-583-7772

MEXICO
Biblioteca Benjamin
  Franklin
Londres 16
Mexico City 6, D.F.
525-591-0244

PUERTO RICO
Universidad del Sagrado
  Corazon
M.M.T. Guevarra Library
Correo Calle Loiza
Santurce 00914
809-728-1515 ext. 343

VIRGIN ISLANDS
College of the Virgin
  Islands Library
Saint Thomas
U.S. Virgin Islands 00801
809-774-9200 Ext. 487

IRS identification number. The Foundation Center carries several past years' tax returns. Look up several years and you can:

- Look for trends in grant size.
- See shifts in funding patterns toward new areas of interest.
- See patterns in funding amounts dispersed among stated interests.
- See geographic granting patterns.
- See if foundation assets are growing and where they come from.
- Look for geographical funding patterns.
- Find the "pet" recipients.

CHAPTER 21

Corporate Funding Sources and Research Tools

Although there are over 2.3 million corporations in the United States, your research into corporations that will fund your project will be simplified and narrowed when the following facts are considered:

- Of the 2.3 million corporations in the United States, only 34 percent make any philanthropic contributions at all.

- Of these, only 6 percent contribute over $500 in a year.

- Of the $64.9 billion contributed to nonprofits by private philanthropy, corporations accounted for 4.8 percent or 3.1 billion dollars.

Since we have already discussed why corporations give, you know that corporate plants and factories or vested interests in your geographic area motivate corporate giving. By drawing a twenty-five-mile radius around yourself, you can identify the larger employers (companies with 100 or more employees) and select the group your project can be most easily related to.

A visit to the Chamber of Commerce will greatly aid in this selection process. The Chamber has information on the corporations near you and will share it, including the corporation's number of employees, payroll, and products.

The Foundation Center Publications sheets (pp. 177–179) are not meant to be an inclusive reference list concerning corporations and you need not familiarize yourself with all of them. A visit to your local public library or college library will prove very beneficial and save you money. Your research is based upon two aspects of the corporation:

1. *Profitability:* when profits go up, corporate giving goes up.

FOUNDATION CENTER PUBLICATIONS

Publications of The Foundation Center are the primary working tools of every serious grantseeker. They are also used by grantmakers, scholars, journalists, regulators, and legislators; in short, by everyone seeking any type of factual information on foundation philanthropy. Copies of all publications are available for examination free of charge at any of the regional collections listed in this volume. Publications may be ordered from The Foundation Center, 888 Seventh Avenue, New York, NY 10106. Please include prepayment and complete shipping address. For additional information or to place credit card orders, call toll free 800-424-9836.

Foundation Directory
For over 20 years The Foundation Directory has been recognized as the authoritative guide to the grantmaking interests of major American foundations. The 8th Edition includes descriptions of the nation's 3,363 largest foundations --the source of 93% of all foundation assets and 89% of total grant dollars. Entries include a description of giving interests, along with adresses, telephone numbers, current financial data, names of donors and key officers, and grant application information.
     See bibliography for ordering information.

The Foundation Directory Supplement
In response to many requests from tens of thousands of Foundation Directory users, updated information on grantmaking foundations is now available between biennial editions of the Directory. Information for 1,752 of the 3,363 foundations in the Foundation Directory has been updated for this Supplement, providing new fiscal data, changes in staff, trustees, and officers, changes in addresses and telephone numbers, and changes in deadlines, application procedures, and funding priorities. Together the Directory and Supplement provide current, detailed information on that key foundation universe which accounts for over 90% of all foundation dollars.
     See bibliography for ordering information.

National Data Book
This is the only directory that includes all of the currently active grantmaking foundations in the U.S. More than 22,000 foundations are listed in one easy-to-use volume with an alphabetical index in a separate companion volume. Foundation entries include name, address, and principal officer, plus full fiscal data--market value of assets, grants paid, gifts received, and fiscal period--and an indication of which foundations publish annual reports. The introduction provides the most comprehensive statistical analysis available of foundation philanthropy.
     See bibliography for ordering information.

Corporate Foundation Profiles
Comprehensive analyses of over 200 of the largest company-sponsored foundations along with summary financial data for over 400 additional corporate foundations are presented for convenient reference in this volume. Covering over 600 foundations in total, this is the most complete source of data on the large

corporate foundations--including information on all of those giving more than
$100,000 annually or with assets totaling more than $1 million. Full subject,
type of support, and geographic indexes are provided.
      See bibliography for ordering information.

Foundation Grants to Individuals,
This is the only publication devoted entirely to foundation grant opportunities
for individual applicants. The 3rd Edition provides full descriptions of the
programs for individuals of about 950 foundations, with up-to-date addresses,
program descriptions, interview and deadline information, telephone numbers,
names of trustees and staff, financial data, and sample grants.

Foundation Grants Index Annual
Lists the grants of $5,000 or more awarded to nonprofit organizations by 450
major U.S. foundations. The 12th edition is the largest index ever, listing
27,000 grants and including an expanded analytical introduction. The volume
is arranged alphabetically by state and an expanded analytical introduction.
Each entry notes the amount and date of the grant, name and location of the
recipient, and a brief description of the grant. Indexes to grant recipients
and subject keywords and phrases, and a combined subject and geographic
category index are provided.
      Annually in April. See bibliography for ordering information.

COMSEARCH Printouts
COMSEARCH Printouts are computer-produced guides to foundation grants published
in the annual volume of The Foundation Grants Index arranged in easy-to-use
subject and geographic listings. COMSEARCH: Subjects includes 78 separate
subject listings of grant informaiton which can be ordered as a complete set
on microfiche or by the particular subject area of interest. COMSEARCH:
Geographic lists grants awarded to recipients in each of four regions, 11
states, and two cities. A new series, COMSEARCH: Super Topics, covers all
grants in 11 broad topic areas.
      Series published annually in May; full list of categories available on
request.

Foundation Fundamentals: A Guide for Grantseekers
This comprehensive, easy-to-read guidebook written by Carol Kurzig presents
all of the facts you need to understand the world of foundations and to
identify foundation funding sources for your organizations. The book includes
12 tables with information on grants and giving, plus 46 illustrations which
take the reader step-by-step through the funding research process. Comprehensive
bibliographies and detailed research examples are also supplied.
      1980. 148 pages. ISBN 0-87954-026-5. $4.95

America's Voluntary Spirit: Readings on Giving and Volunteering
Brian O'Connell, President of Independent Sector, presents 45 of the best
pieces written over the past 300 years on America's national tradition of
giving, volunteering, and not-for-profit initiative. An essential reference
for those who write or speak on the sector's richness and diversity. A wonderful

2. You must be able to relate to the values of the funding source.
    For instance, many corporations have to recruit young execu-
    tives; these individuals have educational desires and you may
    be able to relate to the career goals of employees (or to the
    products they produce, the children of the workers, their re-
    tirees, the health costs of the workers, etc.)
      Since most executives have families that must relocate, the ed-
    ucation system is a big factor in getting the executive to move and
    keeping the employees happy once they have relocated. Culture
    and the arts may be important to corporate recruiting and the re-

FOUNDATION CENTER PUBLICATIONS (Cont.)

gift for trustees, volunteers, and others concerned with the extraordinary
array of institutions which comprise our independent sector.
 May 1983. 450 pages. ISBN 0-87954-079-6. $19.95 hardbound; $14.95
 paperbound

Other Publications

Foundation Today: Current Facts and Figures on Private Foundations: this
pamphlet presents a brief overview of the general characteristics of foundation,
current fiscal status of foundations, and trends in foundation giving.
 1983. 23 pages. $2.00.

Philanthropy in the United States: History and Structure: this pamphlet by
F. Emerson Andrews describes the history of philanthropy in the U.S. with
emphasis on its present structure and dimensions. It describes the various
types of foundations, the fields which have most benefited from foundation
giving, and the effect of increased governmental scrutiny.
 35 pages. $1.50

FOUNDATION CENTER PUBLICATIONS

How To Write Successful Corporate Appeals--With Full Examples, by James P.
Sinclair.
Public Service Materials Center, Inc., 111 N. Central Ave., Hartsdale,
N.Y. 10530

The Complete Guide to Corporate Fund Raising, by Joseph Demer & Stephen
Wertheimer.
Public Service Materials Center, Inc., 111 N. Central Ave., Hartsdale,
N.Y. 10530

The Corporate Fund Raising Directory, by Joseph Dermer & Stephen Wertheimer.
Public Service Materials Center, Inc., 111 N. Central Ave., Hartsdale,
N.Y. 10530

References

Foundation New Magazine
Published by the Council of Federations, 1828 L Street NW, Washington,
D.C. 20036

The Foundation Directory
The Foundation Center, Box FGD, 888 7th Ave., New York, NY 10106

The Individual's Guide to Grants
By Judith B. Margolin, Plenum Publishing Corporation, 233 Spring Street,
New York, NY 10013

tention of personnel. If a corporation has problems with environ-
mentalists, they may be prime to an approach to remove a stigma
or image in the community.

The Dun & Bradstreet and Standard and Poor's materials
(pp. 180–183) are to be used to find out about a company's
profitability, growth, and investment. Many colleges and universities already have one or more of these materials. You don't
need them all—any one of these resources will do.

I suggest that you do not purchase these source books. Use
them at the library. Several directories are available on corpo-

DUN & BRADSTREET'S MILLION DOLLAR DIRECTORY
(See sample on p.181)

This reference tool is an invaluable
source of data on corporations with
net worth of over $1 million.

Entries include the following
information on corporations:

  ° Address and phone
  ° Subsidiary relationships
  ° Sales
  ° Employees
  ° Divisions and products
  ° Officers

They are indexed alphabetically,
geographically, and by product
classification. This makes it easier
to find data on large corporations
in your area.

You can find the Million Dollar
Directory and the similar Middle
Market Directory (listing corporations
with net worth of $500,000 to $1
million in business libraries,
college libraries, and some regional
collections of The Foundation Center.

Dun and Bradstreet's
Million Dollar Directory
99 Church Street
New York, NY 10007

rate giving. Since these directories are national in scope, their
actual usefulness in your geographic area is very limited. Before
you pay $100 to $200 on a corporate directory, consider investing
that amount by purchasing a share of stock in corporations with
plants in your area or in corporations who are current or potential
grantors. The purchase of a share of stock will put you on the
company's mailing list and you will receive:

• proxy statements,

• annual reports,

• reports on shareholder meetings, and

• dividend checks.

```
              D-U-N-S 00-123-8900
        AMERICAN COMMUNICATIONS CO*(NY)
        ACC
        099 Brady Ave., New York, NY  10007
        Tel(212) 897-8888  Sales 58888MM  Emp 877342
        ACC
          SIC 4822 3822 7811
        Communications Holding Company
          *C L Brown          Ch Bd
          *W S Cashel Jr       V Ch B
          *J E Olsen           V Ch B
          *W M Allinghouse     Pr
           T E Bolger          Ex VP
           R R Houghes         Ex VP
           C E Hugal           Ex VP
           K J Whalen          Ex VP
           R W Kleinert        VP
           A vonAuwen          VP
           R E Allen           VP Bus Svce
           J A Bird            VP Network Plng &
                               Design
           J P Billings        VP Federal Regulatory
                               Matters
           E M Block           VP Pb Rl & Employee
                               info
           R J Marano          VP Staff
           H W Clarke Jr       VP Human Resources
           J G Fox             VP pb Affairs
           D E Quinn           VP Network Svcs
           V B Kelley          VP Tariffs Costs
           A J McGill          VP Bus Mktg
           R R Reed            VP Labor Rls
                               Corporate Personnel
                               & Policy Seminar
           J L Begall          VP Financial Mgt
           W H Sharwell        VP Ping & Admn
           A C Partoal         VP State Regulatory
                               Matterd
           L J Clandenin       VP Sis Residence
                               Mktg Sis & Svce
           V A Dwyer           VP Tr
           R N Flint           VP Comp
           H J Trienens        VP Genl Counsel
           F A Hutson Jr.      Sec
           Edward W Carter     Catherine B. Cleary
           Archie K Davis      John D deButts
           James H. Evens      Peter E Hass
           Edward M Hanify     William H Dewitt
```

STANDARD AND POOR'S REGISTER OF CORPORATIONS
(See sample on p.183)

The Register of Corporations is a
good place to begin your corporate
grant research. Entries include:

- Corporate name, adress, and
  phone.
- An extensive list of officers.
  those with asterisks are found
  in Standard and Poor's Register
  of Directors and Executives.
- Sales volume.
- Number of employees.
- Description of products.

In this entry the corporate trademark
is also included.

Standard and Poor's
Register of Corporations
345 Hudson Street
New York, NY 10014

```
┌─────────────────────────────────────────────────────────┐
│              AMERICAN COMMUNICATIONS CO.                  │
│           099 Brady Ave., New York, NY  10007             │
│                  Tel. 212-897-8888                        │
│                                                           │
│ *Chrm & Chief Exec Officer--Charles L. Brown              │
│ *Pres & Chief Oper Officer--William M. Ellinghouse        │
│ *Vice-Chrm & Chief Fin Officer--William S. Chasel, Jr.    │
│ *Vice-Chrm--James E. Olson                                │
│  Exec V-P (Business)--Thomas E. Bolger                    │
│  Exec V-P (Network)--Richard R. Hough                     │
│  Exec V-P--Charles E. Hugel                               │
│  Exec V-P--Morris Tanenbaum                               │
│  Exec V-P (Residence)--Kenneth J. Whaling                 │
│  Exec V-P--S.R. Wilcox                                     │
│  V-P & Asst to Chrm--Alvin von Auw                        │
│  V-P (Bus Services)--Robert E. Allen                      │
│  V-P (Network Plan & Design)--Jack A. Baird               │
│  V-P (Fed Reg Matters)-James R. Billings                  │
│  V-P (Pub Rel & Empl Inf)--Edward M. Block                │
│  V-P (Human Resources)--H. Weston Clarke, Jr.             │
│  V-P (Residence Mktg. Sales & Serv)--John L.              │
│     Clendenin                                             │
│  V-P & Treas--Virginia A. Dwyer                           │
│  V-P (Pub Affairs)--John G. Fox                           │
│  V-P (Pres-Long Lines Dept)-Robert W. Kleinert            │
│  V-P (Tariffs & Costs)--Walter B. Kelly                   │
│  V-P (Bus Mktg)--Archie J. McGill                         │
│  V-P(State Reg Matters)--Alfred G. Hartoll                │
│  V-P (Labor Rel, Cor Per & Policy Seminar)--              │
│     Rex V. Heed                                           │
│  V-P--Bruce G. Schwartzburg                               │
│  V-P (Fin Mgt)--John L. Segally                           │
│  V-P (Plan & Admin D)--William G. Sharell                 │
│  V-P & Gen Coun--Howard J. Trienens                       │
│  V-P (Network Services)--Paul M. Billard                  │
│  V-P & Compt-Robert N. Flint                              │
│  Secy--Frank A. Hutson, Jr.                               │
│  Accts--Coopers & Lybrand                                 │
│  Revenue: $45.41 Bil  Employees 984,000                   │
│  Stock Exchange(s): NYS,BST,PAC,MID,CIN,PSE               │
│ *ALSO DIRECTORS--Other Directors Are:                     │
│  Edward W. Barten           Cathy M. Bleary               │
│  Archies M. Harison         John D. DuBute                │
│  James P. Hannie            Betty Johnson                 │
│  BUSINESS: Communications                                 │
│  S.I.C. 4844;4833                                         │
└─────────────────────────────────────────────────────────┘
```

STANDARD AND POOR'S REGISTER OF DIRECTORS AND EXECUTIVES
(See sample on p.185)

This register, like the Directory of
Corporate Management, is a valuable
tool for determining background of,
and possible linkages with, corporate
executives.

  ° Age
  ° Education
  ° Residence
  ° Other corporate affiliations
  ° Other activities

If, for example, you know someone at
the Massuchusetts Institute of
Technology, you might be able to
arrange an interview with the grant-
making officers of AT&T through this
"interface."

Standard and Poor's
Register of Directors
and Executives
345 Hudson Street
New York, NY 10014

BASHEL, WILLIAM S., JR. (b. 1920 Brooklyn--
  Dartmouth Coll. 1941; (Amos Tusk Sch. of Bus. Admin.)
  1942)--Vice-Chrm, Chief Fin Officer & Dir, American
  Communications Co., 099 Brady Ave, New York 10007
    Campell Soup Co., Dir
    Southside Telephone Company, Dir
    Manufacturers Hanner Corp. & Trust Co., Dir
    Philadelphia Fund Savings Group, Trustee

BASHELL, GEORGE R. (b. 1920 Mansfield, Ohio--
  BPOE)--Secy, Bopping Paines Inc., 664 S. West Street,
  Mannington, OH 44902--Res: 355 Oak St., Mannington
  45654
    Bopping Paines Inc. (California), Secy
    Bopping Paines Inc. (Delaware), Secy
    Bopping Disc Inc., Asst Secy
    Smiths Water-System Co., Secy
    National Construction Sacky Credit Group, Mem

BASHIN, EDWARD A. (b. 1903 Duluth, Minn--Univ. of
  Chicago)--Exec. V-P & Dir (Mktg Sales), Complete
  Controls Inc., 6777 Washington St., Minneapolis
  56654--Res: 5555 Shoreside Ave., Wayzata, Minn 55392
    Fireside Country Club, 1st V-P & Dir

BASHMAN, EDMUND JOSEPH (b. 1936 Rockville Square, N.Y.--
  St. Patrick's Coll, 1958)--Exec V-P & Dir Hoggens
  Mason Wood Walker, Inc., 6 Maple Ave., Baltimore
  32241--Res:7878 A Frame Road, Huxton, Md 88773
    Peacon Picture Services, Inc., Dir
    RFS Financial Services (subs Hoggens Mason), Dir
    Garden Capital (subs Hoggens Mason), Dir

BASHMAN, GEORGE D. (b. 1927 NYC)--V-P (Intl).
  Gordan Guaranty Trust Co. of New York, 23 Hall St.,
  New York 10008--Res: 23 Midwood Dr., Glorham Park
  N.J. 07932
    U.S. Chamber of Commerce Comm. on Import Trade
      Policy, Chrm.
    Import Expansion Comm. of the Bankers Assn. for
      Foreign Trade, Mem
    National Overseas Trade Council, Inc., Dir

BASHMAN, JOHN G. (b. 1931 Columbus, Neb.--South
  Texas College 1953; College of Texas 1956)--Dir Govt.

CHAPTER 22

How to Contact a Private Funding Source

Why

Contacting the funding source before you write the proposal will help you gather information concerning their needs. This contact will allow you to choose the particular approach or method that each funding source will find interesting and tailor your proposal accordingly.

I estimate that you increase your chances of success by 300 percent when you contact the funding source before you write the proposal.

How

Since private funding sources are very short of staff, contact with them is a difficult task. Recent surveys show that there are only 1,500 professionals employed full time by the 22,088 foundations (this includes corporate foundations). Your research will show that many addresses for private funding sources are trustee departments of banks. Your contact may best be accomplished through using your webbing or linkage connections to get you a personal visit with a trustee or board member. The *Foundation Directory* (see the sample and explanation in the section on foundation research tools) contains a cross-reference of board members. If you have a linkage to a foundation in the *Directory*, you can look up the other board members to identify what other foundations they are on. In this way, your linkage to the foundation can introduce you to the other board members and you can discuss the funding programs of the other foundation that person is on.

Personal contact with the corporation or foundation is essential to success. The strategy is simple:

- Write a letter.
- Make a telephone call.
- Go and visit them.

You should evaluate each funding source profile with your project, location, and experience. Then move on to contacting those sources with the highest probability of funding your proposal.

Contact Letters

Some kind of information exchange with the funding-source contact person is desirable. There are several reasons why this correspondence is needed. You must develop as much background information as possible prior to contacting the funding executive (or linkage person) for an appointment. The sample on p. 188 shows how a letter of inquiry type may be constructed. Develop your own and use the one in this manual as a guide.

Your research may indicate that an appointment letter is not what the funding source desires (many state "no appointments" in all literature); they may prefer a letter proposal summarizing your request. Some type of contact with board members is

SAMPLE INQUIRY LETTER TO A FUNDING SOURCE

(REQUEST FOR BASIC INFORMATION)

Use this form when you want basic information prior to writing for an

appointment or after you get turned down for an appointment. (Note: This is

not a letter proposal.)

                                              Date:

Name
Title
Address

Dear _____:

    I understand that (name of foundation/funding source) has an interest in
funding programs that benefit the _____. The ___[your organization]___
is interested in carrying out a project we have developed that deals with
this area. [Brief description of what you plan to do, with an eye-catching
sentence or two pointing out the unique benefits of your project and your
organization.]

    This proposal meets your stated concerns in the _____ area,
while providing our organization with the outside funds necessary to implement
this important project. Correspondence concerning your desired format for
proposals, your current or new priority statements, or other guidelines and
information will be appreciated and utilized.

    Please add us to your mailing list for your annual reports, newsletters,
etc.

    I will be calling you in the near future to discuss our opportunities to
work together. Thank you for your coorperation.

                                              Sincerely,

                                              Name/Title
                                              Phone Number

desired. (In all cases you should attempt contact through webbing and linkage.) The letter they may refer to is not the following appointment letter, but a "letter proposal." The letter proposal follows after the preliminary steps are outlined below.

The Appointment Letter

The importance of pre-proposal contact has already been discussed. The best ways to set up such a meeting are by letter and phone. This sample letter (p. 190) will assist you in developing this personal contact. With so few staff people to assist you, it is understandable that the private funding source may not be able to honor your request.

The Telephone

It is often difficult to get a funding official to give you the time required for a personal meeting to discuss your project. If your organization is a long distance from the agency, it can be inconvenient and expensive to set up such a face-to-face meeting. In these cases, you can conduct a phone interview with the funding official or board member (or webbing and linkage contact).

This checklist suggests a four-step process to go through each time you discuss your project over the phone with a private funding source. The data you want from this phone call (or you want to validate) are:

- the organization's current granting priorities and changes from past priorities;
- specific information on how you should change your project and/or proposal to make it more attractive to the funding source;
- proposal formats (although they may not have formal guidelines, they may be able to tell you what they or their board members like);
- the best grant size to request.

SAMPLE LETTER TO A FUNDING SOURCE

(FOR APPOINTMENT)

Date:

Name (Executive Director)
Title
Address
Dear _____:

    I am interested in meeting with you to discuss an important project that
deals with the area of _____. The need for this project
is _____.

    Since we are analyzing several possible approaches, your input at this
time would be very valuable for our formal proposal development. My research
indicates the ___[foundation's/funding/source's]___ concern and support of
projects in this important area. My request meets your preliminary guidelines
and a few minutes of your time would enable us to more closely meet both your
concerns and our interests in this area.

    Attached is a case statement or brochure on the ___[your organization]___ .
Since we have been dealing with the needs of _____ for _____
years, I'm sure we will have an interesting and productive meeting.

    I will call you to discuss our opportunity to visit.

                                    Sincerely,

                                    Name
                                    Title
                                    Phone Number

Ask the same questions as if you were meeting with the funding source face to face. (see Questions to Ask a Funding Official). Keep in mind these three tips:

1. Refer to Mr./Mrs. Smith's letter of [date]. (This is the letter you have sent.)
2. Ask for five minutes; say you'll call back if it's not convenient at this time.
3. Phone midweek.

Calling a Private Funding Source on the Phone (For Appointment)

The chances that your research will yield the right phone number are much greater for private funding sources than for public ones. But what do you say when you call?

- Ask for the funding official by name (if possible).

- Tell the official you will be in their area and would like to meet with them briefly to discuss a project that your research indicates they would be interested in.

- Ask for an appointment.

If the official's answer is yes, get off the phone. If the answer is no—foundation/corporate policy may dictate that no interview is possible—then try the following:

1. Set up a phone interview then or for a later date.
2. Suggest that you should talk because one of your advocates has contacted his or her board member.
3. Ask if they have a travel schedule and would like to meet you and see your program and the need in person.

If the funding official says that he or she is not interested in making an appointment to discuss your project with you, proceed as follows:

1. Ask why. Changes in interests of funding sources take years to show up in the resource books.
2. Ask who else might be interested. Funding sources know one another and know who is doing what.

3. Ask if they agree that this is an important need that will be
   addressed.
   If you cannot get through to the funding official, then:
1. Use the intermediaries or screens and ask them intelligent
   questions from "Sample Questions Sheet for Interview." (Show
   them you know what you are doing.)
2. Let them know you will call back. Most grant seekers try once
   and give up. You *will* call back.

The Visit

Visiting in person is the best way to get to know the funding
source. But it is also difficult to arrange. Foundations do not have
anyone whose job is to see you and corporations' people are oc-
cupied in important corporate jobs that provide the profits they
need. You are fortunate to get a visit. Use your time wisely.

WHO SHOULD GO

Your credibility will be higher if you take a nonstaff representative with you. An articulate, impressive advocate or advisory
committee member is an excellent choice. Use the information
you collected from your webbing and linkage to choose a close
match to the funding source. Consider age, education, club
affiliation, and other personal characteristics as a basis for your
choice. Dress according to your information about the funding
source or use the book, *Dress for Success.*

MATERIALS TO BRING

The materials needed are those organized in your Proposal
Development Workbook (Swiss Cheese Book). You may want to
bring added materials that document the need in a more interesting or vivid manner. Use simple audio-visual aids that are in balance with the request. A large request ($250,000) can have a short
film, while a $5,000 request should not. Use visual aids to show
need and develop their agreement on the importance of meeting
the need. You have developed several possible approaches to
meeting the need and have the cost/benefits of each approach
outlined. You want to learn which approach they would like, not

to sell or convince them of "the only way to solve the problem." Your Idea Summary Sheet and the Cost/Benefit Analysis Worksheets usually elicit more than enough response to begin a conversation.

Be ready to use the parts of your Swiss Cheese Book for answers to questions like, "Why should we give the money to you instead of some other organization?"

The First Meeting: Questions to Ask a Funding Source

Review these questions to determine which are the most beneficial to you and your current state of knowledge of the funding source. You may want to assign questions to the two individuals going to the meeting and prepare for the visit by role playing various answers.

1. We have developed approaches that are feasible for us to perform. Would you please look at these and comment on which look the most interesting to you (or to the board)?
2. Last year, the amount of funds from your organization to our kind of project was X, and the average size was Y. Will that remain consistent?
3. Our research indicates that your deadlines were — and —. Will they be the same this year?
4. Do proposals that are submitted early help you? Do they receive more favorable treatment?
5. How do you review the proposal and who does it? Outside experts? Board members? Staff?
6. Are these your current granting priorities? (Give copy of research sheet.)
7. What do you think of submitting more than one proposal in a funding cycle?
8. Is our budget estimate realistic?
9. Would you look over my proposal if I finished it early?
10. Can you suggest other funders who would be appropriate for this project?
11. May I see a proposal you have funded, that you feel is well written?

12. Is the amount we are requesting realistic in light of current foundation goals?

Private Funding-Source Report Form

Each time a member of your staff contacts a funder in person or over the phone, he or she should fill in one of these forms and file it (see p. 195).

This simple procedure has a number of important benefits. It will keep you from damaging your credibility by repeating the same questions or having the funder say, "I gave that information to — from your organization. Don't you people ever talk to each other?" Also, it will allow another person from your organization to pick up where you leave off. These forms will show the next person where you or the project director were, and will look good to the funder.

PRIVATE FUNDING SOURCE REPORT FORM

Fill this sheet in after each contact with the private funding source.

Funding Source: (Name) _____

Address: _____

_____

Contacted on (date) _____ By: _____ Phone _____ Personal Contact

Contact Person: _____

Project Title: _____

OBJECTIVE of contact: _____

_____

_____

_____

_____

_____

RESULTS: _____

_____

_____

_____

_____

_____

FOLLOW-UP: _____

_____

_____

_____

_____

_____

CHAPTER 23

Applying for Private Funds

THE LETTER PROPOSAL

Both government and private funding sources have begun using the letter-proposal format (pp. 187–199) as a part of the application process. Public funding sources may call it a pre-proposal concept paper or letter of intent. In some cases they will not send you the applications package (usually the lengthy, difficult forms) unless they like the approach outlined in the concept paper.

Remember, 30,000 private funding sources give away billions each year from these letter proposals. Often, they do not have the staff or the time to read lengthy proposals.

Find out how many copies they "could" use. If they allow you to send them seven copies with attachments, you are more likely to have everything reach the board members. Many funding sources require only one copy, but they have seven board members. If you have your choice of attachments to include, I suggest you use your project planner.

<u>THE LETTER PROPOSAL</u>

Put this on your stationery with letterhead.

Date:

Name (funding source)

Address

Dear <u>(person listed as director or contact person)</u>:

Introduction Paragraph -- <u>state your reason for writing</u>

"I want to introduce you to a project you will find interesting." You
can use your linkage here. "Mr. Smith suggested I write and explain . . ."
Concentrate on the funding source and their interest or relationship to the
need or problem.

<u>Why This Funding Source</u>

You can even ask the question, "Why are we coming to you?" Include your
research on why they should be interested. "You should for _____ has
been an inspiration to organizations like ours for _____ years." Do
your research better than the competition and show it. Analyze the research
and extrapolate from it. "Of the \$ _____ that the Jones Foundation
has contributed, health care accounted for 70 percent of your funds. It is
with this commitment to health that I approach you."

<u>Needs Paragraph</u>

What is the need? Tailor your presentation of the need to the funding
source's biases, viewpoint, and values concerning their geographic perspective.
The use of one or two well-chosen statistics from your needs assessment or
research that hit the funder with impact will help.

THE LETTER PROPOSAL (Cont.)

For example, "As you drive home tonight, of every 8 cars that you pass, 1 is being operated by a drunk driver." 1 out of every 10 children born has _____ "By the time you read this proposal _____ cases of _____ will occur." Be careful, however: too many numbers will only confuse the funding source.

Solution Paragraph

In three sentences or less, describe your approach to the problem. How will you solve the problem you have outlined in the needs paragraph? How will you close the gap you created? You are concerned with the methods, while the funder is more concerned with the results. What will be improved and how much?

Uniqueness Paragraph

Once you have shown the need and outlined your proposed solution, tell the funding source why you are the best choice for "doing the job." State how you are uniquely suited to meet the needs of the clients (or do the research, etc.). "The XYZ Hospital has been meeting the needs of emotionally disturbed pre-schoolers for thirteen years. The trained staff represents over 300 years of experience in this specialized area. The location provides . . ."

Request for Funds Paragraph

Many grant seekers state the total amount of the proposal, but forget to ask the funding source for the money. They expect the funder to figure out how much they want to give. Ask! You could put your request in a form such as:

"With the proven interest you have shown in this area I am requesting a grant in the amount of $ _____ This represents an investment of $1.45

THE LETTER PROPOSAL (Cont.)

for each child we serve." Show the funder what the request equates to per
client. Or say, "Over a 10-year period the equipment you provide will touch
the lives of _____ handicapped persons." Include other donors who have
granted you funds for this project or other sources you are approaching.
This is especially good if you have divided the grant into smaller, more
fundable parts that you plan to take to several funders.

Closing Paragraph

The standard closing refers to your desire to meet with them and have
them visit you. Tell them you will provide your project planner, blueprints,
etc. You may want to use this paragraph to defer the informational requests
to you, the grant writer, instead of the person signing the letter, "Mrs.
Connors of my staff can be reached at _____ for further information."

Signature

You should have your "heavyweights" sign the proposal (even though you
wrote it). You may want double signature; add the board president. Since
it is the board who is legally responsible and not the administration, some
funding sources prefer to see board commitment.

Attachments (if allowable)

You may want to include your project planner, time line, pictures,
graphs, charts, studies, etc. The attachments must be more reduced than with
public funding sources. Include your tax exemption designation and your IRS
number.

If the funding source has a suggested format outline, follow it precisely.
If the funding source does not give you any guidance on format or style but
says "X pages or less," use the project planner and the explanation for how
to write a proposal outline under the section on Public Funding Sources.

CHAPTER 24

Submission and Whom to Contact on Follow-up

The deadlines provided by private funding sources should be observed whenever possible. Since an organization presents an image of being a poor steward of funds if it cannot meet a deadline, try to be prompt, or better yet, early.

It has been the writer's experience that a funding source will often give a few extra days' "grace" period, with proper explanation and the benefit of personal contact.

Be sure to find out if early submission will help and how many copies of the proposal they would find useful. (The directions frequently say one or two copies and they could use five.)

Make note of the following:

- Send the contacts or people you discovered through webbing an abstract or the proposal or a copy of the letter proposal.

- Ask "friends" to push for your proposal at the board meeting or contact their friends to try for a favorable decision.

- Minimize personal contact once you have submitted the proposal lest you be thought of as pushy.

Proposal Submission

When it comes time to submit your request, consider delivering it in person. Solicit an advocate or board member to deliver the proposal. Hand delivery makes more of an impression on funders, and also helps avoid problems with the postal service. You are sure it's there, alas!

If you decide to mail your proposal, send it by certified mail, return receipt requested. This way you will have proof that your proposal arrived on time. You can mail the required extra copies by first class mail or UPS. Check after one or two weeks to make sure they have been received.

CHAPTER 25

The Decision of Private Funders

Private funding sources are more prompt than public funders. They make their decision and let you know the outcome promptly. You will get a simple yes or no. If the funding source says "supportable" but "not fundable," it is a polite no. The easiest way to tell if your grant is funded is by looking for the check. If the answer is yes (the grant seeker's dream answer), you should immediately:

- Send a warm personal thank-you letter to the funding source. One trustee told me that one of the only records they keep on grantees is a list of who thanks them. She said, "We check the list. If you receive a grant and don't thank us, it will be the last grant you receive."

- Find out the payment procedures.

- Check on any reporting procedures that the funding source may have.

- Ask about when the funding source may be interested in

your making an on-site visit to them to report on the grant.

- Put the funding source on your public-relations list so that you send them news releases about you.

- *Important:* ask the funding source for their critique or comments on your proposal—*what they liked or what you could improve.*

If the answer is a rejection of your grant request, make the most of what you can learn, by:

- Sending a warm personal thank-you letter to the funding source. Express your appreciation for the time and effort they spent reviewing your proposal.

- Reminding them of the need for them as a source of funds.

- Asking them for comments on your proposal and if they would look favorably on resubmission with certain changes in the proposal.

- Asking: "Do you know of any other funding sources who would be interested in the project that provides these benefits to _____?"

- Trying again. Successful grant seekers are persistent.

CHAPTER 26

Follow-up with Private Funding Sources

Since most funding sources feel neglected once they have given away the money, you can get on their list of "Good Grantees" by following up with them.

<u>YOUR FOLLOW-UP CHECKLIST SHOULD INCLUDE</u>:

( )   Funding Source in on Public Relations Lists and Will Receive News Releases

( )   Send Articles or Studies Related to Your Area of Concern

( )   Invite Them to Visit You When Traveling Near You

( )   Keep Your Files Up-dated and Have a Volunteer Put in New Lists of Grants They've Funded

( )   Write and Make Comments on How Successful You are Two Years after They Funded You, and Thank Them for Their Farsightedness in Dealing with the Problem, etc.

Grant Resource Bibliography

You may wish to locate a copy of these recommended grant tools before you purchase them. Each type of resource is listed with several locations where you may find both the tool and valuable assistance from staff.

Several institutions have developed joint or cooperative grants libraries to encourage consortium projects and reduce costs.

This bibliography is divided into the following sections:

Government Grant Research Aids
  Government Grant Publications
  Commercially Produced Publications

Foundation Research Aids
  Books
  Periodicals and Newsletters
  Private Foundation IRS Returns
  Directories of State and Local Grant Makers

Corporate Research Tools
  Books
  Periodicals and Newsetters

Computer Research Services

Government Grant Research Aids

Tips

1. Each congressional district has at least two Federal Depository Libraries. Your college librarian will know where the designated library is and will advise you on the availability of the resources listed in this section.
2. Many federal agencies have newsletters or agency publications. You can request to be placed on their mailing list in order to receive these publications.
3. Contact with federal programs to get the most updated information is recommended.
4. All of the government grant publications listed here are available through your congressperson's office.

GOVERNMENT GRANT PUBLICATIONS

Commerce Business Daily
The government's contracts publication, published five times a week, the *Daily* announces every governmental Request For Proposal (RFP) that exceeds $25,000 and upcoming sales of governmental surplus.
    Price: $81.00
    Order from: Superintendent of Documents
                        U.S. Government Printing Office
                        Washington, DC 20402

Catalog of Federal Domestic Assistance, annual
This is the government's most complete listing of federal domestic assistance programs with details on eligibility, application procedure, and deadlines, including the location of state plans. It is published at the beginning of each fiscal year with supplementary updates during the year. Indexes are by agency program, function, popular name, applicant eligibility, and subject. It comes in looseleaf form, punched for a three-ring binder.
    Price: $22.00, subscription price (without binder)
    Order from: Superintendent of Documents
                        U.S. Government Printing Office
                        Washington, DC 20402

The Federal Register
Published five times a week (Monday through Friday), the *Register* supplies up-to-date information on federal assistance and supplements

the *Catalog of Federal Domestic Assistance.* It includes public regulations and legal notices issued by all federal agencies and presidential proclamations. Of particular importance are the proposed rules, final rules, and program deadlines. An index is published monthly.

Price: $300.00 per year or $150.00 for six months.
Order from: Superintendent of Documents,
U.S. Government Printing Office
Washington, DC 20402

1982–83 Official Congressional Directory: 97th Congress, 1st Session, 1,108 pages
Price: $12.00
Order from: Superintendent of Documents
U.S. Government Printing Office
Washington, DC 20402

United States Government Manual, annual
This paperback manual gives the names of key personnel, addresses and telephone numbers for all agencies, departments, etc., which constitute the federal bureaucracy.
Price: $10.00
Order from: Superintendent of Documents
U.S. Government Printing Office
Washington, DC 20402

COMMERCIALLY PRODUCED PUBLICATIONS

Academic Research Information System, Inc. (ARIS)
ARIS provides timely information about grant and contract opportunities, including concise descriptions of guidelines and eligibility requirements, upcoming deadlines dates, identification of program resource persons, and new program policies for both government and nongovernment funding sources.
Prices: *Medical Science Report* $145.00
Social and National Science Report $145.00
Creative Arts and Humanities Report .... $ 80.00
All ARIS Reports and Supplements................ $320.00
Order from: Academic Research Information System, Inc.
The Redstone Building
2940 16th Street
Suite 314
San Francisco, CA 94103

1982 Federal Funding Guide, Jan E. Balkin, editor, 460 pages, 1982
This guide describes programs that provide grants and/or loans to local,
county, and state government, nonprofits and community and volunteer
groups. It includes supplementary materials on President Reagan's
budget proposals.
   Price: $58.95 plus $5.00 postage and handling
   Order from: Government Information Services
                  1611 North Kent Street, Suite 568
                  Arlington, VA 22209

Federal Grants and Contracts Weekly, Robert Zuckerman, editor
This weekly contains information on the latest Requests For Proposals
(RFPs), contracting opportunities, and upcoming grants. Each ten-page
issue includes details on Requests For Proposals, closing dates for grant
programs, procurement-related news, and newly issued regulations.
   Price: $177.00 for one year
   Order from: Capitol Publications, Inc.
                  1300 North 17th Street
                  Arlington, VA 22209

The Grant Advisor
A monthly newsletter, *The Grant Advisor* offers comprehensive informa-
tion for colleges and universities about federal grant programs and fac-
ulty fellowship opportunities.
   Price: $75.00 per year (11 issues)
   Order from: The Grant Advisor
                  P.O. Box 3553
                  Arlington, VA 22203

Grants Magazine
This periodical provides a forum for discussion of the various issues that
affect both public and private philanthropy. It serves both the grant-
seeking and grant-making public by facilitating communication between
those organizations and individuals concerned with formulating grant
programs and those that depend upon philanthropic aid.
   Price: $65.00 (4 issues)
   Order from: Plenum Press
                  233 Spring Street
                  New York, NY 10013

Health Grants and Contracts Weekly
   Price: $167.00 per year
   Order from: Capitol Publications, Inc.
                  1300 North 17th Street
                  Arlington, VA 22209

Higher Education Daily
   Price: $376.00 per year
   Order from: Capitol Publications, Inc.
                  1300 North 17th Street
                  Arlington, VA 22209

ORYX Press
Monthly updates to one main volume.
   Price: $400 a year (approx.) plus $30.00 postage
   Order from: 3930 East Camelback Road
                  Phoenix, AZ 85018

Washington Information Directory, 1982, 930 pages
This directory is divided into three categories: agencies of the executive
branch; Congress; and private or "nongovernmental" organizations.
Each entry includes the name, address, telephone numer, and director
of the organization and a short description of its work.
   Price: $27.50 (approx.)
   Order from: Congressional Quarterly, Inc.
                  1414 22nd Street, N.W.
                  Washington, DC 20037

Foundation Research Aids

Tips

   Many of the research aids can be located in the Foundation Center
regional libraries and in your college libraries.

BOOKS

Corporate Foundation Profiles, 3rd Edition, 1983, 593 pages
This publication contains detailed analyses of 234 of the largest company sponsored foundations in the U.S. and brief records for 701 co-
sponsored foundations with assets of $1 million or more or giving over
$100,000/year.
   Price: $50.00

The Foundation Center Source Book Profiles
This research aid describes the 1,000 largest foundations, by subject
area, type of grant, and type of recipient, including company-sponsored foundations and community foundations. Subscribers to the
series receive cumulative volumes of foundation profiles. Each quar-

terly volume includes *Indexes* by subject, type of support, foundation name, and city and state of both foundation location and focus of giving. *Source Book Profiles Updates* are issued with quarterly volumes.
Price: $250.00

The Foundation Directory, 9th edition, 1983, 761 pages
This is the most important single reference work available on grant-making foundations in the United States. It includes information on foundations having assets of more than $1,000,000 or annual grants exceeding $100,000. The ninth edition includes descriptions of the nation's 4,063 largest foundations. Each entry includes a description of giving interests along with address, telephone numbers, current financial data, names of donors and contact person, and IRS identification number. Includes six indexes: state and city, subject, foundation donors, trustees and administrators and alphabetical foundation names. The trustees index is very valuable in developing linkages to decision makers.
Price: $45.00

The Foundation Grants Index, 12th edition, annual, 1983, 582 pages
This cumulative listing of approximately 27,121 grants of $5,000 or more made by over 400 major foundations is indexed by subject and geographic locations, by the names of the recipient organizations, and by key words. These grants total almost $1.49 billion and represent approximately half of all foundation giving ($3.46 billion).
Price: $35.00 (approx.)

PERIODICALS AND NEWSLETTERS

Foundation News
Each bimonthly issue of the *News* covers the activities of private, company-sponsored, and community foundations, direct corporate giving, government agencies and their programs, and includes the kinds of grants being awarded, overall trends, legal matters, regulatory actions, and other areas of common concern.
Price: $24.00 annual subscription fee
Order from: Foundation News
　　　　　　　1828 L Street NW
　　　　　　　Washington, DC 20036
　　　　　　　(202) 466-6512

Grants Magazine
This quarterly publication provides a forum for discussion of the various issues that affect both public and private philanthropy. It serves both the

grant seeker and the grant maker. The publication contains articles concerning government, foundation, and corporation grants, including information on current programs and trends, the technical aspects of researching sources of funds, and similar subjects.

Price: $54.00 per year (approx.)
Order from: Plenum Press
                233 Spring Street
                New York, NY 10013

Grantsmanship Center News
Each edition of the *News* includes information on obtaining grants, writing proposals, planning programs, managing nonprofit organizations, new fund-raising ideas, and developing resources, as well as information on categorical grant programs and deadlines. Special reprints from the *News* are available and can be ordered from the Center.

Price: $28.00 per year (approx.), six copies
Order from: The Grantsmanship Center
                1031 South Grand Avenue
                Los Angeles, CA 90015

LRCW Newsbriefs (Lutheran Resources Commission Newsbriefs)
This monthly is geared to providers of human services and for keeping up to date on government grant deadlines. It is a thiry-page bulletin of resource material for program development in over 28 subject areas as well as for resource development in general.

Price: $55.00 per year
Order from: Lutheran Resource Commission
                1346 Connecticut Ave., NW, Suite 823
                Washington, DC 20036

The Taft Foundation Information System, 1983
    Foundation Report: This annual directory of the largest private charitable foundations in the United States supplies descriptions and statistical analyses. It includes monthly supplements. Two volumes, 900 pages.

    Foundation Giving Watch: This monthly covers news and the "how-to's" of foundation giving, with a listing of recent grants.

    Foundation Updates: This publication supplies new information on 100 foundations per year.

Price: $400.00 per year (approx.)
Order from: Taft Corporation
                5125 MacArthur Boulevard, NW, Suite 300
                Washington, DC 20016

PRIVATE FOUNDATION IRS RETURN (Available on microfiche from
IRS [50¢ ea.] or free to use at Foundation Center)

The Internal Revenue Service requires private foundations to file income tax returns each year. Form 990-PF provides fiscal details on
receipts and expenditures, compensation of officers, capital gains or
losses, and other financial matters. Form 990-AR provides information
on foundation managers, assets, grants paid and/or committed for future payment. The IRS makes this information available on aperture
cards that may be viewed at libraries operated by The Foundation
Center or at its regional cooperating collections. You may also order aperture cards by state (see price list below) or by individual foundations
from the IRS. To order aperture cards or paper photocopies of 990-PF
and 990-AR forms from IRS, write to: International Revenue Service
Center, Attention; Public Inspection DP-536, P.O. Box 245, Bensalem,
PA 19020.

To order aperture cards or paper photocopies of IRS forms for specific foundations, include the following information on an order: full
name of foundation, city and state in which it is located, the year of the
return desired, and if available, the Employer Identification Number
(EIN). This last item (EIN) will facilitate the filling of the order. Access to
prior-year records may be found at the top of page 1 of Form 990-PF or
page 2 of 990-AR. The cost for aperture cards is $1.00 for the first card
and $.13 for each additional card per foundation. The charge for paper
copies is $1.00 for the first page and $.10 for each additional page per
foundation. Allow four to six weeks for delivery.

Taft Trustees of Wealth/Leaders of Philanthropy, annual
This biographical directory covers private and corporate foundation officers.
    Price: $187.00
    Order from: Taft Corporation
                5125 MacArthur Boulevard, NW, Suite 300
                Washington, DC 20016

Tax Exempt News
This ten-page monthly newsletter keeps up with changes in government
regulations. Sections include: News from Corporations, IRS Private Letter Readings, News from IRS and Treasurer and News from Congress.
    Price: $106.00 a year (approx.)
    Order from: Capitol Publications, Inc.
                1300 North 17th Street
                Arlington, VA 22209

PRICE LIST FOR FOUNDATION IRS RETURNS, 1982 FISCAL YEAR

STATE	PRICE	STATE	PRICE
Alabama	$43.12	Montana	$13.61
Alaska	5.03	Nebraska	33.89
Arizona	33.76	Nevada	8.15
Arkansas	26.48	New Hampshire	37.27
California	457.30	New Jersey	145.17
Colorado	55.08	New Mexico	12.31
Connecticut	132.56	New York	989.00
Delaware	29.86	North Carolina	102.40
District of		North Dakota	9.71
Columbia	65.87	Ohio	274.52
Florida	161.42	Oklahoma	45.07
Georgia	100.19	Oregon	47.15
Hawaii	25.18	Pennsylvania	330.03
Idaho	11.66	Rhode Island	29.08
Illinois	310.53	South Carolina	34.93
Indiana	113.71	South Dakota	7.63
Iowa	60.41	Tennessee	59.11
Kansas	50.92	Texas	269.71
Kentucky	40.00	Utah	29.34
Louisiana	43.25	Vermont	14.39
Maine	35.58	Virginia	92.91
Maryland	84.85	Washington	76.79
Massachusetts	304.16	West Virginia	21.41
Michigan	163.89	Wisconsin	132.95
Minnesota	111.24	Wyoming	8.54
Mississippi	18.03	Puerto Rico	1.13
Missouri	125.54	All Other	20.11
		Total	5,455.93

DIRECTORIES OF STATE AND LOCAL GRANT MAKERS

ALABAMA (184 foundations)
Alabama Foundation Directory, edited by Anne F. Knight. Available from Anne F. Knight, Birmingham, AL 35203.
    $5.00 prepaid

CALIFORNIA (approximately 500 foundations)
Guide to California Foundations, 4th edition, prepared by Melinda Marble. Available from: Guide to California Foundations, 210 Post Street, #814,

San Francisco, CA 94108. Make check or money order payable to Northern California Grantmakers.
$9.00 prepaid

CALIFORNIA (620 corporations)
National Directory of Corporate Charity: California Edition, compiled by Sam Sternberg. Available from Regional Young Adult Project, 944 Market Street, #705, San Francisco, CA 94102.
$32.00 prepaid

CALIFORNIA (73 foundations)
San Diego County Foundation Directory 1980, compiled by The Community Congress of San Diego, Inc. 1980. Available from Community Congress of San Diego, 1172 Morena Boulevard, San Diego, CA 92110.
$10.00 prepaid

CALIFORNIA (45 Bay Area foundations)
Small Change from Big Bucks: A Report and Recommendations on Bay Area Foundations and Social Change, edited by Herb Allen and Sam Sternberg. Available from Bay Area Committee for Responsive Philanthropy, 944 Market Street, San Francisco, CA 94102. Make check payable to: Regional Young Adult Project.
$6.00 prepaid

CALIFORNIA (525 foundations)
Where the Money's At, How to Reach Over 500 California Grant-Making Foundations, edited by Patricia Blair Tobey, with Irving R. Warner. Available from Irving R. Warner, 3235 Berry Drive, Studio City, CA 91604.
$17.00 prepaid

COLORADO (approximately 192 foundations)
Colorado Foundation Directory, 2nd edition, co-sponsored by the Junior League of Denver, Inc., the Denver Foundation, and the Attorney General of Colorado. Available from Colorado Foundation Directory, Junior League of Denver, Inc., 1805 South Bellaire, Suite 400, Denver, CO 80222. Make check payable to Colorado Foundation Directory.
$7.00 prepaid

CONNECTICUT
1980 Guide to Corporate Giving Connecticut, edited by Michael E. Burns and compiled by Anne Washburn. Available from DATA, I State Street, New Haven, CT 06511.
$15.00 prepaid

CONNECTICUT
1979 Connecticut Foundation Directory, edited by Michael E. Burns. Available from DATA, I State Street, New Haven, CT 06511.
$10.00 prepaid

DELAWARE (588 foundations)
Delaware Foundations, compiled by United Way of Delaware, Inc. Available from United Way of Delaware, Inc., 701 Shipley Street, Wilmington, DE 19801.
$7.50 prepaid

DISTRICT OF COLUMBIA (approximately 500 foundations)
The Washington D.C. Metropolitan Area Foundation Directory, edited by Julia Mills Jacobsen and Key Carter Courtade. Available from Management Communications, Publications Division, 4416 Edmunds Street, NW, Washington, DC 20007.
$13.50 prepaid

GEORGIA (approximately 550 foundations)
Georgia Foundation Directory, compiled by Ann Bush. Available from Foundation Collection, Atlanta Public Library, 10 Pryor Street, S.W., Atlanta, GA 30303.
Free

GEORGIA (530 foundations)
Guide to Foundations in Georgia, compiled by the Georgia Department of Human Resources. Available from State Economic Opportunity Unit, Office of District Programs, Department of Human Resources, 618 Ponce de Leon Avenue, NE, Atlanta, GA 30308.
Free

HAWAII (55 foundations and 6 church funding sources)
A Guide to Charitable Trusts and Foundations in the State of Hawaii. Available from Director of Planning and Development, Alu Like, Inc, 2828 Paa Street, Honolulu, HI 96819.
$15.00 for nonprofit organizations
$25.00 for profit-making organizations

IDAHO (78 foundations)
Directory of Idaho Foundations, 2nd edition, prepared by the Caldwell Public Library. Available from the Foundation Collection, Caldwell Public Library, 1010 Dearborn Street, Caldwell, ID 83605.
$1.00 prepaid and $.28 in postage stamps

ILLINOIS (approximately 175 corporations)
The Chicago Corporate Connection: A Directory of Chicago Area Corporate Contributors, Including Downstate Illinois and Northern Indiana, edited by Susan M. Levy. Available from Donors Forum of Chicago, 208 South LaSalle, Chicago, IL 60604.
$8.50 prepaid

ILLINOIS (approximately 1,900 foundations)
Illinois Foundation Directory, edited by Beatrice J. Capriotti and Frank J.

Capriotti, III. Available from the Foundation Data Center, 100 Wesley Temple Building, 123 East Grant Street, Minneapolis, MN 55403.
$425.00 (approx.)

INDIANA (265 foundations)
Indiana Foundation: A Directory, edited by Paula Reading Spear. Available from Central Research Systems, 320 North Meridian, Suite 1011, Indianapolis, IN 46204.
$19.95 prepaid

KANSAS (approximately 255 foundations)
Directory of Kansas Foundations, edited by Connie Townsley. Available from Association of Community Arts Councils of Kansas, Columbian Building, 4th Floor, 112 West 6th, Topeka, KS 66603.
$5.80 prepaid

MAINE (139 foundations)
A Directory of Foundations in the State of Maine, 3rd edition, compiled by the Center for Research and Advanced Study. Available from Center for Research and Advanced Study, University of Southern Maine, 246 Deering Avenue, Portland, ME 04102.
$3.00 prepaid

MAINE (59 corporations)
Maine Corporate Funding Directory. Available from Center for Research and Advanced Study, University of Southern Maine, 246 Deering Avenue, Portland, ME 04102.
$5.50 prepaid

MARYLAND (approximately 300 foundations)
1979 Annual Index Foundation Reports, compiled by the Office of the Attorney General. Available from the Office of the Attorney General, One South Calvert Street, Baltimore, MD 21202.
$5.00 prepaid

MARYLAND (approximately 300 foundations)
1979 Supplemental Information Index to the Annual Index Foundation Reports, compiled by the Office of the Attorney General. Available from the Office of the Attorney General, One South Calvert Street, Baltimore, MD 21202.
$30.00 prepaid

MASSACHUSETTS (726 foundations)
Directory of Foundations in Massachusetts. Available from Associated Grantmakers of Massachusetts, 294 Washington Street, Suite 501, Boston, MA 02108.
$8.00 prepaid

MASSACHUSETTS (960 foundations)
A Directory of Foundations in the Commonwealth of Massachusetts, 2nd edition, edited by John Parker Huber. Available from Eastern Connecticut State College Foundation, Inc., P.O. Box 431, Willimantic, CT 06226.
$15.00 prepaid

MASSACHUSETTS (56 Boston-area foundations)
Directory of the Major Greater Boston Foundations. Available from Logos Associates, 12 Gustin, Attleboro, MA 02703.
$19.95 prepaid

MICHIGAN (863 foundations)
The Michigan Foundation Directory, 3rd edition, prepared by the Council of Michigan Foundations and Michigan League for Human Services. Available from Michigan League for Human Services, 200 Mill Street, Lansing, MI 48933.
$9.00 prepaid

MINNESOTA (450 foundations)
Guide to Minnesota Foundations, 2nd edition, prepared by the Minnesota Council on Foundations. Available from Minnesota Council on Foundations, 413 Foshay Tower, Minneapolis, MN 55402.
$10.00 plus $.40 sales tax or your sales-tax-exempt number

MINNESOTA (598 foundations)
Minnesota Foundation Directory, edited by Beatrice J. Capriotti and Frank J. Capriotti, III. Available from Foundation Data Center, Ridgedale State Bank Building, 1730 South Plymouth Road, Suite 202, Minneapolis, MN 55343.
$250.00

MONTANA (42 Montana and 12 Wyoming foundations)
The Montana and Wyoming Foundations Directory, compiled by Paula Deigert, Jane Kavanaugh, and Ellen Alweis. Available from Eastern Montana College Foundation, 1500 North 30th Street, Billings, MT 59101.
$5.00 prepaid

NEBRASKA (approximately 154 foundations)
Compiled by the Junior League of Omaha. Available from Junior League of Omaha, 7365 Pacific Street, Omaha, NB 68114.
Free, limited supply

NEW HAMPSHIRE (approximately 400 foundations)
Directory of Charitable Funds in New Hampshire, 3rd edition. Available from the Office of the Attorney General, State House Annex, Concord, NH 03301.

$2.00 (Annual supplement, including changes, deletions, and additions, available from the same address for *$1.00*)

NEW JERSEY (321 foundations and 374 corporations)
The New Jersey Mitchell Guide: Foundations, Corporations, and Their Managers, 2nd edition, edited by Janet A. Mitchell. Available from The Mitchell Guides, P.O. Box 413, Princeton, NJ 08540.
  $20.00 prepaid

NEW YORK (approximately 139 organizations)
Guide to Grantmakers: Rochester Area, compiled by the Monroe County Library System. Published by Urban Information Center, Monroe County Library System, not available for purchase. May be used in libraries of Monroe County Library System and at Foundation Center Library, New York.

NEW YORK (185 foundations, 182 businesses, and 42 parent corporations)
The Long Island Mitchell Guide: Foundations, Corporations, and Their Managers, edited by Janet A. Mitchell. Available from The Mitchell Guides, P.O. Box 413, Princeton, NJ 08540.
  $20.00 prepaid

NEW YORK (323 foundations, 362 businesses, and 88 parent corporations)
The Upstate New York Mitchell Guide: Foundations, Corporations, and Their Managers, edited by Janet A. Mitchell. Available from The Mitchell Guides, P.O. Box 413, Princeton, NJ 08540.
  $25.00 prepaid

OHIO (1700 foundations)
Charitable Foundations Directory of Ohio, 4th edition. Available from Charitable Foundations Directory, Attorney General's Office, 30 East Broad Street, 15th floor, Columbus, OH 43215.
  $5.00 prepaid

OHIO (42 foundations)
Guide to Charitable Foundations in the Greater Akron Area, 1st edition, prepared by Human Services Planning Library. Available from Human Services Planning Library, United Way of Summit County, P.O. Box 1260, 90 North Prospect Street, Akron, OH 44304.
  $2.50

OKLAHOMA (269 foundations)
Directory of Oklahoma Foundations, edited by Thomas E. Broce. Available from University of Oklahoma Press, 1005 Asp Avenue, Norman, OK 73069.
  Hardcover—$14.95 plus $.86 postage
  Softcover—$7.95 plus $.63 postage

OREGON (approximately 430 foundations)
The Guide to Oregon Foundations, 2nd edition, produced by the Tri-County Community Council. Available from Tri-County Community Council, 718 West Burnside, Portland, OR 97209.
  $10.00 plus $.50 postage

PENNSYLVANIA (2267 foundations)
Directory of Pennsylvania Foundations, 2nd edition, compiled by S. Damon Kletzien, editor, with assistance from Margaret H. Chalfant and Frances C. Ritchey. Available from *Directory of Pennsylvania Foundations,* c/o Friends of the Free Library, Logan Square at 19th Street, Philadelphia, PA 19103. Make check payable to: Friends of the Free Library of Philadelphia.
  $18.50, plus $1.11 for PA sales tax if applicable

PENNSYLVANIA (194 foundations)
Pittsburgh Area Foundation Directory. Available from Community Action Pittsburgh, Inc., Planning and Research Division, Fulton Building, 107 Sixth Street, Pittsburgh, PA 15227.
  $10.00

SOUTH CAROLINA (203 foundations)
South Carolina Foundation Directory, 1st edition, edited by Anne K. Middleton. Available from Anne K. Middleton, Assistance Reference Librarian, South Carolina State Library, P.O. Box 11469, Columbia, SC 29211.
  Send $.70 in postage stamps

TEXAS (approximately 1,374 foundations)
Directory of Texas Foundations, compiled and edited by William J. Hooper. Available from Texas Foundations Research Center, P.O. Box 5494, Austin, TX 78763. Make check payable to: TFRC.
  $21.50 prepaid. Add $1.00 for sales tax if applicable.

TEXAS (approximately 200 foundations)
The Guide to Texas Foundations, 2nd edition, edited by Jed Riffe. Available from Marianne Cline, Dallas Public Library, 1954 Commerce Street, Dallas, TX 75201.
  $10.00 prepaid

VIRGINIA (approximately 390 foundations)
Virginia Foundations, published by the Grants Resources Library of Hampton, Virginia; not available for sale. May be used in Foundation Centers' cooperating collections in Virginia and at Foundation Center Libraries in New York and Washington, D.C.

WASHINGTON (approximately 968 organizations)
Charitable Trust Drectory, 2nd edition, compiled by the Office of the Attorney General. Available from the Office of the Attorney-General, Temple of Justice, Olympia, WA 98504.
  $4.00 prepaid

WEST VIRGINIA (approximately 99 foundations)
West Virginia Foundation Directory, compiled and edited by William Seeto. Available from West Virginia Foundation Directory, Box 96, Route 1, Terra Alta, WV 26764. Make check payable to: West Virginia Foundation Directory.
  $7.95 prepaid

WISCONSIN (643 foundations)
Foundations in Wisconsin: A Directory 1980, 4th edition, compiled by Susan H. Hopwood. Available from The Foundation Collection, Marquette University Memorial Library, 1415 West Wisconsin Avenue, Milwaukee, WI 53233.
  $12.50 prepaid plus $.48 sales tax or Wisconsin tax exempt number

WYOMING (45 foundations)
Wyoming Foundation Directory, prepared by Joy Riske. Available from Laramie County Community College Library, 1400 East College Drive, Cheyenne, WY 82001.
  Free

WYOMING (12 foundations). See MONTANA.

Corporate Research Tools

The current trend is for corporations interested in corporate giving to establish foundations to handle their contributions. Once established as foundations, their Internal Revenue Service returns become public information and data are compiled into the directories previously mentioned under Foundation Research Aids.

Corporate contributions that do not use the foundation are not public information, and research sources consist of:

* information volunteered by the corporation

* product information

* profitability information

BOOKS

Annual Survey of Corporate Contributions, annual
This survey of corporate giving is sponsored by the Conference Board
and the Council for Financial Aid to Education. It includes a detailed
analysis of beneficiaries of corporate support, but does not list individual
firms and specific recipients.
   Price: $7.50 for Associate and Education Members,
         $22.50 for Non-Associates
   Order from: The Conference Board
            845 Third Avenue
            New York, NY 10022

The Corporate 500: Directory of Corporate Philanthropy, 1980
This volume gives information on the contributions programs of the 500
largest American corporations. Entries include: areas of interest; analysis of trends and priorities; geographic areas receiving funds; activities
funded; eligible organizations; policy statements; contribution committee members; financial profiles; sample grants and applications procedures. Its quarterly updates provide current information. It is published
by the Public Management Institute.
   Price: $225.00
   Order from: Gale Research Company
            Book Tower
            Detroit, MI 48226

Corporate Foundation Profiles, 1981, 512 pages
This comprehensive analysis of over 200 of the largest company-sponsored foundations includes subject, type of support, and geographic indexes. It also includes financial data for over 300 additional corporate
foundations. (Reissued from *Source Book Profiles.*)
   Price: $50.00
   Order from: Foundation Center
            888 Seventh Avenue
            New York, NY 10106

The Corporate Fund Raising Directory, 1980–81 edition
This directory provides information on the giving policies of over 350 of
America's top corporations. It includes name, address and phone
number, contact person, primary and secondary areas of corporate giving, best time to apply, corporate policy on appointments, typical grants,

total amounts of grants, geographic limitations and other relevant information, including guidance and advice to grant seekers.

Price: $19.75 plus $1.50 postage and handling
Order from: Public Service Materials Center
           111 North Central Avenue
           Hartsdale, NY 10530

PERIODICALS AND NEWSLETTERS

Directory of Corporate Affiliations, annual
This directory lists divisions, subsidiaries, and affiliates of over 5,000 U.S. parent companies, with address, telephone, key persons and employees, etc. Included is a separate geographical index.

Price: $267.00 plus $6.75 handling and delivery
Order from: National Register Publishing Company, Inc.
           5201 Old Orchard Road
           Skokie, IL 60077

Dun and Bradstreet's Million Dollar Directory, 3 volumes
The three volumes list names, addresses, employees, sales volume and other pertinent data for 120,000 of America's largest businesses.

Price: Vol. I: $295.00; Vol. II: $275.00; Vol. III: $275.00
Order from: Dun and Bradstreet
           Directories Services
           99 Church Street
           New York, NY 10007

Standard and Poor's Register of Corporations, Directors and Executives, annual
The register provides up-to-date rosters of over 400,000 executives of the 37,000 nationally known corporations they represent, with their names, titles, and business affiliations.

Price: $330.00 for one-year lease
Order from: Standard and Poor's Corporation
           25 Broadway
           New York, NY 10004

Taft Corporate Directory, 1981, 400 pages
This directory provides detailed entries on 300 company-sponsored foundations. Included are five indexes—by state, by fields of interest, by operating locations, by people, and by grants.

Price: $267.00 plus $7.50 postage and handling
Order from: Taft Corporation
           5125 MacArthur Boulevard, NW, Suite 300
           Washington, DC 20016

Taft Corporate Information System
Directory: see above
Corporate Updates: This monthly profiles corporations and corporate foundations that make contributions. $65.00 a year
Corporate Giving Watch: This monthly reports on corporate giving developments. $45.00 a year
Price for the entire system: $347.00 per year plus $10.00 postage and handling.
Order from: Taft Corporation
5125 MacArthur Boulevard, NW, Suite 300
Washington, DC 20016

Computer Research Systems

There is a wealth of information available through data-base and information-retrieval systems. Check with your librarian and your grants office to locate those data bases you may already have access to.

Congressional Information Service Index, (CIS Index)
Congressional Information Services, Inc.
4520 East West Highway
Washington, DC 20014
(301) 654-1550
CIS covers congressional publications and legislation from 1970 to date. It covers hearings, committee prints, House and Senate reports and documents, special publications, Senate executive reports and documents, and public laws. It includes monthly abstracts and index volumes and annual cumulations.

The Dialog Information Retrieval Service
3460 Hillview Avenue
Palo Alto, CA 94304
(800) 227-1960 (U.S.)
(800) 982-5858 (CA)
(415) 858-3810

Educational Research Information Center (ERIC)
This data base provides a complete file on educational materials from the Educational Resources Information Center. Coverage includes reports and periodical literature in education and education-related areas; career education counseling; early childhood education; educational management; exceptional children; information resources junior

colleges; languages and linguistics; reading and communications skills; rural studies; social science education; teacher education and tests and measurements ERIC comprises two machine-readable files which correspond to two separate printed products: *Resources in Education and Current Index to Journals in Education.* Entries cover the period from 1966 to the present. It is prepared by the National Institute of Education in Washington.

Federal Assistance Program Retrieval System (FAPRS)
The FAPRS lists more than 1,100 federal grant programs, planning and technical assistance. All states have FAPRS services available through state, county, and local agencies as well as through the federal extension services. Initially, the program operated through cooperative extension and may have moved. For further information, write to:
1. Your congressperson's office; they can request a search for you, and in some cases, at no charge.
2. Federal Program Information Branch
   Budget Review Division
   Office of Management and Budget
   6001 New Executive Office Building
   Washington, DC 20503
   (202) 395-3112

Foundation Center Data Bases
The *Foundation Directory,* the *Foundation Grants Index,* and the *National Data Book* are each available for approximately $60.00 per hour through *Dialog.*

Government Information Services
GIS FUNDING database with detailed information on sources of federal aid programs, loans, grants, financial assistance, and private sector funding. Other databases are available through the GIS FUNDING system with instant access to *Commerce Business Daily,* the *Federal Register,* and the *Congressional Record.*
   Government Information Services
   1611 North Kent Street, Suite 508
   Arlington, VA 22209
   (703) 528-1082

The Smithsonian Science Information Exchange (SSIE)
   1730 M Street, NW
   Washington, DC 20036
   (202) 634-3933
This is a nonprofit source of information on research in progress received from over 1,300 organizations (about 80 percent from federal agencies of the federal government).

Index

FOR: DAVID G. BAUER ASSOCIATES, INC.
        1205 Ney Avenue
        P.O. Box 130
        Utica, NY 13503
        (315) 797-4441

FUND-RAISING MATERIALS

	Price	Freight

How To...Fund-Raise Manual $49.50 + $ 3.50 _____
       (a complete step by step process to
       evaluate your fund raising capabilities)

MANAGEMENT MATERIALS

How To...Automate $49.50 + $ 3.50 _____
       (a complete step by step process to
       follow answering questions as when and
       how, cost, fringes, benefits, penalities,
       etc.)

How To...Manual for Women Managers $49.50 + $ 3.50 _____
       Over 200 pages of forms, worksheets, and
       checklists to improve your system and styles

Individual Materials
       PERSONAL PROFILE SYSTEM   Per Set $ 7.95   _____

THE ACTIVITY PERCEPTION SYSTEM   Per Set $ 7.95   _____

****

PLEASE SEND MY ORDER TO:

NAME _____ TITLE _____

ORGANIZATION _____

ADDRESS _____

_____ ZIP _____

PHONE _____ (New York Residents Add 4% Sales Tax)

NOTE: Freight charges paid by DGBA when payment is sent with order.

( ) Find my check enclosed. ( ) Charge my purchase.

VISA # _____
                                        EXPIRATION DATE

MASTERCHARGE # _____
                                        EXPIRATION DATE

NAME _____
      Print or Type   Signature

<u>GRANTSEEKING MATERIALS</u>

		Price	Freight
<u>Grants Administration Manual</u>		$79.50 +	$ 3.50 ____
<u>Proposal Organization Workbook</u> "Swiss Cheese Book" (Binder, set of tabs and worksheet forms).	Per Set	$ 8.95 $29.50	____ ____
<u>Proposal Organization Workbook</u> Tabs ONLY	Per Set	$ 7.95	____
<u>SPECIAL 5 sets only $20.00</u> (payment must accompany order)	<u>SAVE</u>	$ 9.75	____
<u>Project Planners--</u> A pad of 25 worksheets -- 3 hole punched (A planning document for developing work plan and budget).	Per Pad	$ 7.95	____
<u>SPECIAL 5 pads only $20.00</u> (payment must accompany order)	<u>SAVE</u>	$12.50	____
<u>Grants Time Line</u> A pad of 25 worksheets -- 3 hole punched for use in proposal planning.	Per Pad 5 Pads @ 10 Pads @	$ 3.95 $ 3.25 $ 2.95	____ ____ ____
<u>Grants Office Time Line</u> A pad of 25 worksheets -- 3 hole punched (for use in the Grants Office).	Per Pad ·	$ 3.50	____

****

PLEASE SEND MY ORDER TO:

NAME _____ TITLE _____

ORGANIZATION _____

ADDRESS _____

_____ ZIP _____

PHONE _____ (New York Residents Add 4% Sales Tax)

NOTE: Freight charges paid by DGBA when payment is sent with order.

( ) Find my check enclosed. ( ) Charge my purchase.

VISA # _____

                                                        EXPIRATION DATE

MASTERCHARGE # _____

                                                        EXPIRATION DATE

NAME _____

        Print or Type   Signature